C000119055

A
DIFFICULT
JOURNEY

A DIFFICULT JOURNEY

A Socio-political Autobiography

MAXIMO SERRANO HERCULES

Copyright © 2019 by Maximo Serrano Hercules.

HARDBACK: 978-1-946801-70-8
PAPERBACK: 978-1-7334214-9-2
EBOOK: 978-1-946801-71-5

All rights reserved. No part of this publication may be reproduced, distributed, or transmitted in any form or by any electronic or mechanical means, without the prior written permission of the publisher, except in the case of brief quotations embodied in critical reviews and certain other noncommercial uses permitted by copyright law.

Ordering Information:

For orders and inquiries, please contact:
1-888-375-9818
www.toplinkpublishing.com
bookorder@toplinkpublishing.com

Printed in the United States of America

CONTENTS

AUTHOR'S NOTE

To the reader of this book:

This book was written and published first in Spanish, therefore, the translation may be a bit different and may lose some of its content but I will try my best as possible.

For instance, the poems written were translated but will probably lose some content, feeling or meaning and of course, its rhyme.

You will find several local words used in a particular region in Central America; some words come from Mayan dialects spoken in El Salvador, Lenca and Nahuatl.

I hope the readers will have a better understanding of these passages - an autobiography, and enjoy it the best way possible.

From the writer:
Maximo Serrano Hercules

DEDICATION

I dedicate this work to my parents. They are unforgettable and always loved. I will always have them in my heart.

I also dedicate it to my people who suffered and to the fraternal people; to the people who fought for the minimum livelihood; to all third-world countries that must fight against an empire, and to all those who are exploited, decade after decade, century after century.

To those who are victims of racial discrimination in their own country or in foreign lands; to those who are discriminated because they are of a different race or have another culture and to those who feel their lives are miserable because of this.

To those heroes who have already left; heroes who sacrificed their own lives to give the next generations a better future; to those who are remembered by people; those who will never be forgotten; those who fought against misery, injustice and exploitation - who gave their lives. The unforgettable heroes who have already passed away but will, never, ever die...

FOREWORD

For as long as I remember, my life along with my family was marked by neocolonialism. Although my parents had a little land they had inherited from my grandparents on both sides, they wanted to live that experience of being settlers in a landowner farm. My father was almost enslaved and in many situations he had to go to work in the farm during weekends or at night without payment. All of my siblings and I were born in that farm. Life was pleasant and nice until my father had to leave that place and resort to the inheritance my grandfather, his father, had left him to make use of and live there with us.

My childhood was very hard. However, I would like to live it again because it was, at the same time, very naive. There was very little development; so as the rural life at that time in my country. The greatest crisis time was when El Salvador was at war with Honduras. The whole country was in extreme poverty; many people had absolutely nothing to eat.

Remember that children from five to twelve years old wandered in their villages, naked or half-naked, dirty or stained because they did not have a place to take a bath, begging nickels to buy food. At least, in the farm there is an advantage that rural people go to the mountains to get fruits or wild vegetables, and to find any edible bug to hunt and take it home to be cooked by the mother in the family.

From my childhood I also remember that it was common to suffer from fever and diarrhea, to be full of pinworms and to get sick because of many tropical epidemic diseases. My mother always had to take care of us alone because my father was in the farm.

Then, school time came. We had to walk along the bog, and if the student wore a dirty uniform the teacher would hit him with a stick.

And when we helped our father in his work, we went to school dirty with earth and green hands due to grass and we were also hit.

Later, the other times arrived, the beginnings of a war, and there was a lot of uncertainty among people. The bourgeoisie, supported by the United States, used its money and power to manipulate rulers as if they were puppets. There was a lot of corruption.

However, nobody could not imagine how it would be the time to come - having to sleep in caves in the chasm to avoid being killed when military convoy came; flee into the ravines; people murdered people heaped in a pile; shootouts and bombs exploding everywhere dropped by airplanes and helicopters that attacked peasantries, valleys and villages, both during day and night.

The military fought over political and military power. As an old woman who still had his small store in the market of San Salvador said, "They fight like dogs and cats. We know that they are all alike. During their political campaigns, they said,

"Exploitation of man by man will soon end", but when they come to power, they are the same. Promises are just to deceive people, and they remain puppets of both the rich and the United States administration."

El Salvador has suffered greatly from natural disasters such as hurricanes and earthquakes. Hurricanes have caused floods and the most affected people are always the poorest ones. There have been many major earthquakes that have obliterated villages and entire communities, which have led many poor people to their deepest misery. In my country, the gap between the rich and the poor is huge. Once, I read a book where the fourteen richest families in the country are mentioned - the Regalado Duenas family has a total of 176 million dollars in the country. In that very poor country, there are so wealthy families.

The country is very small but it has great potential because it has a lot of domestic industries, foreign and transnational capital industries and many workers. Because of war, many of them have emigrated; it is considered that only in the United States there is an average of two million Salvadorans after Mexicans, they represent the largest group of immigrants in that country. For many years El Salvador has been the country that sends more money per head to their families. There is no doubt that before this war many people from many countries of the world do not even know of the existence of El Salvador, which by its geography it is called the Tom Thumb of America. Nowadays, global statistics say that at least a Salvadoran can be found in every single country. The world realized the existence of this small size country but big in many historical, political, geographical and social aspects.

The adventure through foreign lands gave me a lot to learn. I started in Guatemala, in Tecun Uman - I lived together with indigenous people and only a few spoke a little bit of Spanish. Their way of life is totally different from ours, and they are absolutely conformist, they live in more extreme poverty than ours, but they are satisfied with that life. During the time I lived in Guatemala and I worked in Mexico, I could see well the difference between both countries. Then I came to Michoacán, near the Mexican territory, with its own culture different from the southern one. The accent changes, people belong to other ethnic groups. There, most are Ladinos or completely white, of either Spanish or European origin. Indians live separately. After that, I worked in Guadalajara, Jalisco, which is the second largest city of Mexico. Later, we were involved in the hardest part - avoiding being discovered by immigration agents and reach the north; they question even the Mexicans and asked for their documents. In the north of the country, Chihuahua and Sonora, I worked throughout the process of the grape. Wine grapes plants are foreign and their products fly to other countries. People suffer and do not benefit from nothing; they just earn money to survive. The struggle is constant in those places.

After several attempts, I finally got to know the United States. My first jobs were in agricultural fields in Arizona, and then I went to Wyoming where I worked with beets.

I had the experience of being imprisoned for my illegal situation and then I was deported. Had it not been for relatives in the Army, I would have been killed. And I had to be in the Death Squad, it was the thing I hated most, unable to do anything about it. I saw my parents suffered from this situation, and they were also threatened.

Then another adventure heading north came, and with different ideas, living and knowing different people and cultures. The experience of being undocumented and not knowing the English language is most depressing thing when you are in the United States. In addition, there is racial discrimination. At work one has to do his best, twice or even more than any not undocumented person would do so as to deserve the employment and prove that one's worth as a worker. Even so, one is humiliated, insulted and despised by workmates, especially white people, who have prejudice most rooted both in their hearts and in their minds.

In that period, the fact of working voluntarily in the organization we have founded helped me a lot morally and psychologically. Feeling you are doing something for other people who are in worse conditions than you fill one's heart. And, of course, one worries that our loved ones never lack their food and basic needs in their homes, especially our parents who brought us into the world.

AS A SETTLER IN A HACIENDA

Rural Life

Swallows cast away the air with concern.
Trees swayed their branches with purity.
The river in its course restlessly, slowly.
And flowers dried up, lost their smooth complexion.

Dawn with its red glows repainted the morning.
Roosters with their singing took over the dawn.
Sporadic barking of a dog that maybe needed
Caresses his master gave him in the mornings.

The farmer prepared his oxen with the yoke
Because he plowed. There, at the top, furrow after furrow he cultivated
Sowing the seeds he longingly left,
For his family foodstuff, whom he loved.

Dressed in green Spring, the stubborn weeds to sprout.
Beans or corn green fertile ravine,
Where the tortillas will come up and scandalize for its smell,
That housewife makes harmoniously with love

The sobbing days for the winter.
Aggressive clouds spouting their crystal.
A hurricane or a tornado that would come.
Our sustenance depended on the natural phenomenon.

At their home chickens bother
Clucking in the threshold
The children were crying, asking.
A pig that roared and rain coming.

The mother gathered and fixed clothes.
Washed in the stream that was close to his shack,
thinking about her husband dinner (what would she prepare...?),
He would soon return from work.
Their children wondered if his father was about to arrive.
Thinking about his life and the daily rest.

The farmer returns with little to say.
Their huaraches, almost finished; his shirt, already smashed.
He takes off his hat, eats a tortilla,
And think about the morning, the day after day routine.

He watches the sunset very slowly.
Some bold gray hair are noticed because of the sun,
Withered wrinkles begin to invade him,
Afraid that one morning he would have to leave.

In a small square of San Salvador there is the monument of
TOROGOCEZ, it is a newly built square and the bird is our
Salvadoran national bird.
"The *torogoz* or turquoise-browed motmot".

I barely remember the time when my father was a settler in San
Antonio farm. According to some people, the farm was called that way
because its first owner's name was Antonio. Without any doubt it was a
Spanish who emigrated from Spain in colonial times. According to what
had happened at that time, that person also contributed to an episode
in the history of El Salvador during the colonialism period and, in one
way or the other, he took over the nine hundred hectares farm.

Most of the lands of this farm were in lowland. It shared boundary
in the west with the Sucio River, where there was very fertile land. There
was a lot of wood in various parts of the farm. The mountains were
virgin, they hadn't been touched. In the hills there was a huge variety
of big trees, where timber was removed to build houses.

The owner, Mr. Alfonso González who was the grandson of the
landlord who supposedly came from Spain was more interested in
livestock farming. Thus, he began deforest part of the farm to cultivate
pasture for livestock. In one part they had already planted coffee trees
and sugar cane. The farm was surrounded by fruit trees like mango,

avocados, zunzas trees, sapote, various kinds of oranges, lemons, etc. And, of course, they had a great number of different types of bananas including; plantains, banana trees, red bananas and others. At that time, the banana was much sold on the town's market. All this make a farm or ranch nicely decorated with fruit trees.

Mr. Alfonso - who, as I said before, was the Spanish heir, and at the time I remember was the owner of the farm, was a tall man, with light brown or swarthy skin and he was about sixty years and he usually had a gentle character.

This man was the one who chose my father to work in his farm. There were family ties between Mr. Alfonso and a cousin of my father's father, that is to say, my paternal grandfather.

And as this gentleman had very few people on the farm or settlers to work there, and because he thought cultivate in a more intensive way, then he spoke to my paternal grandfather as they already knew each other.

My paternal grandfather lived in the outskirts of that farm, in a small valley where he had installed a hamlet that would have about thirty families at that time, called Agua Fría -Cold Water- because water is usually cold in there. Only country people lived in the small village. It was a slope area, with some hills, that is to say, broken land, and the people who lived there were families of low economic resources.

Also I have to say that when my father was born and raised where it was no schools in the country side in El Salvador, but my dad knew how to read and write very well and math he knew more than anybody who had 9th grade of school. He could figure out easy how much lumber a log of a meter in diameter was going to produce. He loved to deal with numbers all the time when he had to do furniture, a house, lumber or anything that involved math. I never asked him how he learned. He read the news in the papers very often when he bought them in town.

Some farmers had their small piece of land to work in. Others had no land, and in order to sow they had to lease, either with money or rent, which means a swap or barter system - half a hectare of land was left to work in exchange for some measures of corn (grains) when the harvest was ready.

They also sought land for a cow they might have because it was necessary to have it around to go to milk it every morning. Many also had their horses for everyday use, as they used horses to go to the village to bring things they bought, as a means of transportation, to fetch firewood to cook food, to haul firewood, to herd cattle in pastures and to bring the harvest home. At that time, the horse was a totally necessary service when it came to transportation.

That was the small valley of Agua Fría, where my paternal grandfather, who was one of the first inhabitants of the place, lived. He had acquired a small piece of land of about six blocks with many efforts. This block measure was brought by the Spaniards: 1 block is 10,000 square yards (1 yard are 33 imperial inches), equivalent to about 8,700 square meter, about 2.2 acres in all.

It was also known that in my grandfather's family there were carpenters, the whole family had inherited this trade. They were all sawyers, because they could cut the wood between two with a saw in the air. The trunks were mounted on the beams; they were trunks of more than one meter in diameter and five meters or even more in length. Planks, beams or rules were made to build houses. These gentlemen, in addition to cutting wood, made the caisson of a house or rather they built the house lines and even made fine furniture in general.

For all the people it was a profession that guarantees the supply of the family, and this was the reason why Mr. Alfonso called my father to work on his farm. In return, the employer would give a piece of land that he could work on.

According to many people, the response was immediate. It is said that several settlers reached the farm together with my father and they made a small hut on a small plateau near a cliff from where they could see the river at the bottom of an abyss. In the place there had already been houses, but nobody liked that place because it was very dark, and distant.

It is said that took some wagons with beams, clay or mud tile and other materials, and within a week the hut was finished. It was made with thick wooden posts of fine wood, raw wood from trees taken from the mountains, plump beams from pitchfork to pitchfork with plump wooden beams to put the tile. The walls were made of jaraguá grass, a grass that reaches a height of about two meters. They used bamboo for the side chains and they covered in mud the side where it was supposed to be the kitchen. The floor was dirt floor, because only the grass had been cut, and that was it.

It turned out that when heavy rains came, water flew in the house, so it was no longer necessary to go to the stream to fetch it, because there was water for weeks.

My father and his life partner, my mother, were already settlers in San Antonio farm. I can remember that we lived in a small hill. As Salvadorans say, "That is where my umbilical cord rested."

In that place there were some fruit trees and the remains of a house. Hurricane winds blew very strong because it was a little high, and they always came from south to north, they came by the river canyon north and due to the fact that in the north we had the mountain, hurricanes collided with it. The mountain was quite tall and had huge trees.

It was also said that in that place there was something that frightened the settlers. The previous inhabitants had left the place for that reason. They said that a rooster sang at midnight in the vicinity or at the top of the mountain. Others claimed they heard the Siguanaba, a woman who cackled at midnight in the middle of the mountain. The Siguanaba is a ghost, and in almost all Latin America believed that it really exists.

On that mountain there were also many dangerous animals such as large snakes that could devour dogs and even small baby cows, and they meant a threat. In addition, people could not have chickens because there were wildcats. My mother could keep neither chickens nor chicks; hens with all chicks were eaten. Those cats were similar to lynxes, as big as a dog, and there were others of the same size, but more like a small lion. They would eat a whole chicken and were still hungry for another.

The only found fun in summer time. My mother went down the river to wash clothes while we learned to swim. My older brothers taught to swim but I do not remember exactly what my age was, I guess maybe about three years old.

By that time, it was a larger river than it is today. The water was purer, clearer, and less polluted than today. Years later with the establishment of many factories upstream by the proximity of the town, it became the dirtiest river in the region. The coffee mills were used to get rid of coffee pulp, and it really stunk when you walked the vicinity. When they cleaned the sugar mills they were killing fishes, then they opened a US factory, Kimberley-Clark. This factory often polluted the river, and there was a foul smell because of the dead fishes.

Since then people could no longer wash clothes and less bathe in its waters. Water pollution was one of the things the United States caused in El Salvador because of industrial exploitation. This happened with all kinds of industries that American settled in third world countries, since it is not a fact that it has only occurred in our country.

In brief, under those circumstances, my parents were already tired of living in such a dismal place. It was hard to breed chickens, ducks, turkeys or any other small animal because predators devoured them.

In addition to this, it was an ugly place. In winter it was a little scary to live there, standing at the foot of the mountain. When there were hurricanes with wind, tree branches flew long distances through the air; the tiles also flew away and broke. Storms at night or early mornings were the worst; we felt sick and we suffered from fevers, colds or flus. At that time, we were four siblings, all young. Most of us were about eight years, and I was six. When there was a storm, in the morning my father had to fix the roof, sometimes there were no tiles left to do so. Once, one side wall flew too.

Living there in winter was a real pain, so my father spoke with Mr. Alfonso and told him that if he gave him another house elsewhere, he would stay at the farm, and if he refused to do that, he would leave.

After a few days, the employer told him he had a house down the river through the valley, in a beautiful place. There, the river took a turn, and there was a land of about four hectares of plain.

The problem was, in that nice place a man named Juan Guardado had lived for many years. The boss had been told that this man did not want to work there any longer because he was wealthy enough. He had many animals such as cows and other livestock, although some of them were not his property, he fattened them for others in exchange for some of the money the owner received when the animal was sold.

Suddenly, this man came to know that the employer wanted him to vacate the farm house. The man refused to leave and said that not even the National Guard would make him go somewhere else. He had already become fond of the place and besides, he was making money in other ways. However, after about three months, with the help of other legal sources, the employer managed to get him of the house. From there, that man became my father's enemy for the rest of his life, but as the boss said, it was not my father's responsibility, it was the farm that made the decision.

One spring day, before the start of the winter, we moved into the new house. I remember that my uncle, my father's brother, came with his pair of oxen and his wagon to carry our belongings. As it was not far, we did it in a day.

After living in the old house, we felt we had reached a castle. The house was large, about fifteen meters long and eight meters wide. There was a separate kitchen, three bedrooms and a large living room. There were two corridors, one on the north side and another one on the south side. All walls were made of adobe and the floor was made of bricks, so it could be mopped up. The ceiling caisson was made of sawn timber, well regulated, and the ceiling was made of tile. The corridors had based cement pillars.

Around the house grew a beautiful grove of fruit trees only - coconut palms, mangoes of various kinds, oranges, lemons, bananas and others. There was also a beautiful shaded area for animals, such as poultry and other animals that could be kept there.

Beside it was a tract of land large enough to plant corn and other vegetables. The land was fertile, and because it lacked rocks it could be plowed with tractors.

The family's daily life harmoniously developed in the field. My mom took advantage of the conditions of this house, surrounded by fruit trees, and had animal husbandry. She had managed to have over a hundred hens, so she had to travel every four days to the town to sell eggs, sometimes to take a pair of chicken. From there she brought home the things we needed.

She also bred ducks, turkeys, guinea hens and some pigs to fatten and then sell. Likewise, we already owned two cows that were in the pasture. I remember one of them was gray and we called it Scarf. The other cow was called Chiltota (spot-breasted oriole) because it had a reddish color, like the bird of that name. I think the name of this bird comes from the Mayas. In Mexico it is called Calandria. This bird has a very harmonious and beautiful singing. It makes its nests in the tops of the tallest trees, with fibers found in the stems of trees. Nests are finely woven, shaped as a bag that looks like a sock of about forty two feet long, and they can be seen rocking in the wind on top of the trees.

The cows did not give much milk, only four to six bottles each per day. Either my dad or my mom milked them from five to six am before the boss goes to work. In the afternoon, my mother first took out the cream, then cheese and finally cottage cheese. Pigs ate the buttermilk coming out at the end in order to fatten faster.

This type of cattle is called Castilla because it is supposedly brought from Spain. These animals eat almost anything and they can live even on the most difficult terrain. It's the kind of cattle that usually has the peasantry because it is also the cheapest. When used to work, they are good for heavy loads, either to pull the wagon or plow the land. Thus, they are highly linked with the peasant and farm's economy, so they used to have dozens of yokes. Farms used the yoke to plow the land where the tractor did not work because of the stones, so they had to pay laborers that will plow it with animals.

The weekends my dad did not travel to town he stayed with us and after breakfast we went to the river.

Sometimes, he already had some scrub ready for us. He built it as follows - he chose a place where the water was gentle without strong current, and approximately one meter deep, then he made a lair shaped burner with big stones. Then he put thorny tree branches on top of it, thus, he formed a sort a den. So we just had to throw chingaste (grinded corn) every day, during a week. Finally, he enclosed the place with nets or driftnet and began to remove the branches until we caught all the fish that were trapped there. At that time there were still a lot of breams and guapote fish in the river and it was the most fished that way.

That was a way of living, making use of natural resources but in those days all that ended and survival was more difficult for someone who had to find his own food.

Sunsets were beautiful there with the river noise. Then they turned gloomy. I remember seeing my father at sunset walking down the slope of the trail of the hill before reaching a stream that was about two blocks from our house. I remember watching him carrying the two meters long saw on his right shoulder. The three eldest siblings went out to meet him at the stream. Then we helped him with the gourd, or canteen, or with his backpack. But the thing we liked most was the ration they gave him on the farm, which consisted of fried rice with boiled beans in a cajón de tusa -maize leaf-. In our country we called cajón de tusa to the sheet remains after the corn cob is removed; employer used it to wrap the ration that was served to the laborers on the farm. We loved that food, but maybe my dad was already bored of it and my mom prepared something different while they talked about the work of the farm and his partner, mashtro (master) Manuel, with whom he worked about ten years.

That man was an expert in removing the wood from a tree, he knew very well the product a log could give and so he was called '*master*'. He often visited our home and he loved us. Sometimes he had dinner with us and after dinner we sat on the house yard, in the moonlight where he told us stories, such as the tiger and lion's story, the coyote and rabbit's story among others.

At that time, a working day of eight hours of a hand was worth a colon, but as the head of the house did a more technical work, he gained 1 colon and 25 cents and all earned, fried rice with boiled beans.

Every day the butler passed through the work fields. He travelled in a cart pulled by a yoke of oxen and he carried his conch that he whistled to announce his presence, and then distributed the food to all the workers. Some laborers cleaned the cane field, others the coffee plantation, others repaired the barbed fence for cattle not to go to the beans or corn field, etc. Others worked in the stables, milking and taking care of the cows.

During autumn days, they cut the cane and processed it in the press which was operated by one or two yoke of oxen (trapiche). The press is a kind of mill, and it was used for juicing up the cane. Juice falls into cauldrons where it first becomes a sweet honey and then it becomes raw cane sugar for sale. They put it in wooden round moulds to make it brown sugar. In those days it was also the coffee harvest, and I remember that every day it was taken to another place to be processed. Sometimes the boss came to see the progress of the agricultural work. He came from San Salvador, in a jeep or several because sometimes he brought his family.

Jeeps should have mountain pinion so they could move in bad roads. Mr. Alfonso lived in Escalon Colony where all the rich people of the country lived and in many other farms he had in other countries.

Some farm butlers knew his house, and they said it was a very healthy and luxurious mansion. Sometimes his two daughters went to the field to horse riding. They were very cute and little proud with people since both of them occasionally spoke with the farmers while a laborer pulled their horses. All the boys watched them with admiration, knowing it was useless to think about them. They lived in a different world from ours, they did not know the suffering and extreme misery many human beings suffer. For them, "life is a delight from birth - they just have to ask and they have everything at their feet," said a man named Fermín who looked after the oxen, horses and donkeys that were used for transporting milk from the farm to town every day.

Mr. Alfonso also had the manager's daughters and to some farmers' daughters as maids. Their drivers and gardeners lived in the farm. In the '60s, of course, it was not easy to find someone who reached the sixth grade, and that was one of the requirements. One should have the appropriate skills and most people could neither read nor write.

Before the '60s there was not the slightest possibility of an attested professional education. There were no schools, especially in rural areas for Salvadoran citizen, and if there was any (Casita) little shock where young people learn to read and write at least their names was on the initiative of the same peasants who proposed it. Perhaps there was a place for ten or twelve villages nearby and all the inhabitants were illiterate.

Farmers who had economic resources sent their children to town. That involved investing money in admission expense, school and maintenance because students usually had to live in the village.

My father told me that back in the '30s, when he was ten years old, in that region there was not a place of learning or a teacher, and no one could read or write. For this reason, everyone had to sign with the right thumb to get their personal identity in the municipality they are in.

If any of them knew a little, with a second or third grade, he was assigned commissioned by the municipal government. He brought and take orders from the valley to the town hall, he told news - like a death, a murder or an accident, he carried the correspondence and was at the service of the community. However, he was working without pay, they called it voluntary work - but it was not so voluntary. They had to do it when there was an emergency; they had to leave their work and go to the mayor or, if it was a death, he had to go to the National Guard of the Treasury Police. And, usually, they were not well treated; they were treated with great contempt and discrimination when they were in front of a guard lieutenant or a sergeant.

In addition, these commanders and cantonal commissioners as they were called also recruited adolescents. They took thirty men who were under their command to recruit young when there were festivities or to take them to the barracks. So when there was recruitment, which was always forced, young people stayed at home, and those who went out sometimes were recruited. On many occasions, those who could write and read were used for that purpose.

During the days close to Easter, a trip to the beach, Acajutla port, was organized. It was the second time we went there in a group with all the farm settlers.

It was, of course, a distraction or entertainment trip as people of this little place were not accustomed to go out on trips, but as they had done it once before and they liked it so they decided to do it again. It was very nice. All settler families prepared food and other supplies because it was a two night's stay in the beach.

I remember there were dozens us, adults and children gathered at the farm at four in the morning to start the two hours walk to town. Once there, we waited for the train in the little station where tickets were bought. At half past seven the train whistle was heard, coming from San Salvador to Sonsonate.

It was a steam train; the one that still use firewood. It's working strange and extraordinary. Trains operating in Central America are narrower than the trains of Mexico and the United States. The railway line has approximately just one meter wide and wagons are narrower.

When we travelled, we filled two train cars. We were happy and calm. The adults talked about the farm works and we, the youngest, played during the trip and bought sweets sold by peddlers. We enjoyed seeing the places we got through. The train had to stop at about fourteen stations. In summer, which is the dry weather of our country, we watched irrigated plantations of all kinds - banana, coconut grove, papaya trees, canals, cabbage plantation, cornfields, pineapples, tomato fields, etc.

Meanwhile, in the curves of the railway line we could see the little steamed machine with its black smoke coming out and we could hear that outdated whistling sound.

In Sonsonate City, once after lunch, we all went out to visit San Antonio, a saint that many people are devoted. He is in a church situated in a tiny town called the same way, adjacent to Sonsonate. The church is very beautiful, you can buy many religious things, and people pray their rosaries to San Antonio. There are also some devotees who perhaps have asked for a miracle and they ought to go.

After that walk, we returned to Sonsonate. We arrived at the station from where "two engines" as they called a powered carriage that was on the railway line set off. They were oval and they could carry a hundred people. We travelled to the beach by one of them.

We went to a beach called The Bishop, and it is on one side of Acajutla port. The port which enters the sea about three kilometers and is very beautiful was built by the Japanese with high-tech after the '60s. At that time, at The Bishop beach there was a wooden quay, it was the old pier. At one time, this quay had been used to unload imported goods. When the modern port was built, the old pier which was badly damaged and it was only used by fishing industry, there we copied the maneuvers we did in Sucio River.

The whole community of the farm enjoyed the trip. Adults took baths on the beach, ate seafood, they drank their spiritual drinks and rums with coconut water and rented the palm made huts on the sand where they would sleep. The little kids bathed, chased crabs that live in the sand; we played and watched the sunsets on the beach and listened to the sound of the waves. It was nice to soundly sleep on the beach sand when the tide was at dawn; the water was up to our feet, inside the hut where we were sleeping.

Of course, after those trips, one is satisfied and motivated. And sometimes, after such happiness come unexpected things.

It turns out that my mom was pregnant and she was expected to give birth in the next few weeks and in those days, a pest called '*the accident*' came. This plague killed all the hens, dozens died in an hour or two. This had happened before and in three days all died. Even the ducks and turkeys died, and the pigs became ill. My mom cried in anguish, because we would have nothing to eat without those animals, there was only a little corn and beans and some cows that still gave little milk.

A few weeks later, my mom got sick for that reason - she was pregnant and very delicate. Another son would come, and she was in bed. My dad went to the other side of the valley, where my grandmother, my mother's mom, lived. As she knew of births, she liked to be present, especially with her daughters.

A lady came with them; she was a great woman within the community. She helped dozens of women in labor in all the villages; I'll talk about her later. Her name was María Orellana, and I remember her very well. She was present helping my mom during my birth. Nowadays she is well remembered. No matter the distance or the time she was always there.

This time, it was a rainy midnight. Two ladies came down on the sidewalk in the mountains along the cliffs that was beside the river. They were carrying a candle in their hands to give light in the darkness. Finally, they came to the house and found my mom almost dying in bed. While my grandmother pulled a few thorns and cleaned the blood of her hurt toes because of walking barefoot, she constantly asked about her daughter. We were taken out of the room and locked up in another place. Few hours later we were told our sister, "the girl who was on the plane, was dead."

The next morning, while the ladies cooked something for my disturbed mother and us, my dad went to his brother's, who lived in the valley. He had to request some boards to make a box to bury the child, because my father had no money and he would bury his little daughter next to the house. According to the country laws, you could not bury a child in this way, because before that you had to register the baby at City Hall with a name, etc., and pay five or six colons I think but my dad did not have that money, he only had one colon. Then, right there, my mom, my dad, my grandma and Mrs. María christened the baby with the name of Juana and she was buried under the trees of the farm house.

Silence takes over our home for a while. Finally, my mother was restored. It came the time to reconnect, to keep her emotions and turn her affections on the reality that surrounded her and what made her want to live. She should forget what had happened; it was already in the past.

Time to go to school finally arrived. It turns out that a teacher named Abraham had come to the village of Agua Fria paid by the municipal government, and he was enrolling children in the house of a neighbor called Pedro Dueñas because there was no official school to study. My mom took the three oldest brothers - Tere, the eldest, Francisco and I, who was only six and a half years, the youngest. The professor said that he would not matriculate me because I was supposed to be not ready to attend school because of my age.

Furthermore, the current mayor in the town was a great friend of Mr. Juan Guardado, the man who had left the farm some years ago, and both had the idea of taking possession of Mr. Eugenio Canjura's house.

Mr. Eugenio was a humble farmer who had a wife and children. At that time he and his family were living out in the open with their beds and other belongings under the trees. He hoped to recover what he had lost: not only the house but also the land. These two men, with their contacts in the village, were decided to take the property he had inherited some time ago. The family was, indeed, a close to my parents, and we knew what was going on.

Mr. Juan, for his part, was leader of the Conservative Party, which at that time, was the National Conciliation Party (PCN). As he was at ease in that place and, as we say in El Salvador he already "snored heavily" in the valley, he was trying to humiliate the poorest peasants. He had done this maneuver to use the house as a school so his children did not have to go to town to study. This decision, coupled with some selfishness, was a ridiculous thing. After much litigation in the courts and in the municipal government, and with the help of a lawyer, things were clarified and Mr. Eugenio won the case.

The mayor made this move because while fighting the case, his time was over, and he had already received money from the Ministry of Education and from the city to build a school. We, the students, were attending school in that house and the Canjura family was living in the outdoors.

It was an adobe house with corridors at sides, tiled roof, pillars and floor. It was large, and had enough room for about sixty students. Then, more students came because all parents want to send their children to school. That's where the boys began to interact and know each other.

The Ministry of Education had sent Professor Mr. Abrahán, and then they would send another one. He was very gentle and very collaborative with his students. He slept in a farmer's house, Mr. Pedro Dueñas.

He also ate there, and he only went to town on weekends. As it is known, in our country we are accustomed to work on Saturdays, what we traditionally call it: "Spanish week" so he had to teach until Saturday at noon, and then he went to town. In the morning, until noon, he taught first grade, and in the afternoon, second grade, which was formed by those who had already studied in town or in other schools in the region.

Later, they sent a teacher. She was named Josefina and she took part of the Republican Party and fought her position as trustee of the village. She was a very strict woman.

The teacher brought his son, called Amílcar. She sat him in the front of the class and during the exams, she whispered him everything. It was not easy for him to learn. She beat us unmercifully with a bamboo stick. I remember she asked us questions like this: "Four by four...?" when we were learning the times tables and she put the end of the rod on our cheeks to the point of bleeding. And when it was a punishment, she gave us three blows with a stick on the legs, and they turned purple.

After seeing how teachers treat their students in developed countries, I realized that she committed abuses with us, but we could not do anything about it.

Another problem was the fact that we walked barefoot, without shoes. Some of the children had shoes; others did not. If we went to school in the afternoon, during the morning we helped our father to weed the field. So we arrived at school with dirty nails and stain of the mountain and we were punished because the teacher checked our hands. It was also a problem the uniform we had to use: men had to wear blue pants and white shirt, as the flag of our country; and women had to wear blue skirt and white blouse. We were punished when we did not wear the uniform.

The small village School in Agua Fría, where I spent my first two years of study. The roof of the school was pulled up several times by hurricanes, but the community repaired it without the town hall help. All inhabitants worked voluntarily together to keep the school always open.

My parents had just bought one uniform for each of us. When the uniform was dirty, it had to be washed so we went to school with other clothes and that meant an inevitable punishment.

Finally, with the help of the Ministry of Education and the mayor, and the work of all farmers, a school was built about four blocks from the house where it was the previous one. The land was granted by a man who had a large property and gave a bit to build the school. The school had three classrooms where three degrees could work. The walls and floor were made of clay brick, and tin roof placed on rod trusses. When it was raining and we are in the class room it was so loud that sometimes the teachers had to stop the class and water got in to the class rooms because on the sides the school only had chain link fence on half of walls.

I do not remember the name of the person who donated this place, but he did a good deed. It was between the peasantry valley and the "San Antonio" farm; and although the owner did not have much land he made a great gift to the community. The school was named "Rural Mixed School 'El Agua Fría' ".At least once a month, parents have to attend a meeting to give donations that were like demands: parents had to give money to help pay the teacher -because the Ministry ordered it- and to help pay for materials. At that time, the farmers usually gave only one colon and although it was not much, it was a work day in the labor of that time. Rural areas conditions were critical because the villages were almost incommunicado with the other towns. There were no proper streets, and only the carts with oxen and horses could pass through there. In winter large bogs were formed and there were a lot of stones in the streets, so only on rare occasions a four-wheel jeep could be seen in the street. For the teacher, it was not easy: she came every day on foot from the village to that place, so she had to get up early because she had a two hours journey. The same happened on her way back in the afternoon.

As the school was new, there was another problem when winter came. Grass was put in the playground because it was full of loose soil. Parents were not organized to do the work, therefore, the teacher suggested that for a period of time all students should take a piece of grass every day: it was an order by the professor who said: "Woe betides you if you do not bring grass until the project is completed". Not everyone wanted to do that, but we feared being punished with her heavy hand.

After a few months the project was completed and we could play football, the most popular game in our country. Girls played baseball as it had been established by the Ministry of Education.

I remember we also suffered for nicknames. Some classmates did not like to be called by a nickname and they always fought for that. Whether we liked it or not, we all had a nickname. If somebody did not know the name or nickname of someone else he would make up one. And, as always there are '*rabbles*', they did not care about their fellow. There were always fights for that reason, and it was more common among boys. I think the teacher was a bit sad because of things like that and due to the fact that there were many children, the situation was almost out of control.

Regarding illiteracy, in some cases the system was not the only responsible but also the inhabitants themselves. On several occasions I heard some farmers saying "Why do I send my child to school? I do so in order not to be a lady boy". And if the child was female, they said that the girls had to learn to read and write in order to communicate with their boyfriends when they were older... among many other excuses.

Because the system people were alienated and ignorance had endured so many people did not care whether there was school or not. Furthermore, as the old farmers had never gone to school they wanted their children to behave in the same way because they could not find a sense of achievement in such a thing. We know, in fact, that this was a terrible mistake and that because of the system there were many ignorant parents. This was a problematic conviction of the working class: instead of moving towards to a better world, they just did the opposite. Instead of seeking development they held underdevelopment ideals.

Other farmers did not send their children to school because they did not have money to buy books or pencils. Some parents usually bought all the supplies and uniforms, but many other farmers lived in extreme poverty, with six, eight or even ten children and perhaps half of them could attend school. Instead, seven year old children had to help their family, especially the father, to work in the cultivated field. Besides, they had to give breakfast and lunch to their fathers and elder brothers who were working.

For girls it was the same thing: they had to help their mother to cook, do the washing and take care of their younger siblings. That was one of the reasons why parents did not accept school: they had to put their children to do daily household chores because they needed it. There was no hope for the future of these adolescents rather than work on the land till get old and, if it was a female, marry early -from sixteen onwards-and become a housewife and have many children. In those days it was common to see a family with ten, twelve or fourteen children.

I remember a lady who had been our neighbor in the valley, and years after we had moved she was thirty-five years and she already had had seventeen children. Three of them had died and fourteen were alive. Of course, none of them went to school, because they lacked clothes and at the age of six all kids walked completely naked.

Many farmers were not aware of the importance of studying, and they lived in a different world. Moreover, no one knew that future decades would bring more technologies and more development, and that it would be necessary to have certain skills. All this is due to the subjection in which our people have lived since colonial times till present.

Now, coming back to my story about the farm, I remember that Mr. Alfonso the owner sometimes visited us. He occasionally came with his two jeeps since it was the only mean of transportation that could get to the farm and then to our house. There was a street for carts, but these vehicles were good and had mountain pinion just in case the way was in bad condition.

The owner came with her daughters, their suitors and other family members. They liked to bathe in the river in the beach. In drawers clinging to the back of the jeeps they brought fruits like coconuts, oranges, limes, mangoes, etc., and they talked to my father. Meanwhile, the girls played with us and sometimes they gave us a three or five cents. They studied in Miami and only came to El Salvador on certain occasions, and gringos sometimes came with them.

Mr. Alfonso enjoyed talking about his business: he spoke of his livestock, crops, farm, etc., and of course, he spoke about the people who were making houses, the couples of sawyers who worked for him, those who did the adobe and the people in charge of manufacture tiled.

One day, Mr. Alfonso appeared with a gringo. The gringo had his own helicopter and they landed on an even near the ranch, about five kilometers from our house. Time they arrived, there were already two persons in charge of the farmyard waiting for them with horses. So, they took them to the farm, where were my dad and us because it was holiday time.

After arriving, the owner told my father: "Look, Juan, take Bob for a horse ride through the plains"; such was the man's name, Bob. My father then took him to several places in the farm. The man did not speak any Spanish and he pointed with his hands in different directions as he spoke in English, and my dad just answered "Yeah... Uh huh..." to all the words the gringo said.

What was the difference between an English-speaking gringo and a peasant? One Saturday day, on Christmas Eve, the owner Alfonso Gonzalez came to the farm. It was time for grinding sugar cane in the mill, and he told Mr. Silverio Ruiz, the farmer in charge of the work, he wanted to eat the honey that was boiling in the cauldrons.

Mr. Silverio Ruiz was the '*pointer*', he was called that way because he was an expert in knowing honey points during the process: first comes the honey called table honey, then the one called finger –with which delicious handmade shakes are made, and finally comes honey for sweets. This last one is put into molds where hardens and then becomes raw cane sugar. Usually, even today, rural people are used to make coffee with pure coffee, and they throw a piece of sweet while boiling, instead of using sugar. Sweet is also used for all kinds of canned food made of fruit or vegetables, such as pumpkin, jocotes, sweet potato, mango, cashew, nance, etc. People came from different valleys and they gathered in the farm waiting for honey points to buy it and use it at home.

That Saturday, came the employer to pay the laborers. There were many who worked for the day that is for eight-hour day but at that time on the farms there were several laborers who were paid a salary. Usually, these last ones were the people responsible for the maintenance of animals: they had to be available overtime, the six days of the working week, from morning until evening, and they usually earned even less than the others. That time, Mr. Alfonso gave each peasant one sweet lees. One lee corresponds to two tied bundles, which are four raw sugar canes, and weighs about five pounds. He also gathered the farm settlers to tell them that in two weeks later he would return and he would talk to all of them.

This is run by oxen spinning around, A man inserting the sugar cane into a three cylinder machine, the juice goes into big/huge pots where the honey have different stages that are very tasty/rich through the process while boiling until gets to the point of brown sugar.

Meanwhile, in corn, sorghum and beans sowing time, etc., my father always accommodated a boy known as a pawn. The pawn's payment as a colon and my mom gave him food. Many peasants paid the pawn only seventy-five cents, so pawns preferred to work for my father because they also liked my mom's good food: for breakfast they ate cheese with refried beans, fried eggs and bananas; for lunch, she killed a chicken or did something good to satisfied them. My dad had twenty-five cents of his daily wage left and he was faithful to the farm.

He also had to seek help when it was time to harvest the crop, and due to that, his brother came occasionally with his children. The house corridors were filled with corn cobs, sacks of beans, sorghum, etc. Our family had overcome some setbacks occurred throughout the entire stay at the farm. There was so much joy to my dad gave his brother a young beef bull of those who had already grown our cows' litters, so he did it ox, in gratitude for the help he had given him.

But unexpected news came: the meeting that the employer wanted to do was to tell us he would move all settlers to another place. Two weeks later the owner came and sent four peasants in different directions to ask other farmers to attend the meeting. The peasants began to arrive within two hours as some had to finish their work day. Meanwhile, Mr. Alfonso ordered some coconuts because he wanted to eat coconuts in honey: they threw coconuts in boiling kettles. They were very tasty.

Finally, when all the settlers arrived, he said, "From today onwards, all the settlers of this farm will have to move to other houses, and there will be a rotation every two years." The peasants looked at each other, and did not like the idea of being changing houses, because they already love them. They also were upset because they had to move their animals and they would lose some; hens, for example, disappeared: hens walk around without enclosure and when unknown the place they disappear. So many left the farm in search of other direction where they would build a small hut for their families. Some had the money to buy their piece of land together with a friend or a relative; but others had to continue living in the farm because they had no choice and they had to face the situation.

Mr. Alfonso had a list with the names of all the families and where was supposed to move every settler. Our family had to go across the farm about an hour from where we lived. The place, because it was awful, was called '*the chambers*'. The house was very ugly and it was located in a totally bare ground, treeless, so hurricanes flew the ceiling every single year. There was no chance of breed animals, which was a source of life for the peasant, and it was far from the school and town to walk up to them, because we had to go through the whole farm. Besides, some streams blocked the passage in winter when they were overflowing, and in the paddocks there were many bogs, so it was almost impossible to walk on the sidewalks. Therefore, those who had no shoes were suffering much from food rot. During the whole winter we had foot fungus, and our feet were always inflamed from walking on the mudflats.

The people noticed years later that the government passed a law that farm owners having settlers for over two years in a single house, the settler could fight for the house and the lot where it is seating.

IN THE VALLEY

My father and my mother made a decision - after almost ten years of living on the farm, they no longer wanted to live there by setbacks with work and school for us, and there was no hope of prosperity.

We would neither have the river nor see the crabs coming to the house when the river was overflowing. We would not live in our loved house.

Our grandfather had died a few years ago, and he had left a legacy of about six hectares of land. There lived my father's brothers with their families. Concerning the property only half of the land was for crops and the rest was still a virgin mountain that had never been exploited. He had to share everything between the three brothers.

Before we left, almost all my mom's hens were dead due to the plague and there were only a few sick ones out there. My father had to sell part of the basic grains products because we needed to survive. In addition, they had to get rid of the cows they had, firstly because of need and secondly because we moving.

So, we reached *Agua Fría* valley. My dad made a small shelter to live in while preparing everything to settle better. The shelter was made of grass and *jaraguá*, and had bamboo beams. It only protected us from the sun, because when it rained our beds and everything else got wet. At least we moved in during the summer and it was dry. During Easter, we are located on one side of the terrain next to other neighbors. We could hear their family problems and we had to adapt to the change of life. On the other hand, my mother was pregnant again. The only advantage was that the school was close and we did not have to walk long distance to get there, we were in second grade.

By that time, the conflict between El Salvador and Honduras had already started. The President of our country was Fidel Sánchez Hernández, from the National Conciliation Party (PCN), a conservative party that had remained in power for many years manipulated by the military leadership of the country and that only advocated to the rich and to the United States.

It was 1969, commercial, diplomatic and political relations between El Salvador and Honduras were over and both countries had their troops already on its borders. Relations were resumed in 1984. Because of this, our country has nothing but scarce, no money and nothing to buy.

We had absolutely nothing to eat, not even a pound of beans or corn to make *tortillas*, we just had a little salt in the kitchen.

My mother sent us to the mountain to see if we found something like *chufles* – wild Salvatorian flower, wild vegetables and fruits. The paternal and maternal family helped us because they sometimes had some supplies like rice, corn and beans, especially my mom's siblings who were still single. They gave us some of corn and from time to time, we borrowed corn that would be payable when the harvest came.

In September of that year, a war between the two countries began and even where we lived the earth shook; we heard the bombs dropped by aircraft exploding in the battle lines, on the border. Meanwhile, my mother gave birth to a baby girl; she was the last sister we had.

At that time the Supply Regulating Institute (*IRA: Instituto Regulador de Abastecimiento*) existed in the country. I do not remember if it belonged to the government or to the rich, but the institute would buy basic grains to the banks - when the peasants paid debts to the bank with grains and hoarded them to sell to people when they were in crisis. Also they sold products abroad and the country was in need of buying, they imported although the products were not the same. Thus, during the war they brought from abroad yellow corn that came all torn to pieces and people even got sick when they ate it. In addition, they brought a bean they called monkey beans; when it was already cooked it felt slimy and people do not like to eat it, but there was no choice. The IRA had already sold the products produced in the country and had bought those products to be consumed, of course, at higher prices.

With what was gained in one working day, only one pound of beans could be bought and sometimes not even that, something that was not enough for the basic needs of the population, especially because families were formed by six or eight members, even more, and only the head of the family worked to support it. What he earned was not enough to buy beans or corn. People had to manage to survive, making use of natural resources on the field.

The media would tell people that the cause of the war was the victory of El Salvador on Honduras in the CONCACAF soccer qualifying for the World Cup in Mexico that would be played in 1970. It was a real taunt by United States.

This is a real shame for us Central Americans that in the past I have seen the jeopardy on TV when comes out the question when two countries in Latin America they got in a fight/war for a CONCACAF football game in 1968 to go for World Cup in 1970 to Mexico.

The reality is that: It was a General Treaty on Central American Economic Integration signed by Guatemala, Honduras, El Salvador, Nicaragua, and Costa Rica.

Central American Common Market, (CACM), In Spanish was called the" MERCOMUN". Putting these two countries in a war in the region this treaty wouldn't function and that's what Richard Nixon did with his administration in 1969 to keep the people down with it's dreams of development.

To destroy the treaty of getting ahead with the plans of John Kennedy; using the excuse of a soccer game.

Others said they were fighting for the Meanguera Islands, which are located in the Fonseca Gulf, a place where the three countries - El Salvador, Honduras and Nicaragua share maritime boundaries. The islands belong to El Salvador for geographical and historical reasons but according to some, they were proclaimed by Honduras. In addition, all its inhabitants are Salvadorans and are registered in that country. It must be understood that when the people does not accept a proposal this cannot be carried out. The truth is that the army of Honduras entered the islands, invaded them and mistreated people even killed some people. I remember what was reported in the news.

"The real truth" in some media, it was also said that the war started because of the treaty of "Alliance for Progress" that had prompted President John F. Kennedy in Costa Rica at that time. Kennedy wanted to get Central America out of the hole, after the loss of Cuba. People were really confused and the truth was that the whole problem would only affect the poor and peasant classes.

Finally, Fidel Sanchez Hernandez, President of El Salvador raised the warplanes five minutes ahead of the time that was ordered against to the brotherhood country and destroyed the military air force base of Toncontin, in Tegucigalpa, Honduras with its war planes. General Oswaldo Lopez Arellano, President of Honduras another puppet of the region.

Our army and planes came to Tegucigalpa, capital of Honduras, and destroyed the warplanes. The fighting continued on the borders between the two countries, the military combats of both countries every day. The treaty between them was canceled. The military, the rich and the United States did not care. They made a war between two puppets in the strip of the continent isthmus. What is certain is that the conflict led countries to an even more extreme poverty.

Richard Nixon in 1969 brought these two countries into war just because he wanted to break the relationship between the countries by all means - social, diplomatic, politics and diplomatic relations were gone. That way Kennedy's treaty is over to industrialize Central America and to bring more social and economic development to the region. Richard Nixon closed the doors to this treaty to happen.

On the other hand, there were many Salvadorans in Honduras since Maximiliano Hernández, general dictator and CIA representative made a coup to the current government in El Salvador in 1931. Maximiliano Hernández killed more than 30,000 farmers in the insurrection or rebellion in the west of the country in less than a week. In 1932, he sat in the presidential chair and there was so much repression, many Salvadorans left the country and went to Honduras in search of better horizons.

In Honduras lived, then, thousands of Salvadoran families trying to overcome with land, livestock and daily crops, and because of the ravages of war mentioned before there were more people migrating over there.

Honduras was deserted and Salvadorans were picking up even in the ravines of the region.

Many Salvadorans told they had no place to live or even families around. A large majority had to go to work in the banana plantations in Honduras, as the United Fruit Company, an American company that had its workers in slavery-like-conditions. There were snakes and tropical diseases, malaria was one of the most common, and all people were stripped-off their belongings, tortured by the Honduran military and even killed.

Finally, they had to abandon their few possessions and return to the country with nothing more than a basket with clothes in their hands - all the rest of their lives were lost, it had been left behind.

This was used as an excuse, but the truth is that it was a maneuver led by the United States. When it was signed in Costa Rica the treaty to industrialize Central America, it was called "Alliance for Progress". At that time it was known that President Kennedy had started to build some schools in Costa Rica and it was thought that, thanks to this treaty, years later all Central American countries were supposed to be industrialized.

In fact, it was signed to counteract the triumph of the Cuban revolution and avoid political disturbance in the Central American countries that constantly arose due to hunger and exploitation. However, some official sources said it would help to take them out of extreme poverty with more jobs, more development, more opportunities, and that would encourage the creation of a common market among these countries, which were considered brothers since they had been a single country until they were separated in the 1840s due to the interests of a few, "Creoles with their industry and land possession."

However, those who had wealth did not agree with this treaty. The rich from Honduras could not compete with the Salvadoran industries. Coffee growers and those in the sugar cane industry in El Salvador, those who had in Honduras tobacco industries and other agricultural industries, especially the United Fruit Company of the United States were impassioned.

The heart of this American transnational is in Honduras. It is one of the richest companies in the world and nowadays throughout Latin America. If I am not wrong, its first purchase was in 1913 when James Monroe was President.

The most important thing was that if this treaty was implemented, people would have a higher level of development, more studies and more comfort; they would wake up and would have more political awareness.

In order not to see certain things, they should instead be kept politically asleep and immersed in illiteracy, which meant a great weapon for the conservative sector.

At the beginning of 1969, Honduras began expatriate Salvadorans who were in its territory. Even though most already had laws in that country and they had papers, they were sent back to El Salvador and stripped-off all possessions, such as land, crops and livestock. They tortured, mistreated entire families, and went to El Salvador with nothing. In the radio and television's news and in newspapers, only that was commented. Mothers came crying because they had nowhere to start their homes again. In our valley about two families came and told us the vicissitudes they had gone through the last days in that country.

So, El Salvador began to do the same with the Hondurans who were in its territory, although there were not many Hondurans in our country as Salvadorans in Honduras.

By that time, Richard Nixon had assumed the United States presidency, and while carrying forward the war in Vietnam, he also ordered harder policies carried out in our region. Since then, the Organization of American States (OEA) could no longer do anything in The Haya (note that the United States does not take part, then, in this diplomatic body).

They were looking for destabilizing the relationship between countries, especially in relation to trade links, not to carry out the treaty, so they began the war. Salvadoran troops crossed the border and entered Honduran territory. They invaded around a third of that country. They killed opponent troops and even citizens. They reached the capital, Tegucigalpa, and destroyed Toncontín airport.

The war was fought by air and land, with heavy artillery. El Salvador lost three aircraft in combat and Honduras, seventeen.

I remember some time, at midnight, in which all the Salvadoran territory was alert and unlit so that the people were not detected. Honduran aircrafts arrived to bomb the capital and the Pacific ports but they were brought down with anti-aircraft.

Meanwhile, troops were starving at the battle lines. David Marroquín - a neighbor whom I will speak later and his brother had been in the army.

He told us that the experience had been very hard. He had seen many of his comrades fall next to him, pierced by bullets. They passed through villages abandoned by their inhabitants, where people had left the warehouses, shops, etc. Occasionally, they found some guy and if he opposed, they had to kill him; elderly and children's lives were respected but the towns were usually deserted. He also told us that when the helicopter did not come to throw them food, they killed a cow and put pieces of meat on their metal hats, with the heat of the sun the meat got cooked and they ate it. Her mother had gone to look for them till the front line.

Many people also became rich thanks to this war. As the troops advanced into the country, many Salvadorans freely crossed the border because there were no Customs Officers and the border crossing was not controlled. They went by trucks to loot shops, stores, white goods and agricultural products stores. They also killed many farmers in the area to steal their livestock.

When the war ended, Salvadorans were satisfied and happy because our country had won. It was celebrated with rockets and parties, but the reality was that we all had lost. The damage was great because the enmity between the two countries emerged. Even while we were at war and as Honduras was losing, it was said that Nicaragua was going to fight at its side and that Guatemala, however, would fight along with our country - there were four countries in conflict. We must be grateful that none of this happened.

Two cemeteries were made in El Salvador. One is located in a city called Aguilares, near my home town, and the other is in the east of the country where fallen soldiers were buried. In each grave there are sixteen veterans due to poverty.

The crisis took over our country; people did not have any for their daily sustenance. In rural areas, the situation was depressing; there was neither money nor grain commodities to buy. In marginalized neighborhoods the situation was alike; children walked naked and barefoot, asking for a penny to eat. The country was in extreme poverty just before the war, and after that, it wallowed in misery even more. There was no friendship at all nor did trade exist between us and our brotherly country.

This was one of the reasons why internal political problems arose in the next period during the seventies. There were many inevitable uprisings because poverty, hunger and exploitation had surpassed any limit. All peasants and workers sector echoed a new ideology which included the search for a structural change in the country.

Now I return to the story of our life after we left the farm. A few months before the war began the construction of a new school was finished, "Rural Mixed School, La Loma del Espino". One hectare terrain was donated by Dr. Fernando López. The building had three classrooms and pit latrine for boys and girls, but as there was no water, it was not septic. There was a space to play and one place where agricultural experiments could be carried out. The piece of land was part of the large farm that years later bought the landowner Mr. Vicente Escobar.

Again we had to carry grass. All students had to carry a handful of grass and plant it until all the ground was covered. The lower part was arranged to make threshing ground of vegetables such as radish, cabbage, tomatoes, etc., and to make agricultural practices because, as I said before, teachers gave student some theoretical introductions and practices regarding agriculture.

When classed started in1969, there were three teachers and each taught two grades. There were three grades in the morning until noon, and three in the afternoon until four in the afternoon, six days a week. Because teachers taught until sixth grade many had not to go to town or to other distant schools. As we already had to go to third grade, we had to go to this school, because the school in Agua Fría had only second grade at that time, with one teacher.

Teachers were friendlier and helped students.

I remember Mr. Manuel, whom we called Mr. Meme, because he liked being called that way. He was the Director and taught fifth and sixth grade. Mr. Mauricio taught third and fourth grade, and he was also a good person; and Mr. Julio taught first and second grade. Mr. Mauricio and Mr. Meme are still alive but Mr. Julio was killed during the war.

The Independence Day on September 15, was a big celebration. Parents and other people came to witness acts.

School was decorated with blue and white ornaments; pictures of dignitaries that supposedly free Central America from Spain "they

31

were already Spanish and Creole", cultural events took place such as folk dances, theatrical acts, etc. there was also a parade with all pupils dressed, of course, in blue and white; the flag rose while the National Anthem was sung with the right hand on our chest, besides, we salute and sang flag prayers.

To perform this civic celebration, several raffles and fundraisers must be done between parents because the Ministry of Education gave us nothing, the whole community effort was needed.

In addition, some students' moms sold bread with meat, stuffed tortillas, soft drinks and sweets for the school benefit. This was done for the Independence Day and for the farewell of the year, in early November, when graduations were carried out.

I also remember that years later, teachers changed a bit the way of teaching because the Ministry of Education said so, and we got a sports day - Thursday was the sports day, and we went to the soccer field. All grades came from morning to play; boys played football, girls played softball. We did those activities on the football field where Mr. Vicente would later built his huge mansion that was about half of the soccer field.

At that time, as we were bigger, at early summer after finishing school we went with my mother to other farms for coffee harvest. The first farm which started going every year was Tutultepeque situated in San Salvador department. My mom left my older sister in charge of my father and little brothers' food while she and the two biggest of us went to the harvest.

We had to walk a couple of hours to get the coffee plantations. I remember we received 38cents of a colon per arroba which were 25pounds, but as always, the heavy ones were altered and once again workers were robbed. They gave as a ration of two poorly made tortillas with some beans and salt. People did not like them much because corn was badly bruised, sometimes they were raw and a bit rough, sometimes there whole grains inside but as we were very hungry we had to eat them anyway.

Many poor people came from different places to work in these farms, and they had to sleep in sheds or coffee plantations in the open, where everyone used those places as bathrooms.

This farm was immensely large; there were many coffee plantations, sugar cane and cattle. They also had a lot of tractors for sugarcane because there were thousands of hectares to be planted every year, and tens of yoke of oxen for corn seeding and other tasks. During the cane and coffee season there were thousands of people that settled, but throughout the year there were a lot of people working too. For this reason, large farms were the best option because there was no shortage of work.

The coffee harvest owners hire about ten to twelve crews consisting of thirty laborers or families who were looking for work. There was a foreman in charge of controlling the work and that there was not a grain lying on the ground.

This work was based on an estimate of five arrobas cut per day, that is there was a payment calculated to be paid if five arrobas were cut during an eight-hour day, but usually people cut less than five arrobas, and rarely the coffee plantation was good and people worked more. They also had "the seventh" which was an additional equivalent to five cut arrobas the pawn got only if he did not miss a single day of work during the two weeks, which was the time between a payment and the other.

This farm belonged to a millionaire family in the country - the Bustamante.

They own four farms or haciendas in that place, "Tutultepeque" and "Tacachico" which were lands for sugarcane and "Las Marias" and "El Aguacate". In all these farms there was a foreman with settlers. They had electricity for lighting and mills to make the dough for tortillas and for agricultural machinery.

They also had phone line taken from the north trunk road that went through all the farms to communicate with employers.

Tutultepeque farm had two foremen, one for sugarcane and livestock and the other to take care of coffee plantations. There was also the administrator of the four farms. Payments were full parties, because all farms were paid there. People had to walk long distance to receive their payment, and they gathered. So payment was every two weeks; it began on a Saturday afternoon and did not end until Sunday dawn. Many had their businesses to sell food at night, others gambled money, some got drunk and usually ended in fights and some ended wounded, even killed.

A cousin of ours, named Juan, took care of Bustamante's Doberman pinscher. Our cousin's work was only taking care of the dogs and gardening. He was older than us and he told us he knew the mansions employers had in the capital and in some other even larger farms in the department of La Paz, which is in the central part of the country. I never met the owners. I worked several years there but they rarely went there and they never showed among workers; only clerks, foremen or managers knew them.

Years after the '70s, I had to work on these farms cutting sugar cane, cleaning cane fields and coffee plantations and cutting coffee. At that time, underage people (somebody who was under eighteen years) were paid the same as women - an established regular salary because many women went to work there doing cane or coffee plantations cleaning chores, and usually women worked in those plantations because they saved money by paying lower wages. At that time, they were paid 2.25 colon. The salary, not even a dollar a day was not enough for daily sustenance and with a weekly payment workers could buy neither a shirt nor pants. Shoes were even more expensive, so to get new clothes and shoes, people had to work during a whole season on the farm.

I also remember there were crews of 'miqueros'. The role of those 'miqueros' was to remove coffee plantations after the harvest. The work of the 'miqueros' consisted of removing shade to the coffee plantation because the coffee tree needs to have half shade; there must be neither excessive sunlight nor shadow for the production to be effective.

The 'miqueros' walked all day cutting unnecessary branches of trees which were lowered by rope to avoid damaging the coffee tree. Each 'miquero' had and assistant responsible for cutting branches and arrange them in the middle of the furrows. These workers often were accidentally injured or they fell from trees and sometimes even died. When they were just hurt, they were paid their average wage until recovered; if the pawn died because of falling from a high tree of the farm, they bought the box for burial and gave little money to the family of the deceased.

Some farms had a small first-aid kit with some bandages, aspirin, cotton and alcohol. Moreover, there was a person who could put serum and injections even though he was not graduated. However, they were not well prepared. When someone suffered serious injuries, they had to take him to the farm and then saddle a couple of horses so another man could move him to town where he could receive medical care. If the patient was seriously injured, he would be carried in a hammock. This was too hard because a dozen men should be gathered to carry him.

Usually, there was no ambulance in the villages so they had to call the Red Cross of the capital to send one to move the patient to a hospital. Patients sometimes died on the way.

Naturally, the coffee harvest occurred earlier in the lowlands of the country than in the volcanoes and summits because it is warmer, so the two elder brothers and my mom started our work on Tutultepeque farm and then moved to the San Salvador volcano to finish the season. Our prehistoric ancestors called this volcano Quezaltepeque that means "the hill of the quetzal" because in those days there were a lot quetzal on the volcano, and even today some of them can be seen at the peak, and there is still much monkey. In this area there are many farms and production is much better than in the lowlands because the weather is suitable for coffee production. We went there for the season and returned here when it ended.

I remember the first farm we went to was called "El Carmen". Cordova Alvarez still owned the farm. He has a chain of farms in the volcano and down in the shallows of the country where they have coffee processing plants. There were three plants of this type around my village. The Álvarez Cordova is one of the fourteen richest families in the country. They have billions of dollars because they are major coffee exporters. It was difficult to get work on these farms because many of the people who went there either knew somebody or have connections. Thanks to some common friends of my family and the owner we got numbers and my mother, one of my brothers and I went there.

The gang, as I said before, consists of thirty numbers. The farms were trying to avoid putting "added" to the crew numbers. The assistant was a laborer or pawn who worked in the gang unofficially, that is, somebody who did not receive his payment directly. The assistant's payment was made by a number pay; the representative of the number received the payment together with the assistant's, who then received the corresponding part. Thus the hacienda avoided paying the assistant the seventh, holidays and food. He only got sacks to put coffee in and to sleep in them.

Regularly, people would not get the appropriate payment. They had to talk with the clerks because the accounts were different in the forms and arrobas were missing. All workers wrote down their daily arrobas, but the same thing always happened.

On many farms, the coffee was weighed on a scale, but it was altered. It only pointed full and half arrobas, if half a pound was needed for another half arroba, then, that half arroba did not count. In other farms the coffee was measured with a one and a half meter ruler that was numbered about six inches. They put it into the coffee bag to the bottom, the unlawful things was that the bags were thirty inches in diameter, and they did not accept another type of bag because the bag had their label, and if one measured eight arrobas with that rule in one of those bags it possibly weighed from eleven to twelve arrobas in the scales. So after they finished weighing or measuring they made the reweighed to calculate what they were not taking into account and that meant an extra benefit for them.

I also remember that in this finca or farm there was only one shed to sleep. It only had tile roof and a wall on one side which was falling. The floor was made of brick, and about two hundred people slept there. There were people who did not have place to sleep under this roof, and they went to sleep under the coffee plantations. The settlers' houses also were filled with people. There was nowhere to cook, so some cooked in the ground.

Due to the difference between the climate of the lowlands and the area of the volcano, people got sick with flu - the epidemic and the cough infected everyone. In the volcanoes there are no streams or water springs; water was accumulated in huge tanks during the rainy season. Water tanks reaches houses through gutters. Mostly tanks do not have a roof to cover them and people do not put chlorine in them, then water contaminates, turns yellow and algae appear.

I remember that a whole family died because a slug entered the pot of beans that had been left on the floor.

While they were working, the slug fell into the pot. In the afternoon they came back and ate beans, and then died.

The foremen, clerks and other residents who already have a certain economic level on these farms also took advantage in these seasons. Some owned their small grocery and vegetable stores, outsiders sold them at high prices - a tomato or onion cost three or four times more than in the town.

The foreman had a shop handled by his wife and children; they distrusted at high prices products such as butter, oil, grains, vegetables, etc., until the payment date. Moreover, the lady sold tortillas to customers. I remember that at that time, when we were back on the farm and already had dinner at seven in the evening, my brother and I, we were thirteen and fourteen years, asked my mom for a dime each to go to see Combat - Germans against the Americans. The foreman had in his home a black and white thirteen-inch TV, and as we loved watching that show, we paid a dime to the owners and we watched the combat through the window with other outsiders boys like us. At that time only few people had a TV and we believed that those images we watched were true. They also had a small ballroom and during weekends musicians played the marimba and other instruments. They played waltz, which at that time were still heard and people loved to dance.

After summer, we went back to school. It was 1972, presidential elections approached and teachers only talked about that. They belonged to the National Opposition Union (UNO), which had been formed by the union of three parties and it represented the working classes.

In the afternoon a young man came to talk with them in the shadow of a fig tree in the school. This young man named Roberto was a college student. By then, he was already a militant and spoke about the steps the student movement was giving. Years later, he was the first to become a revolutionary and guerrilla in our place. Teachers loved him, and a large rock that was in the school it was painted the emblem of the UNO for the community to see it when walking to the town.

In March of the same year the ratings took place and they were won by the UNO with engineer José Napoleón Duarte as candidate for president and Doctor Guillermo Manuel Ungo for vice president were conducted. However, the National Conciliation Party (PCN) - the conservative party of the rich, took the win.

Colonel Arturo Molina, who was the leader of the PCN, was president; as always, colonels and generals became presidents, "*The puppets*".

I also remember that the PCN paid trucks that went to rural areas to find people to vote; in that way they won votes. At that time, the entire government leaders were the military, as well as military representatives of ministries and the diplomatic corps. When we heard in the news any comment from a ministry it was always said that the general or colonel so-and-so... All had some bone thrown to them rich. Of course you should have money to study at military school in "Gerardo Barrios" and the poor were only private or corporal; they did not become superior officer; they rarely became sergeants.

As we know, from that moment onwards people no longer believed in voting. That was when people took to the streets to protest against the Conservative Party and the rich - catches, tortures and against the people began. The National Guard and the Treasury Police (PH) began to terrorize nationwide.

The National Guard was fathered by General Maximiliano Hernández in the days when the dictator was president. He hired Germans to come and let in El Salvador a copy of what Hitler had founded in his country. That is why their uniforms and discipline resembled the German military. In his helmet or cap they had the Salvadoran flag on one side and the Germany flag on the other. It was the most frightening body of the country. Then there was the Treasury Police, which was similar. The role of the two bodies was to humiliate peasants.

Shortly after, college students and teachers launched a nationwide strike. The strike took place throughout the country. Teachers were organized in the National Association of Educators of El Salvador (ANDES); students with their student movement.

Teachers demanded better wages and better living conditions; students expected better government facilities. For example: for the study and demanded freedom for political prisoners (who were already in prisons), freedom of expression and freedom of organization.

In our school there were no classes for about two weeks. Then the Ministry of Education sent other teachers who might not have a degree, but they belonged to ORDEN, the reactionary party that years later collaborated with the Death Squads. These teachers were unfriendly with people and with students. People did not want them because they also instilled the student political ideologies that were contrary to the interests of the poor, "reactionary, anti-revolutionary therapy."

Old teachers came to school and sat under the fig bark that was in the play area. They had grown a beard and were there as a form of protest. The country people gave them to eat during the day and offered them their moral support. After about a month and a half, women, men and children from the valley could not stand that situation and went to school to protest, saying "We want the old teachers! The New let them go! ". Days later, after a strong repression that took place in the cities against students and teachers, the issue died down, and some old teachers returned to their schools.

Later, José Napoleón Duarte, with some military support, spoke on the radio asking people to support a coup in the country, but the maneuver failed and Duarte was imprisoned and tortured in clandestine prisons. He was left blind in one eye and they cut off a finger. Then, he was expatriated and exiled to Venezuela.

A WOMAN FROM THE
COMMUNITY

María Romelia Orellana. We will always remember this woman, whom all valleys and villages loved; she died in 1976.

I want to add a few lines about a great lady, someone who brought so much to our community – Ms. María Orellana, "a great midwife."

We know she received her degree in recognition of midwife in the Health Unit of Quezaltepeque City, and although her husband, Mr. Francisco Flores, provided little data (due to his advanced age), it was very relevant. Mr. Francisco Flores told us that in war days, while Death Squads and the military made a general search in the area looking for weapons and youth to kill or recruit them, they searched his home and took the title of Ms. María as well as her photos and other documents her husband kept.

Ms. María was a rather tall lady, very sociable and talkative, she was happy almost all the time though she felt worried inside her. Her family was very Catholic; she did not show proud to anyone and thus was very popular. Although she did not go to school because there were no rural schools at the time, she showed great intelligence.

When I was a little boy, my mother took me to town and sometimes we met her on the trip, walking on foot. She talked to my mom about some work that had some night or days before in a lady's house in the valley or the surrounding villages. I remember some time that one of our neighbor had given birth a few days before, and when Ms. María met my mom she asked: "Well, and... blew that hill?", so I could not understand because I was too young, barely a teenager. This lady helped almost all women in all these valleys when it was about pregnancy, because the country conditions were extremely underdeveloped at the time regarding transportation and it was not easy to enter a hospital.

Mr. Francisco told us that sometimes he had to carry her on his mule to other valleys away, and that to arrive there they had to cross rivers and streams in those mountainous areas, sometimes at night, under the rain, crossing mudflats formed on the sidewalks.

At that time the maternity hospital was new, and was the only hospital in the country that attended those cases. The Social Security Institute of El Salvador (ISSS) was for industries employees; only a few workers and middle-class people went there, but rural could not. Maternity hospital had no capacity for many patients and full almost all the time because the turnout was too much; sometimes they had no bed to give birth in. Rural people usually did not dare to bring their women to give birth to this hospital because they often were rejected; they told them that there was no room, and because money was needed, but at the time there was no time, neither money nor a means of transport.

In my home village, there is still the hermitage that was considered the center of the community, about two blocks from the school. Opposite there is a fig tree, and from it hung a piece of rail - when there was a wounded or sick person, someone went and beat it so that neighbors knew there was an emergency. When there were ten or twelve men together, they took the patient home in a hammock and led him to the town. The streets were stony and there could be so much mud, so it took several hours to reach the town.

Then, in the city of Quezaltepeque – it was already a *city*, they had their small clinic, though sometimes there was no doctor, no ambulance and they had to call the Red Cross of San Salvador.

As I said before, the Red Cross picked up the patient and took him to the hospital for medical care, but it was not strange that the patient would die halfway.

In view of these setbacks, country people usually did not take their women to health centers like that. Ms. María Orellana was the *midwife;* she was called that way. No matter how far it was, the time or climate, when a peasant came asking for her help, she went with her oil lamp for those bogs to help the woman, and did not accept to be paid except for a donation if the person had something to give.

She assisted at least ninety percent of all pregnancies in the area. She was a real expert, despite her background. Although the patient was having trouble giving birth because the baby was in a bad position, due to her intelligence, her wisdom and her beautiful hands she managed to do it well. My mother had eight pregnancies, and this lady was present in each of them, including the writer of these lines birth, and I say this because it is a great honor.

None of the women assisted by her had to undergo the Cesarean section in giving birth; nowadays, in the modern world, with all the technology that exists, undergoing through the cesarean section is used whenever a birth becomes complicated.

My friend Juan Ovidio Orellana, one of her sons, has helped me get this really important data for me.

Ms. Maria Orellana died at age of fifty two. I do not remember the exact date, but it was in 1976. She left eleven children, including two twins who were still teenagers. Our family attended her funeral; there were a lot of people who accompanied her until the last moment of the funeral procession. I remember all the women of the valley and the villages around wept with pain with the death of this great lady, and nowadays they still remember her. The procession was from the valley to the village, about eight kilometers distance on foot. Four men carried her remains in a box, and a great multitude (the bigger I saw in my life in the valley) accompanied them and prayed while all women were crying the loss of this great lady.

Juan Ovidio Orellana told me some things related to María's illness and death. He says her family took her to Rosales Hospital, where they often helped very poor people, but they did not find her any disease. Then, after twenty days she was taken to another hospital called San Rafael located in Santa Tecla city. Unfortunately, after fifteen days, they haven't founD anything. There, however, they gave the family a reference for her to be admitted in Santa Ana hospital, called San Juan de Dios. As they found nothing there, she was discharged.

"And this is how we could not detect my mother's illness" my friend Ovidio told me. She felt very rare symptom and had a severe stomach ache. We did not believe in witchcraft, but after visiting three hospitals we had to think about something else. By chance, there was an old woman in the city of Quezaltepeque that was smart and knew about hexes. When we got to know about her existence, continued Ovidio, we went to ask her for help to cure our mother. Once we arrived at her home, she said, "If you had brought her yesterday, I would have paid attention to her. Today I would not". She continued, "I know you do not believe in these things, but somebody had put a hex on her." A lady named Inés López who exercised the same 'profession' was suspected to have done it because of envy and selfishness; mostly it happens in those cases.

Her husband, Mr. Francisco Flores, knew how to respect the memory of Ms. María Orellana, because she was his dear wife and mother of his children as well as the privileges she had gained in the community. Ms. María left a significant mark, thanks to the love she sows among the people of the valleys and surrounding villages. Nowadays people have her in their memories. Where a woman and a child struggle with death, many people still mutters wishing her presence with her title of *"midwife"*.

Mother

You, mother, who embrace the last dream
In the twilight shadows, with the star of the night;
You call her in the dark for a little heat.
Proud, she arrives; loving, without reproach.
Who gave you the light? Who gave you the sun?
If, by force, lost, she no longer seems who is...
If the pain of a mother as soon has been lost,
Why many believe you, in the world, insignificant,
To have male chauvinism, including up the surname?
Why, if you're the life of an infant,
You have lost the privilege and last name?
And you are the mother of all; no one else has felt it.
Mother, owner of pain and lost tears,
I name you in my adventure... I can no longer exclaim...
What I feel in my heart I need in life.
Now, it is difficult I mutter because of society.
Who holds you in your bed?
With freshness, while you weep and groan,
She kisses you; she gives you a smile...
And makes your sleep deep and sublime.

AT SCHOOL

Another year ended. We, the three eldest, finished sixth grade - the biggest requirement to work as a laborer in a company. Meanwhile, the three smaller ones were still in school.

Mr. Meme, the director, summoned my parents. The three of us had been the best students in all grades during school time. My sister got the first place; my older brother the second place; and I got the third place. Two other students who had obtained the fourth and fifth place were from third, fourth, fifth and sixth grade.

My sister was very smart. She participated in theatrical and cultural plays when there were school events, and she has always been the best. My older brother and I did things with wood - we learned it from our father, the head of the house, how to make yokes, plows in small, and we presented those things at school.

Our parents were very proud of us.

When they went to the meeting with Mr. Meme, he told them we should not end our study right there, and he asked them to make efforts to send us to continue studying, but my parents were of great the poverty that they could not afford further education for us in town.

My brother and I still walked barefoot. We had no shoes. In seventh grade schools upwards, barefoot students were not accepted.

That end of the year we went with my mother to the coffee harvest to the finca we had already gone the previous year, "El Carmen", while my sister stayed again at home to care our younger siblings, to cook food for them and my father.

We work for three or four fortnights. I remember they paid 58cents per cut arroba. When we cut the coffee, my mom told us, "This time, you are going to wear shoes, after the season."

In February of that year we returned home. When we arrived, my mother told my brother and me, "Let's go to town to buy shoes" and we did it. My brother and I were so happy and excited about the shoes that we went forward, towards the town. Halfway we waited for my mother who was not coming, and then we returned after a couple of hours.

To our surprise, when we returned we got to know that our mother had a pain and had decided to stay in her mother's house. We found a lot of men including my dad carrying her in a hammock. Because of the force she had done in the coffee harvest her hernia exploded. She was almost dying but she reached the hospital and recovered after the surgery. She was taken in the Rosales Hospital, which is the general hospital in the country. That was because she had somebody who was a godfather who worked there in the hospital; otherwise, maybe she would have died.

She was there for a month because the problem was delicate.

During that time, the wife of my dad's brother came home to cook for us. All the money earned in the harvest was spent on healing of my mom and there were no shoes that year. We continued going barefoot to school, and we waited what the next year would hold.

I remember the early days at school when we were taught this first stanza:

Hear how gaily the bell,
In this school sounds,
She calls us with its ringing,
Always saying 'ding-a-ling'

La Loma Del Espino School, today.
Eventually, many repairs and renovations were made.

Opposite there is an area where we put into
practice agricultural work and where men played
football and females practiced softball.

Girls wearing typical clothes because they
perform dances of our *Cuscatleca* land.

A small act of our rural schools - September 15,
El Salvador Independence Day.

I studied the last four years in this school, traditionally known as the "Mixed Rural School of *La Loma Del Espino* village." So called because it was located there; however, this place has its own history. *La Loma del Espino* was a village in *"El Cantón de las Mercedes"*. It is said that a woman named Mercedes, belonging to a family of Spanish colonizers or Spaniards Creoles had this great land that stretched from my village to the Lempa River. It was a tract of land of many kilometers away within my department. Note that in this place there was not a school until 1968 when it was founded.

The first appointed teacher to work at this place was Manuel Figueroa Bonilla. Then a second teacher came named Mauricio Enrique Canales. Together, they undertook the noble work of teaching and instructing children in this beloved place.

At first, they encountered many obstacles to carry out their noble task; one of them was how to create a school center to resolve this situation. For that reason they began to do their work in a place known as "La Ermita" which was inadequate because it was a religious center. It was a small church where people go to tell God their prayers. They worked there for a while but after some time the attendance of children who wanted to study become too big. So they realized it would not be possible to stay there. Some ideas for planning the construction of a proper school center that meet certain conditions arose.

To carry out this idea they should gather all parents and tell them.

They were lucky, after a few days the meeting took place and parents supported the idea. Parents, students and teachers were organized. The work plan was to conduct activities to raise money for the purpose they had in mind. Raffles, dances, field trips were made; in short, many things. Finally, in less time than expected, they started the construction of the school center. The López Dueñas family donated the site and the school is still there.

It is noteworthy that this achievement was possible, thanks to the teachers' efforts, they were the promoters. Parents and students joined them because neither the government nor the Ministry of Education provided fund to achieve this work.

I also want to mention an American that contributed to build the school center. This man's name was Lloyd Radinton; he came from

Chicago, Illinois and was a bricklayer. He worked closely with people, other construction workers and peasants.

Thus, he spontaneously made his contribution to make this work. We still remember him; he was about thirty five years old, very tall, blond and cheerful. He liked to talk with students while practicing his Spanish. Since in our country people are shorter, we saw him even taller. To honor him, a bronze plaque with his name was put in the front of our school.

In this way, teachers achieved their dream about the school, and were happy with the achievement. Of course, it had not been easy to conclude such a great feat. Parents and students were amazed and happy because they could have a school and they felt confident that the work was finished.

However, teachers still saw that there were essential things ahead, and continued with some other school arrangements to make it look prettier. Among some other things, they painted and planted fruit trees within the site and they constantly took care of them. When spring came, we brought grass to have a property ground where sports and other recreational activities would take place.

In addition, teachers planted *maquilishuat* trees. This tree is one of our two national trees. Colloquially, we call it *maquilihue*. The other tree that represents our country is the *balsam*, but it is more difficult to grow in the lowlands of the country because the weather is very hot; however, it grows a lot in the volcanoes area. The *balsam* is a medicinal tree. Its resin is used to make creams, ointments and other things. The seed is also used to make a great variety of medicines. Many agricultural practices were also carried out at school.

Teachers included in the teaching plan of Genetic Study of Plants. We had to carry plants with roots to study them, and in an area of the site we began to make a series of threshing soil for vegetable crops such as cabbage, tomato, onion, cucumber, radish, eggplant, corn, lettuce, green beans, beans, etc. This was done during the winter as it was the rainy weather. We were organized in groups of three or four students to work in a threshing floor and were assigned the plant we would grow that year. It was very beautiful to see the piece of land all planted with vegetables.

For us it was a moment of relaxation and joy when we had agricultural lessons outside the school building. He had to weed, fertilize and prepare the land. We also had to discuss the problems and try to solve them. Of course, the teachers were always there since they graded this activity.

When we got the crop, we made a small celebration and exchange products. Given the area where we lived, it was necessary to learn the peasant farming system as it was a tool for us, children of small farmers or peasants who fought for their crops.

Teachers also organized a kind of craft lessons which were then explained. Some of us presented paintings, works linked to our ancestors' art, wooden objects like small yokes for oxen, band saw-cut maps, puzzles, animals made of wood and clay objects. Girls made cloth embroideries that represented the beauties of our *cuscatleca* earth as bouquets with coffee leaves and ripe beans, peasant houses with tile and mud roof, flowers of this land, etc. The atmosphere was harmonious and it strengthened the value of our culture within the student social life.

My older sister was very good for theater plays and folk dances. She was always the best at school and this merit appeared in her notes by the end of the school year.

Remember the times I spent in that school, sometimes gives me joy and then I would like to relive those moments. For instance when we played soccer with peers, ran to each other a game we called "free play" and the one who better ran won, the marble, with the spinning top game and we had spare time for the yo-yo and cup-and-ball.

There were many students who were unscrupulous in games; others were fair and honest. I remember a fellow named Santos, alias Polín. This boy always wanted to take advantage when it comes to games and as sometimes we bet five or ten cents, whether it was cup-and-ball or spinning top game, this boy became very restless. During the break he liked going to other classrooms to drink other students' water or juices. They took from their bags whatever they had brought to eat or drink, and consumed it. It was not just him; there were many other students who did the same. I remember him saying, "I am already thirsty, I'll go and see if I get something" and he went into the classroom, and after he left someone without water, he returned satisfied. He was naughty and he enjoyed disturbing others students or fight with them all the time.

In addition, he and other students bothered and fought with girls if they did not allow the boys to copy from them during monthly exams. They were engaged in perversity, but they were bitterly punished as well. Teachers called their parents to school and made them see how their children behave.

Once, some students created a way to hurt birds, especially the *torogoz* or turquoise-browed motmot, which is very quiet and peaceful - the national bird of El Salvador. It is a splendid bird with brightly colored feathers that gleam with sunlight. It is from the family of Guatemalan Quetzal.

Its body is about nine inches and it has a very long tail formed by three long silky tip feathers. This bird makes its nest in the cliffs, walls, etc. Nests are caves in the earth of three or four inches in diameter and a foot or two of depth. They make them that way to protect them from snakes that eat their eggs or chicks.

These students then had begun to cover the caves with stones. Obviously, the birds died together with their eggs or chicks.

When the teachers heard that, they told the students to respect the national bird and if they knew that these things happened again, they would punish them very hard.

On the way to their homes, many children covered the birds' nests built on the vertical cliffs of white earth or volcanic ash.

Other students reported this to their teachers, and they punished the naughty students and made them know they were collaborating with the destruction of the country's wildlife.

In El Salvador, when I was growing up, when the teacher had to punish a student she used a stick. Every teacher had one, thick as a finger, about three feet or ninety centimeters long. With that stick she punished the student with two or more hits on the thighs or in the back below the knee. The number of strokes the students received depended on what they deserved according to what they had done. Of course that was legal in the country.

In other schools there were teachers who were a little wilder - they hit the student with the edge of the thick and heavy rule.

Furthermore, all teachers named their clubs. My teacher called his stick '*rasquincito*'. So when a student committed an offense, the teacher would say, "Now you won two or three strokes with '*rasquincito*'" and called him. That happened often in school. Sometimes the whole class went through *'rasquincito'* because maybe we didn't make the homework or something else, or we all misbehaved. Our legs became purple because of the lashes, so when there was a threat that if we did not do something, we would be hit by *'rasquincito'*, we did it right away, because the threat then was fulfilled.

Many older students who were eighteen years old, sometimes wanted to reveal against teachers and to fight them because they would no longer tolerate being punished and sometimes some problems arose because of this. But there were also parents who had received complaints about the bad behavior of their children, and they told teachers they could punish them harder because they were dumb and wicked, and they would not straighten out.

Some parents, however, complaint about punishments. The teachers said that if the children misbehaved, then parents should correct them at their homes or they should not send them to school. Mr. Meme, as the school principal, was the one who spoke to the parents.

I do not know how teachers managed to raise funds to celebrate the anniversary of our school. I remember that day there was a tournament in the community soccer field, several teams from the surrounding areas were invited and we played each other a trophy. People from those places came to see who the winner was. In addition, ring races were made because at that time there were many horses in the area. Everybody liked to see who would win the best bands and the best prizes. *Piñatas* were blown out for children and there were soft drinks and sweets.

There were also artistic events. *'Los Madrugadores Del Chiltaco'''* sang. It was a group formed by the students who played acoustic instruments. Representations of our ancestors and comedy acts were performed.

All of us enjoyed the sack race. It consisted of running and passing obstacles along a path within a bag and jumping like a kangaroo and carrying a spoon in the mouth with an egg in it. When you reach the goal, you have to eat an orange as quickly as possible and burst a bag. The winner is the one who finish it first.

In brief, students felt very excited, people had fun and spent really great moments. Everything was organized by teachers to keep the memory of the beginnings of our school.

Another big party was the traditional celebration of Children's Day. When we celebrated it, our peers performed unequalled acts. They made things in wood such as carts with oxen, a plow with oxen plowing the land and horses carrying two water jugs. In addition, there were exposed paintings on wood or cardboard where the history and the beauties of the country were represented. There were also theatrical plays, music and folk dancing like the dancing called '*El Carbonero*' which is considered the second hymn of El Salvador.

The Race Day was also a date to celebrate - the day when people say the liar of Christopher Columbus discovered America, though in fact, it was Américo Vespucio - another Italian, who got up earlier than he who discovered the continent. That day was also a public holiday in our country but it did not attract people. We knew nothing, so we were taken up with lies, because the mere reality is that in this land there was already a great civilization that lasted for thousands of years - the Maya empire.

We also celebrate the Independence Day on September 15, 1821. The love we felt for our country and heroes is indescribable. Anyone would wonder if we really loved our homeland or if we were totally deceived by the system arbitrariness but the fact was that we had to wear in blue and white and went to school and celebrate.

Celebrations were made in commemoration of our heroes. Their pictures were put on the wall and their names were mentioned by their achievement of 'free our countries'. 'The blue flag is raised and the national anthem is sung with the hand on our chest, with the sight on José Matías Delgado and the Aguilar brothers. However, it is painful to see our history after we realized the whole truth.

Our national anthem is very nice. In my opinion, it is the third best national anthem in the world as far as its lyrics and music is concerned. It was written by Juan Aberle and José Simeón Cañas. It speaks of the beauties, traditions, cultures and everyday works of the country. We also have the Flag Prayer, which names the beauties of the country, its volcanoes, lakes, beaches, crafts, traditions and culture, and of course, the daily dedication to work of its people.

It was said by those who were our heroes and those who gave the country independence – independence for them, a few, because they were the owners of the land. They were never taught who the oppressors and chiefs of our people were. They did not tell us about the great idealists of the country who were killed as Farabundo Martí, Feliciano Ama, Cayetano Carpio and Juan Chacón either. Going further back in history, in the previous century there was a man, Anastasio Aquino - the first rebel Indian in our country who in 1833 fought against the Spanish armies to free his people from slavery subjected to by Spain and Creoles. He was killed after taking power in the country; he remained in the memory of all the people of *Cuscatleca* land.

At that time, the field conditions were extremely underdeveloped and the streets were too rocky and muddy, so the horses had trouble passing through them. Just four by four jeeps dared to go there, but they also got stuck in the rocky and heavy clay land. Teachers also had to make use of that street, they arrived in a pickup truck that took them every day and one of them even had a motorcycle in which he carried the others in turns in that damaged street. Teachers then decided to organize people in order to repair it.

In addition, they thought of the need for some kind of medical care and asked the Health Unit of Quezaltepeque a first-aid kit containing basic things and medications to treat common low gravity illnesses. But there was no response from the Ministry of Health or from the village clinic. Health requests were never heard by the government.

In countries like El Salvador - a tropical country, epidemics are very common, especially during rainfall time. Diseases attacked mostly young people. Water consumed in these areas is from streams and contains many bacteria. In the rural areas of El Salvador there was no child who had not been infected with worms; I suffered from them on many occasions. Due to that, other diseases attacked children's life. Dengue and cholera were really serious illnesses.

The Health Ministry has never been concerned, so far, to have clinics in these villages, in these rural areas where it is estimated that lives roughly half the population. As we know, in these third world countries, peasant life is very common and although they live without water, without electricity and without forms of communication, people often lead a more natural, relaxed and peaceful life.

In those ancient times, as I said before, a dozen men had to gather to carry ill patients in a hammock, those who could not be attended in the villages. Many died while waiting for an ambulance or on their way to San Salvador, as it happened to my uncle Andrés, my mother's brother. After work, he felt sick, so they looked for people to take him in a hammock to the village that was about eight kilometers away. In the village there was no ambulance, they called one to come to San Salvador to move him but when they were halfway toward San Salvador my uncle died. Many people died the same way across the country. My uncle was twenty six; he was single and had more chances than us, when we were in need he was there to help us. For this reason we really noticed his absence. And so it should be noted that in our country we also have people who offered themselves when volunteers are needed, especially when it comes to these cases.

So they organized all parents to see if there were potential human resources available for the plan: start doing, as always, dances and raffles to raise funds because they had not obtained the necessary support from the mayor or from the Health Ministry.

So they set to work bringing together parents and others in order to fix the street and get a well-stocked medicine first-aid kit.

So teachers insisted on the subject telling all students that parents should not miss meetings because there were plans to have a small first-aid kit and a possible medical care in the village, for this reason they needed the support of the entire community. Besides, they talked about the need to work to repair the street. It was amazing, but true: when these meetings were held, they had to gather outside the classroom and many times because there were too many people. Though some parents did not have their children in the school they were interested in the street. When parents could not attend the meetings they sent the older children to know what had been discussed.

Dozens of people cooperated with the activities carried out to raise funds, such as dances, raffles and selling of homemade food prepared by the ladies. These events were very popular among the village, and there was always a little place where anyone could do something. Many young people competed in horseback ring races. I remember girls participated as queens carrying a gift for each runner; they helped their mothers to cook and had fun at dancing time. Jokes, stories, anecdotes and poems, piñatas, tape horse races.

The peasants came with their horses and began to earn the sashes and gifts the queens had, Queens were mostly young girls from school.

When one could catch a tape with the pencil or tip his holds in his hand while galloping on his horse, he won a gift and a sash that the Queen herself took off to give it to the winner. A bouquet of roses, carnations and izote flower (this last one is the national flower of the country) was given.

There were dozens of gifts of that kind. Of course, the participant had to pay to enter the contest.

Ladies, mothers of students, played a good role in these events: selling traditional foods such as stuffed tortillas, pupusas (the main traditional dish of El Salvador), and breads stuffed with chicken, stuffed peppers and fried yucca with sauces and fresh vegetables. They also prepared fried pies: they were made with corn flour dough, folded, filled with ground beef or chicken and vegetables, and then fried in a pan. In addition, they served lemonade, almond milk drink of various flavors and other homemade and very healthy drinks with ice. The aim was always to raise money to improve the school.

There were football tournaments in which between twelve and sixteen teams took part. In this case they also earned a trophy and the money they paid for admission was destined to school too.

And finally dancing - girls do not have to purchase a ticket so there was even more public. The money paid by the gentlemen was also to the school benefit. We enjoyed these parties. People came from all parts of the area and appreciate the peculiarity of our school; it was unique compared with the surrounding valleys.

Teachers also created 'The amateur's time'; in this event we made different presentations of art, we sang and played with guitars and other instruments, recited poems, told stories, allegorical stories, anecdotes and fables, we shared jokes and riddles. Through that we discovered our artistic qualities and we developed socially and culturally.

As part of the same event, we traveled to Sucio River to swim.

We practiced different styles, competed with the schools in the city and other places. Fortunately, we also achieved good places in school competitions. These competitions were held in a resort called "La Toma' in Quezaltepeque", where there are swimming pools. People took advantage of the trip to the river; they got crabs in the caves, under the rocks and in giant tree roots. Many of us were very good at that, also in fishing bream and other fishes.

You can be certain that these ideas and actions were an initiative of the teachers who had no support from the Ministry of Education, the municipal government or any other government entity, neither from the councilor. There was no one who promoted or directed such a thing. Town councilors, even if they wanted, couldn't do anything: they were freeze and alienated by the system in the country.

Everything was done with the cooperation of parents. Meetings were organized for parents to give a small financial contribution (as it was very little what they could give). The most productive thing was when teachers organized dances made in the same school where youth went to dance, made raffles and gave them to student for selling. Teachers formed a board, membered by parents, both men and women, who were responsible for fundraising. Ladies organized everything related to food for the events. Men were in charge of sports and dances. Everyone participated. It was a duel against poverty, a struggle to bring up their children in school.

And finally we had a better first-aid kit, it was a "mini clinic," not only for students, it was also for parents who came with their sick children that requires attention. There was nurse who generally offered her time even though she hardly gets paid. At the same time, they organized some mothers and other volunteers to vaccinate and treat patients with minor problems such as children with diarrhea, colds, fever or vomiting, and, of course, adults with injuries and other minor illness. They achieved a healthier community with the cooperation of some young girls volunteer from the valley. Others worked in repairing the street leading to town where farmers and students went.

We also managed to save money for a few trips to the pleasure grounds of the country. We went to 'La Puerta del Diablo' (Evil's Door), 'Los Planes de Renderos', the Labyrinth (where you get lost) and to the zoo.

During the time I was in school, we had two trips in a hired and extremely beautiful two buses (I cannot forget them) with some parents, we went to beaches and to Boquerón volcano. We saw birds of many colors that do not exist in the lower areas of the country. After the trip, the teachers asked us to do an analysis of what we've seen in a chronological narrative of the journey.

Everyone admired the school, so beautiful and full of charm, it attracted the entire community atmosphere that surrounded it. It was like this that we had a better school and better desks.

At first we had seats donated by churches, eventually, we got a lot of individual desk. They had a stand to support the pen and a drawer below to store the supplies.

We were extremely happy that we had the desks, which we always dreamed of. Students who liked to copy answers or notes from others could no longer do that, it made us even happier. However, the last classroom does not have desks yet. When we finally got them, we also got better blackboards and better health services.

We made a great Salvadoran coat and a large national flag that was raised during our Independence Day.

The same flag in his white stripe says "God Union Freedom," though we are far from that...

As mentioned previously, at that time the country's teachers had to manage to make money to continue working for the student and take him forward. The Ministry of Education and the government only contributed materials; teachers had to teach anything that was against the conservative system. Sometimes they sent advisers who sat in classes and observed. During break time they asked students how the teaching went and they looked over our books.

Before these agents or advisers arrived, teachers tells us we should have a tidy school, property well-maintained, to be very neat in our notebooks and books well-kept so that the teachers will have a good image and us too.

Teachers sent later from the Conservative Party, just spread adversary politics that favors the government, the military, the rich landowners and the oligarchs. By fueling all this internal structure of the country they became a threat to the community. They began with adolescent students, asking them if any of their relatives, friends or acquaintances were involved in political issues. They worked for the oppressive system. They were sent to the cantons, valleys, villages, etc., to find out how the student organization functioned in schools, and if they did not like something, they report it to the town and that teacher gone.

Our old teachers told us why we lived like that in the Salvadoran communities, especially in rural areas where peasant people used to be poorer, and, of course, where families tended to be larger. For example, most students from sixth to ninth grade walked barefoot. Only few students began with shoes, but then their parents could no longer buy another pair so they also went barefoot. The other children were teasing and said, "Your shoemaker has died." Students were embarrassed to go to school without shoes. More so as we had to help our parents, the seed and the thorns were very hard, we always had injuries in our feet. The hardest thing was in the winter where we walked in mudflats; our feet get filled with fungi. Feet swelled up, we could no longer walk, so we had to resort to medicinal plants and rub our feet with herbs from the field.

Thus, teachers gained people's love. Whenever we hear the sound of the first bell of strikes, demonstrations and strikes by university students and teachers, all progressive teachers suffered from hunger, humiliation, and torture and even those who disappeared, the most radical and progressive country teachers - people supported them due to all their humanitarian works, and they are still remembered.

A BAD LANDOWNER

La Loma Del Espino is a small village located in a valley at the top of the hills. Peasants who live there own small plots that are worked only during rainy season since the place is dry and has no irrigation system.

On one side of this valley is a cattle ranch formerly called *"La Merced"*, 1,500 hectares of land owned by the granddaughter of Spanish Creoles who came in the days of the conquest –an heiress of the colonization era. She hardly ever visited the place. The manager leased plots to peasants to work on. The woman owned few cattle, which her men took care of, apart from sowing corn, beans and other products.

In addition to land for cultivation, there were also many mountainous areas, where lots of wood were removed to build houses and to use as firewood. Most of the woods were sold to potteries, both in town and in the capital since in our country it is still widely use clay products. Many people are not used to cooking in metal containers and continue to prefer clay pots or mud. They say that tortillas and beans taste better when cooked in a clay pot, and tortillas when cooked in a hotplate. That is why the pottery industry is very important in El Salvador as well as in other Central American countries.

About 150 families lived in the farm where they made their houses according to their economic outreach and rented land from farm owners for their crops. Somebody who had no money gave a percentage of the crop as payment for the land use. However, to pay for housing they contributed working days to the farm. The overseer and his bailiffs took control of the administration of these agreements. Many farmers had their yoke of oxen to plow the land and others had their cows, they also paid a monthly fee for having animals that feed from the grass in the farm. In this sense, all people carried out a balanced peasant life.

I remember that on the street leading to the village there was a soccer field, thanks to the collaboration of all the peasantry. In that soccer field, teams played with other teams that did not belong to any league, they were from other neighboring valleys or surrounding villages. It was played for money. The field was very nice and it had an entire valley around it, all the surrounding valleys also chose the field for the championship tournaments. The tournaments involved thirty or forty teams from different places. They were full parties. A great amount of food, beer and moonshine were sold to delighted fans watching the games. People also played cards and dice apart from soccer. Things changed few years later. The owner of the hacienda decided to sell the property to avoid having more problems with it. Apparently, the foreman appeared to have kept most of the income of the farm. People rumored that the foreman, Mr. Ramon, liberally robbed it since there was no one to oversee his dealings. Even the foreman himself said it when he was drunk; he said he had money stolen from the farm. With that money he also supported many women and when someone needed a product he put a price on it, sold it and kept the money. He also sold many animals that were raised in the farm, he put them in his records and when they're already grown up he sell them and never reported it as an income of the farm. In short, the man used the farm as if it were his property; but the owner was well aware of it that is why he put it on sale. The woman (the heiress of the colonization era) was very rich and did not even enjoy going there; it was an inheritance with little importance to her.

Shortly afterwards, a cattle farmer with his eight children came to see the farm to buy it. This man was Mr. Vicente Escobar, a sixty year old, tall and white-skinned Ladino Spanish Creole. He has many bullet and machete scars on his face, chest and arms.

This man had sold his farm because all neighboring farmers in Chalatenango, province/region where he came from, wanted to kill him because he and his sons were extremely dangerous. People said that in the region of Chalatenango, a farmer left him almost dead in the sidewalk. He was hopeless but he survived. His children were very bad. They put a gun to any peasant's head; they were murderers, rapists and thieves. They stole cattle and horses.

It was also known that he had become a millionaire during the war between El Salvador and Honduras. At that time, this man lived near the border of the two countries, he took advantage of the war and entered Honduras where Salvadoran troops passed through and exterminated all living being with their own and rented trucks to seize cattle and whatever he found in the fields and villages.

Mr. Vicente also had several farms in other parts of the country and was one of the leading producers of milk and beef. He often appeared on the newspapers front page when it came to farming.

A couple of months later, the big news came that this gentleman bought the farm "behind closed doors", that means to say that everything in the farm belonged to the farm and only human beings could get out of there. Farmers would lose, for example, the materials of the houses they had built with their own efforts, the barbed wire to fence their plots and all the equipment that was there.

Mr. Vicente then appeared with a group of National Guardsmen and farm police to drive all people out. Most had nowhere to go and asked for a little time to get their products and animals such as hens, pigs, cows, oxen and horses, and undo their houses to remove the material and find a new place to live. But the man did not give them any time and wanted everyone out of there immediately. People begged the guards to not repress them, but they began beating them with the butts of their rifles and killing the few animals they had. Some peasants' houses were burnt, and with them all their belongings. After all this, worthy of barbarism time, they turned away, warning they would return. Moreover, he also appropriated the soccer field, which had already been donated to the community, and said that he would his farm there.

The situation of the peasants was desperate: the old man came with his sons, all on horseback, with belts loaded with bullets and guns hanging, and they threatened all who crossed in their way. Girls were abused by the man's sons and there was no way to do anything with the laws because they had bribed the village "security forces".

Days later, people went to complain to the poor prosecution's office in San Salvador. They were hundreds of people, because there were about 150 families, among which was also mine as they also had things to lose. The next day the news about the protest appeared on the front page of the newspaper *La Prensa Gráfica*. It was mentioned a group of peasants, including women and children, calling for justice, for being respected and being heard since they wanted to recover their belongings that were still in the farm. Most people had lived there for ten to forty years because the previous owner had donated land to build their shack but now that land was difficult to recover: the new owner had said he did not want "moles within his property."

A couple of weeks later, the National Guard went bothering people again. There was a widow and already quite old lady named Adela whose job was to buy pigs, cut them into pieces and sell the meat to the farmers to live and support their grandchildren who were orphaned. She told Mr. Vicente and his sons that she was disgusted and would not leave the property. One day the Civil Guard appeared: they beat her in front of her children; they took her things out her hut into the street and arrested her for a few days. When she was released, she was told that if they do not leave immediately, she and her children would stay in jail for a long time.

As a consequence, most people went to the town hall to ask for a place on the banks of the street to make their hut as there were free parts. Days later, the edge of the street was full of *champitas* in the widest parts, built with cardboard, grass and old sheets.

My aunt, María Hércules, she has lived forty years in
the street lands and says she is happy there. There are
considerably wider pieces of land to make a house with
bamboo walls, roof of grass with bajareque, typical houses
built by farmers in our country using rice[1] or *jaraguá* grass.

I also remember that this gentleman, Mr. Vicente, started fire in
his land during the driest times. The fire destroyed the little plantation
left. He accused eight peasants in the valley to have burned the paddock
whose names he obtained with the help of a local farmer. So, the
National and the Judicial Guard came for the eight denounced people
to arrest them and bring them to the cell in San Salvador. They were
kept in prison and tortured for several weeks. Everyone felt a great
hatred for this man, Mr. Vicente Escobar because of all the things he
caused the people of *La Loma Del Espino* valley. Many peasants built
their little adobe or brick house with so much effort, they had already
lost and it was so difficult to recover. People who left the place cried
their misfortune. Many were parents of young children who were naked

because their grass houses had been burnt along with everything they had. What was not burnt by the fire was destroyed by the old man. When it came to roofed houses, he went there to steal it. Housewives and elderly gentlemen said that this man would pay God for all they had suffered and what they had been stolen from. People slept under the trees for several months while doing something to cover them in the outdoors. The so called poor lawyer's office did not intervene and said they could not do anything because this man had much money and was respected; and to people who lost their things, they said "they were sorry but they could do nothing".

In the summer of that same year, in 1972, Mr. Vicente built his farm exactly where the soccer field was. It was a block long house with a room for each of his eight children and for each of his two unmarried daughters, a large main bedroom for him and his wife, a room for the maids and another where some workers they brought would sleep in. There was an area where milk was processed to make cheese; another where they only had long and short caliber guns, saddles and equipment related to cattle and horses, and a sleeping place for a dozen dogs trained to work with cattle. The huge house also had two rooms opposite a large corridor and on the other side was the cellar where work trucks, automobiles and electricity generator were placed; there was no electricity back then. They did not have that problem because they generated their own electricity twenty-four hours a day. The point is that the place where once was the community soccer field, but now fully covered with buildings and opposite the farm, crossing the street leading to the town, the landowner built the barn for milking cows and a riding stable for horses.

Time passed, after a few months, people managed to stabilize in other paths of bitterness and suffering while Mr. Vicente threatened of death to anyone who walked by their properties. This part of *La Loma Del Espino* is a fairly high area and in summer there is shortage of water, all streams dry and for three valleys that bordered on the farm the only resources were two small water sources that were in the field of this old man. The only other option going to the river was three times farther, so people risked walking through the grounds of the landlord to get water. To reach this place people had to walk an hour and a half; to go to the river even more.

Mr. Vicente and their children had the time and the evil heart to go and stand on their horses with the gun in their hands, to wait peasants coming along the paths, down the cliffs to get water, to threaten them. His sons raped many girls: most of them were girls they allow to fetch water, and when inside their property, they seized these girls or women by force. Others were seduced: they told them that they could go to get water and other things to gain their trust, but if they did not succeed, they ended up being raped and severely beat. They enjoyed going horseback while pointing at somebody their guns, even ladies, until they came out of their land by the same way they had entered. Mr. Vicente was responsible for checking the fences and seeing where the people crossed their land.

Then people began to bring their water at night or early morning when it was still dark, because at that time they were starting to milk their cows, they had thousands of milking cows and many cattle or fattening cattle. Sometimes I could see how these Escobar's brought cattle from another farm they had in Santa Ana, an area on the border of Guatemala, it was amazing to see so many cattle they brought! The street was full of cattle for a whole stretch of about five kilometers.

In the valley lived a man named Margarito López, a poor peasant who was very old and had to move on his mule because he could hardly walk. With someone's help, he sat in the chair, once mounted he could not go down without help because of his age and his suffering from arthritis. Once then, Mr. Margarito mounted his mule and thought of going across the ground of Mr. Vicente as the road was three times shorter, but to his bad luck there was a man watching women going down to fetch water from the source. The old man was taken down from the mule; held at gunpoint and beaten so mercilessly that caused him deaf and disoriented during his last days of his life: he died a couple of months later.

The same old man said that he was beaten with the butt of the gun and left unconscious, lying in the road.

Days later, Mr. Margarito's son-in-law outraged by what they had done to his father-in-law went to monitor Mr. Vicente and their children for revenge. He was popular and a very good person in the valley. He never wore shoes; he walked barefoot and always wore his good slingshot to kill pigeons. His name was Esteban, but as he did not wear shoes, he was named *The Cat*, and he liked to be called so. One day he met Mr. Vicente hidden in the bushes waiting to see someone from the valley entering his property but Esteban won the lead.

"Do not move, son of b*tch, because I'll kill you!" shouted Esteban from about five meters away.

The old man was surprised because who aimed him did it with just a slingshot rubber, but he could really kill him. Mr. Vicente was so frightened that he could not answer, trembling with fear, he carefully took out the gun and threw it to the ground. Esteban wanted to kill him, but he failed because he lacked courage, and while aiming him he told him to leave people in peace and stop bothering. After a few seconds, he lowered his slingshot; he did not have the courage to kill him. He told the landowner he did not kill him because he was sorry. He told the man to stop bothering his family and that his father-in-law had died due to the beating. Esteban made the old man drove back, raised his gun, removed the bullets and threw them in a gorge. Terrified, the old man could not say a word. He went to the cliff to pick up his gun, mounted his horse and galloped away. When he was riding away, he shouted that Esteban would pay for that later.

In cases like that there were no local laws to make justice; there was nothing to put a limit to this man. The laws remained silent when a farmer came to official sources to report such cases – because of this Esteban wanted to take the law into his own hands.

Later, when the first political revolts began, Mr. Vicente's sons walked with the Death Squads "putting finger", pointing at and killing people. In April 1980 they came to kill Esteban and other people in the village. I went to see the bodies of my friends who were massacred; there were four bodies covered with a white blanket that had the initials DS, "Death Squad". Esteban was not with them. He was stabbed about two hundred times and did not die immediately, but managed to drag a block to his home, where he had been taken naked at midnight. He died while he was been carried in the hammock to the town for medical care.

Soon after, the Escobar's bought another land. They were several hundred hectares adjacent to the land they already had, only that they were across the Sucio River. As the river also divides towns' jurisdictions, this land belonged to another settlement. They said they owned the river because they owned several kilometers of land on both sides. According to the law, in El Salvador certain amount of meters on both banks of a river are national, or free and they cannot be owned, and there anyone can fish or do any activities. But these men up for that reason beat up, mistreated and humiliated peasants. And although there were some complaints against them for abuses, the law does not reprimanded them at all, - for that reason it was dangerous to walk along the riverbanks where the Escobar's strolled with their guns. They were tall and white, dressed in cowboy hat, denim shirt, jeans, and cowboy boots. Walked with their riffles and automatic guns full of bullets (they really looked like actors from movies of the West) and treated people violently all the time. Peasants fear them the most.

After buying that land, they tried to take little pieces of land to two families whose properties were adjacent to the one they had already bought. In the past, the land had been the street leading to town; previous mayors sold these small plots to peasants in the area, perhaps corruptly, but the owners had their legal papers. A new street was opened elsewhere and the old one was in the hands of the town's municipal mayor. Thus, these peasant families had acquired their properties. Mr. Vicente, together with his lawyers, tried to take over these plots as he succeeded to do elsewhere, leaving the peasants in misery. The old man was obsessed with stealing pieces of lands. Many of them were next to their farm and, as it seemed, they had been separated in previous times so that he wanted them back.

This is the problem that exists in our country: a person who has money buys power, the bureaucracy and the official forces. People said the old man was very bad but they were afraid to do something against him. These peasants were saved only because they had friends with a little social influence, otherwise, they would have lost everything because the man had already intimidated the whole area and assured that he would rob farmers and all land next to his.

My mother and father were a little worried because the small inheritances that each of them had, shared a border with this old man's farm. The worry was such that many people looked for a lawyer to explain him each case. Lawyers also took advantage and robbed the peasants' money without doing anything in return, besides they often made them sign papers without knowing what's in it, most of them could not even read.

I remember once the old man was with some of his sons repairing the fence that separated their property from the small plot my father had and where we lived. It was about nine o'clock, the man walked with his hammer hanging, cutting trees to make posts. I went to fetch water from the stream on our property, when I returned I saw the man cutting a tree that was within our plot. He already had so many hectares of land to cut trees. My father went to see what was happening and he found the old man cutting another tree, always within our plot, so my father intervened.

"Repairing the fence, Mr. Vicente?" My father asked.

"Yes! " Said the old man, "I'm cutting these trees here on your property because on my side people already stole me a lot of wood"

"That cannot be avoided" my father said, "but there is no need to cut off those trees that are just growing and will be of good wood. You have trees that are better for that kind of use" he explained.

The old man murmured that in his farm people have been stealing wood and he cared little. He was already stroking the butt of his gun.

Finally, my father let him do what he wanted otherwise he'd only encounter problems or death with this old man. It was true that peasants and people who had no firewood to use for cooking stole wood from the old man's farm but that wood was at the verge of rot or dry. Some of the neighbors went to collect some wood and cut the branches or dry shrubs. Despite those reason, Mr. Vicente did a lot of abusive things.

Years later, when we were grown up, the man's sons were a little friendlier with people. They knew that nobody liked them, but as they needed laborers to harvest, they had to show a hypocritical kindness. Minority wandered on different farms to seek work, if they did not find it, they arrived at the Escobar's farm. There was much need to earn a few pennies, especially in the winter when expenses are multiplied when farmers are doing their crops. Although they did not want to work for the Escobar's, they had to and face the old man.

Once we went with some friends to ask him for work. We crossed the gate that was at the entrance, facing the street. We started to walk a hundred meters away to get the house, about a dozen of German Shepherds and Dobermans began to attack us. Mr. Vicente was standing in the corridor, as the house was on a higher part he could see us very well, yet he did not yell at the dogs to leave us alone. We were five guys and we all carried *machetes* to defend ourselves, so at last the dogs were afraid. The old man was smoking tobacco in an eastern pipe, while he smoked his pipe he saw us approaching shyly, until he finally said, "What do you want?" We answered that his son Antonio told us the day before that had cut rice work for us and that we had to come that morning. The old man came down the steps slowly while he grabbed the pipe with his right hand and smoked heavily; he stopped a couple of meters from us. He uncaringly stared at us, one by one, and after a while he told us that his son was not there and we should come back later.

Usually, they paid us a colon less than in other farms: if in other farms the owners paid five colons, they paid four colons for an eight-hour work. Because of the need to earn money we had to work at any price. That time I closely see the man and the number of scars in his face. As he was wearing his shirt unbuttoned I could also see the scars in his chest; and when he breathed, a small whistle came out from his inside.

From all of his sons, Antonio was the best employer: he was the most considerate and communicative, although sometimes, after finishing the eight-hour work day he sent us to water the grass seeds for pasture; those hours were not paid, and if we refused to do so, we would not get the payment for the whole worked day. Employees were not paid hourly wages, but eight-hour workday; this forced the labor to finish his workday to be paid. Some employers paid a half if the hand worked half a day, but that was optional, not compulsory.

I, my cousin and some friends went back to look for work with the old man. His son, Antonio, told us the previous day, his father had a job consisting of cleaning grass and plant the sorghum used to pasture cattle. When we reached the place the man said: "Here's this sack of sorghum: first water the sorghum and then weed it so it can born. Measure the tasks form ten to ten strokes each".

A task of ten to ten strokes were about six hundred square meters, and the grass that had to be removed was about one and two meters high. It was difficult to fulfill those tasks, although we were determined to work, it would be very difficult. Yet, we began assessing tasks with a rod; my cousin did the cut and measuring since he was taller than me.

We already knew that the old man would come back and measure it again when they were ready; the man was taller so his rods were longer and we had to satisfy him, otherwise he would not pay us. But the sun hid and we did not finish. We returned the following day to finish our work. Then we went to call the man to check our work and the measure we had taken. When the old man came, he stared at the work we had done while he smoked his pipe.

"These are not complete tasks" he said, and began measuring with a bigger stick he had, so those tasks lacked two or three meters from both sides. Then he added: "If you want to get paid, finish the task"

"Look sir ", said Jose Lino, my cousin, "I will not do anything else, because that rod you brought is bigger than usual; and if you want to pay me, do it; otherwise no".

"Well, I will not pay you!" answered the old man in a bad mood and he turned around to get back to his home.

While the old man was leaving, my cousin was very angry and he said, "Maybe you can use that money for candles."

Mr. Vicente jumped when he heard what my cousin said. He took his the gun out and pointed at him, to kill him. We shouted at the old man because we were scared.

"You are alive because your nana is a maid in my house, otherwise I would kill you right now!" the old man said furiously shaking while scratching his head.

My cousin went home embarrassed over the incident. He was really lucky that the old man did not kill him. Partly it was because his mother worked in processing the cheese made in the farm with the milk that did not go to the factory; they had all the necessary equipment. Meanwhile, the four of us set out to complete the tasks to get the payment; otherwise we would not receive the four colons the work was worth and was almost done.

A year later, the street leading to the village was almost totally destroyed due to the rains. Water ruined the ditches and ran in the middle of the street, even the horses had difficulty walking on it. The community usually repaired the street after the rainy season to make it more accessible in summer time. All who became mayors in the village, during their political campaigns, promised they would restructure the streets well; build bridges and bring electricity to that place. There were thousands of families living in the area without electricity and almost not able to communicate, the streets were no longer accessible and good for horses because it was eroded by rain stones. It looked like a dried-up creek. It was necessary to make, at least, new waterways (with picks and shovels as they were accustomed to do it there), lift them a bit and throw some ballast over a dozen kilometers.

David Marroquín was the man who spoke to the town municipal government for help to repair the streets. This man, who worked with pick-axe andshovel next to the other laborers, was the leader of the organization - responsible for our valleys, *La Loma del Espino*, and *Agua Fría*.

David was about 35 years and a trustworthy man. He looked Caribbean because he was tall, had kinky dark brown hair, one would even say that he was half Black and half Hispanic. He always smiled and always in a good mood; everyone liked him. He always made a good impression and had a suitable character for leadership. People treated him with great respect. When it came to community things, everyone chose him; he was very popular and good at speaking. He had fought in the war with Honduras in 1969. Sometimes while we were working, we asked him to tell us something that existed in the fighting. He fought together with his brother; he told us what they experienced and how he saw many countrymen fell wounded by Hondurans bullets.

As always, the help was denied, so we had to do it on our own. The mayor's office no longer cared about such thing. People had to do something about it, so workers organized meetings, held in central locations in the valleys and villages of the area. Each valley designated a couple of farmers responsible for keeping track of those who worked and what was up to each. The person who could not help because of no time must pay a labor. It is so evident that this kind of action is typical in our country. Communities had to solve the problems with the streets, water and other needs.

After these people were appointed and determined who would provide work and who would pay a labor, it was also spoken of wealthy landowners in the area and those who were almost be considered landowner for their economic position and because they had enough land, who also used the street with their trucks and jeeps to go to their properties. If, for example, farmers who made money carrying agricultural products to the town, especially those with ox cart were asked a week of work, all the more reason it was fair to ask rich people to cooperate too.

A group of peasants were selected to go and talk to the representatives or managers of those properties and asked them to offer assistance by giving two labors for a couple of weeks, and if they wanted to provide more help it would be welcome. They also talked to some trucks owners (people that when the street was good took people from the valleys to the towns) to see if they could provide some ballast trips; on one side the village there was a hill that was a red volcanic crater, and they asked them to take four up to six laborers with shovels to fill the truck. Permission from the mayor's office must be obtained so as not to imprison the truck's owner, and fuel expenses ran to his office. They asked peasants, farmers or ranchers who could donate money for collaborations to buy cement, at least fifty-pound bag.

To raise funds the community began to perform dances during weekends in the three schools that were along the street leading to the town; sound equipment was rented and local musicians participated. Moreover, there were raffle draws. Farmers who were better off donated bull calves to be awarded; with the money gained they bought materials to build small bridges and culverts.

Several days later, groups of peasants were seen working in the streets with picks and shovels, digging ditches and throwing dirt into the streets. Peasants' wives or daughters brought lunch to their husbands, parents or siblings, oddly rural dressed.

A group of three or four men asked those responsible for the farms and farmers for help, which was often denied. Sometimes they did not want to give a labor for a week. It was frustrating for the community. Peasants cooperated despite their poverty, and many who have money did not do it although they also need the street. However, most people contributed at least a bit, either with labor or with some bags of cement. At that time Mr. David Marroquín invited us to go with him to ask Mr. Vicente Escobar's help.

After a very tiring day, we went to visit Mr. Vicente to ask for his cooperation. That day we worked hard, after four in the afternoon we hang our water bottles and bags on our shoulders and we went to the farm.

"Let's go and see this man" said David; "maybe he will give us some labors for a few days or a few bags of cement to build sewers. If he gives us money, it will be better, we can pay more labors", and with an optimistic smile, he added "Where it is not expected, it comes", people say.

David, seven workers and I were on our way to the old man's house. We were about half a kilometer away. As usual, when we opened the gate leading to the big house, the brave and aggressive dogs appeared. As the sons were there marking some iron with calves in the farmyard, they shouted at the dogs in order not to bother us. In two minutes we were in the house, and then the old man came out.

"What do you want...?" he asked us.

"Excuse us, Mr. Vicente because we have come here to bother you" replied David, "but the purpose of our visit is to ask you cooperation for the streets; whether you send laborers give us some bags of cement to build sewers to drain water, or provide some money which for the payment of a pawn".

"My Trucks and my horses do not need the street to be repaired to reach the village" Mr. Vicente very coldly interrupted.

A while back, a large truck belonged to Escobar's had gone out of one of the garages because it had been left in neutral and without brakes, it gone down the slope, downhill. As this incident happened at night and no servant was near to stop it, it broke some fences. Finally it stopped in the street. In its rounds it had destroyed a cement sewer that drew water out of the street. David even asked him whether he would cooperate to repair the sewer but the old man refused. David was upset by the answer, though he did not show it and continued talking with humbleness, "but, note that if we do not do something now, the street will be completely destroyed and the thing will be worse".

"Beg the fuck!"- He interrupted. "Go away... Go away from here and I do not want to see you again in my house", he added, he then took out the gun and pointed at the three of us who entered his property.

We turned around and walked slowly toward the exit; the old man followed us with the gun in his hand. We were a bit shaken by the man's attitude. Julio and I were practically frozen. David was also frozen, but not because of fear, but because of anger, he felt a cold running down his back, a kind of tingling, and he remembered the war days while he was walking with the old man aimed at him in his back. It was unusual to see him angry, but this time he was very angry. David never left his weapon either, but he did not want to pull it out because he said the gun should not be drawn by taste. Obviously, Mr. Vicente was a complicated man. His sons only watched from the pens few meters away.

When we went out into the street, David said that for a moment he felt like leaping on the man.

I think- he added- that those men may not detach from the gun even when sleeping.

And it was probably true. Also the two daughters had guns in their belts when they walked out of the house, wearing jeans and boots and mounted on their horses.

Since that time, the whole family had the goods on David. They hated him so much that, days later, the old man's sons stole him a pair of Creole bulls that were in his field. They did it to inflict harm, not for necessity. The Escobar's had rented an adjacent field to David's field and they had cattle in it, so it was easy for them to break the siege to move animals. They put their iron mark; legalized them in the registry and sold them in another village in the area. They also robbed several registered cattle to other farmers and sold them through contacts, overnight, the beef or meat were already in pieces in the markets. David consulted a lawyer because he had evidence that they had sold the beef, but those men had more influential lawyers, he could never win the case. The Escobar's hated him even more.

When we left the owner's property, we felt much better. Those who were waiting saw how we had left the place. David only shook his head and murmured:

"I cannot believe how this man is...! I cannot believe it!" and he took off his hat to fan him.

Then, the eight of us walked back. We walked in silence thinking about the ugly scene we had with the man. David, for his part, felt upset and disappointed.

In those days, I remember quite well. It began a disastrous age that no one will forget. People's discontents were extraordinary. There were rumors of the people's struggle.

As a wave that devastates everything, so came the noise of political incorporation of the masses - all the peasants spoke of the Popular Revolutionary Block (BPR).

Mr. Vicente continued getting involved with people. One of his older sons had killed a boy and as his relatives had more money than Escobar's, the case went pear shaped. The victim's family paid their lawyers a lot of money to apprehend Erasmus Escobar who evaded justice while he was being judged as 'absent'. The young man had several girlfriends. In the valley, peasants' daughters he conquered helped him hid from the law for a while. Then he went with the revolutionaries to be safe from the law. A few months later, he passed to the side of the far right wing with the Death Squads, since he knew many people in the area could betray several farmers; he continued to escape the murder case which was still in force.

Around the same time, three other children of the landowner were persecuted by the law. It was said that the three of them were returning from a party in the city of Santa Ana, the second capital of the country. They were travelling in their Cherokee, drunk, driving down the Pan-American Highway when they saw some girls walking along the side of the road. They tried to get them into their car, but as they refused, they let them walked about two blocks and then aimed the car at the girls. It was said that one girl died and the other two were seriously injured. It was never known how they fixed the issue, because then the political problems appeared and they had to leave the place.

The revolutionary movement wanted to enlist the old man. It was vital to have people of influence and good economic position in the process, but this man was far right wing, and it became difficult to achieve such a thing. People from the movement went to throw papers in front of his house, he was threatened to take part in the revolutionary process, and otherwise, he would be killed. The old man prepared his sons and those who served him very well. He insisted that he was not moving anywhere. "Only dead I will leave this place," he assured.

That summer a big demonstration that reached the city of Quezaltepeque was performed. People came from other towns: El Paisnal, Aguilares and other surrounding places. There were about thirty thousand people protesting outside the village mayor. The city was filled with people carrying placards and megaphones, shouting things such as "Revolution or Death" and "The people united will never be defeated." They demanded higher wages for peasant laborers; that factory employees were entitled to be represented by unions, etc. After two days, they left the city but they also left people's demands. It was a mark that lasted for all the years during the time the country was in conflict. All of El Salvador was involved; political movements had national scope. Everyone talked about the revolutionary unity, and so began to raise awareness in the masses. They demanded the freedom of political prisoners who were in clandestine prisons, basic rights for farm workers and a series of demands, including "Out US intervention."

Meanwhile, Mr. Vicente remained stubborn in his position: he neither wanted to unite the process nor leave the place. He said he did not fear a sad peasant who had nowhere to sleep. The old man brought about thirty national guards from the barracks and put them around his property, well-armed with automatic G-3 rifles. All the time they care for the Escobar's welfare. At night, those guards disguised themselves as common people and went to farmers' houses in the area and killed them. They massacred elderly people, ladies and girls and they also raped women. They tortured and killed them immediately. Mr. Vicente's sons were in those paramilitary groups. When they started killing people, they left the bodies wrapped in a white robe with the initials D. S. in color red. As peasants had no weapons, they did not react, but were aware of what was happening and they were getting ready. Many people had already lost their sons, daughters, husbands and wives. In many cases, if they were to find a family member but could not find the person they were looking for, they killed another family member instead. Everyone feared them, and while all the time they walked with their faces covered, they were recognized by their voice. The old man's sons and their guards were pleased by all these misdeeds.

Meanwhile, *"The boys"* were unifying to pay Mr. Vicente a visit in his house. A few days later, about three hundred armed revolutionaries went to the farm, shooting lasted several hours. In those days, the popular paramilitaries only had pistols, revolvers, carbines and short range rifles, but still they killed some of Mr. Vicente's guards. It was during nighttime, so they managed to get very close to the house. Guards were there, they threw stones and bullets to the building. They damaged the roof and the walls made of brick. Later they completely burned it.

The old man began killing people in an uncritical way, and this was happening across the country. The thing went from bad to worse. The Death Squad was looking for David Marroquín to kill him. Mr. Vicente's son, Antonio, was stabbed and killed in a canteen. Days later, Vicente's oldest son was also killed in another city, and in later years, almost all of his sons were dead.

Mr. Vicente's civil guards abandoned their headquarters. Perhaps they were afraid to lose all "security privileges" and so they left the old man alone with his sons. This time, "*The boys*" attacked the property and left it almost totally destroyed. They took what they found on their way.

We did not kill them because they managed to escape to a house they had in the village. Days later, they threw bombs at that house and they also exchanged fire. They were ambushed in the street; they were attacked when they went to see if they could recover animals or collect some belongings. Some of them were wounded. They threw grenades and shot them with machine guns.

They then went to the capital. The old mother was still alive and lived in Colonia Escalón, where only millionaires live. In that same place, the old man died of cardiac arrest in 1983, caused by dairy problems. His sons joined the Death Squads, cooperated directly or indirectly with them. They satisfied their desire to kill, that was what their father instilled in them since they were little boys. The great David Marroquín was killed by a Death Squad while he was working on his plot.

Mr. Vicente Escobar, who lives by the sword will perish by the sword.

THE BEGINNING OF THE WAR

The peasant

Beautiful Jayaque summits
Where only grow green coffee trees:
You are witnesses
Of the major fatal crimes.

Volcanoes, so rich in production
That made from a town a move.
The human right to live...
a life, but not as a rich miser.

Peasants who picked the coffee,
Peasants who harvested sugar canes,
For you, decomposed tortillas that distributes the owner
And for the stingy rich, the whole capital.

They reached the last corner
massacring the working poor,
Whose face reflected sorrow...
That was the life of the poor peasant.

On July 19th, 1979, the Sandinistas took power in Nicaragua. This event generated much joy and motivation in the region. In our country, people were very excited and wanted to fight for changes in the country as well. But the differences between the two countries had to be taken into account: as it was known, in Nicaragua there was less military force than in El Salvador, and, on the other hand, at one point the

US administration had taken its financial support to the Nicaraguan dictator, Anastasio Somoza de Bayle

On October 15th, 1979, President ('puppet' or dictatorship), Carlos Humberto Romero in El Salvador was removed from power through a coup sponsored by an American movement. This president had put in place several decrees. One of them was the guarantee of public order, which allows anyone to commit atrocities against the people. The scariest were committed by the body of the Death Squads, with the cooperation of members of ORDEN, which were also called ears. Political corruption closely linked to the rich. The military, the government and the United States, were at the order of the day. Broadcasters conveyed chain letters so all the people would listen. All government bodies were military and the group of powerful families who exercised power (about fourteen) had their 'puppets'. Of course, in those days they wanted to prevent the world to understand the atrocities happening in the country.

After the fall of General Romero other leaders assumed power with the idea of pacifying the country. The new Government Revolutionary Assembly, as it was called, was composed by Colonel Jaime Abdul Gutierrez, Colonel Adolfo Arnoldo Majano Ramos, Engr. Ramón Mayorga, Dr. Guillermo Ungo and Engr. Mario Andino.

But the Army had the support of the National Association of Private Enterprise (ANEP), and behind them was the founder of the Death Squads and CIA representative, Roberto d'Aubuisson. This man gave the report to Washington as representative of Central Intelligence Agency. He was the intellectual murderer of Archbishop Romero of the American nuns as well as many other Catholic priests.

Dr. Guillermo Ungo was the first to resign. The high command of the National Guard was the Gen. Vides Casanova. At the same time, Gen. Bustillos became the head of the Air Force designated by Gen. García, and then defense minister and who truly commanded the country had all the control. The repression, the disappearances, the tortures and massacres continued. This made civilian renounce power.

On January 9th 1980, the second Government Revolutionary Assembly was formed. It was composed of Colonel Jaime Abdul Gutiérrez, Colonel Adolfo Arnoldo Majano Ramos, doctor Héctor

Dada Hirezi, Dr. Antonio Morales Erlich and Dr. Jose Ramon Avalos, but because there were no structural changes, this time it was Dada Hirezi who resigned and was replaced by Engr. Jose Napoleón Duarte. So the third Revolutionary Government was shaped. They failed once again, the country was even worse.

In late 1980, Enrique Álvarez Córdova, leader of the Democratic Revolutionary Front (FDR) was murdered along with other party leaders in the famous *Puerta Del Diablo* (Evil's Door). They were participating in a public meeting in a Jesuit church high school. When they left there were two hundred soldiers who had surrounded the place, they were killed. Juan Chacón was also murdered. The place is attached to the capital in Los Planes de Renderos. So, Rubén Zamora and Guillermo Ungo assumed the leadership of the party and joined Farabundo Martí Front for the National Liberation (FMLN), this union was renamed FMLN/FDR. The FDR began operating as a diplomatic body in guerrillas in El Salvador; it had diplomatic relations with France, Mexico and other countries. It acquired merits in the international arena, but had to face a great empire. On January 10th, 1981, the first insurrection against the national oligarchy and the United States happened. They had the idea of taking power in the country, but they failed.

People rose up with arms saying "It is enough!" Tired of so much political, economic and social injustice, people grouped in the streets and began to form assemblies. In my place, the Union of Rural Workers (UTC) and the Revolutionary Popular Block (BPR) were formed. The masses were moved by Popular Liberation Forces (FPL) born as an armed wing of the revolution.

On the farms, settlers organized and declared national strikes and rallies. They demanded better wages and benefits for the peasants who work the land; that land distribution was more individually equitable and that health services should be improved. In El Salvador most people were uneducated: there were problems arising from this situation up until this day.

The rich left their farms in the hands of the Government and fled the country. They formed the Salvadoran Institute for Agrarian Transformation (ISTA), a body that allowed the Government to run the farms. Under its control, there always work for the peasants, whether in sugar cane or coffee plantations. They also sent troops to all farms and recruited peasants to form Death Squads.

Well trained by military bodies and experts in revolutionary militants from these groups they were engaged in killing people at night. If they did not find the person they were looking for they killed the whole family. They had clandestine cemeteries in coffee plantations, and they buried people a few feet deep to the point that dead bodies were unearthed by dogs.

A few months earlier, the farms had been occupied by peasants demanding better wages. In my home town and around the farms were burned, as well as tractors and agricultural equipment; all grains, fertilizer and other materials, wineries, oxen and other livestock were stolen. The farms were taken by force for several days; there only remained demands written by the people and, of course, everywhere you'd see the image of our great internationalist comrade (Che Guevara). This was happening throughout the country. The crowd gathered on the farms: women, children, elderly and young people. Political talks with megaphones were heard: they talked about the crisis affecting our country and they called for justice. The salary earned by the proletarian did not cover the basic basket of home. Independence of political prisoners who were in both legal and clandestine prisons was demanded. They also claimed for freedom of expression, the demolition of Death Squads, etc. Moreover, they demanded the stop of forced recruitments frequently made throughout the country. Everywhere, on roads and neighborhood streets, were checkpoints escort of soldiers seized buses, trucks and some other means of transportation of young people to recruit, even if the young man had physical disabilities: nothing mattered.

In these days, El Salvador was starting a new stage which radically changed the life of the peasants: the humble worker who only derives a living from plow and machete became a man with a rifle and dreams ready to realize his ideals. He was no longer a property of those with power and money. Thus, days of great uncertainty came throughout the country.

Napoleón Mira Hernandez.
This boy was an instructor in the valley in 1979.

In those days, the teachers and students formed an organization called: National Association of Educators of El Salvador, ANDES 21st OF JUNE, where teachers and students of universities of the country marched in the streets. More oppression came as a wave of the political crisis. This boy that is in my book and his brother were killed to shot down the voices against oppression. The killing and disappearance of teachers and students was very popular in the cities of the country.

In those days in 1979, we went to receive political doctrine to a small valley adjacent to ours; we also received military revolutionary training so later we could participate in the popular militia ranks of national liberation. My older brother and I had to attend, it was said that who did not go would not be secluded from the revolution. People felt a great enthusiasm for the revolutionary movement. Peasants were organized and had already BPR leaders holding meetings in the valleys and in farms where farmers were informed about the reasons why it was necessary to organize and why the gun would be used. It was already known that the adversary was the rich with armed forces: they only crushed and there was not the slightest hope that changes were peacefully achieved. Conventional control goes from the propaganda to weapons: it was necessary and indispensable to unite and fight to defend people's interests. People first thought it would be a totally peaceful political change; no one expected or imagined what was coming. People still had no weapons; trainings were with clubs or sticks. On the other hand, they tried to hide the events occurred in 1932 with Farabundo Martí. Most of us learned about what happened from old people, who told us what they remembered: people relived the story and took a lot of literature that kept the national university and left-wing groups. We rebelled against the capitalist and imperialist system. Years later I realized that it was illegal even in school to talk about such subjects; teachers could not talk about it with students. Teachers who were politicized could talk about these and the reasons for a radical change, but other teachers lied to us to the point of telling us that Christopher Columbus was Spanish. Overall, all Latin American people had been deceived.

People also feared the Cold War between the United States and the Soviet Union. We all thought that those countries could not get into our business: we were an independent country and worthy of a democracy. However, the United States (which had economic and political interests in the region and did not care that people were being exploited) began to support the military, and with them are the capitalists, the powerful, and the monopolies' owners. Also, an issue that helped capitalism and imperialism was that the communist said that he did not believe in God, and our people are believers.

Labor unions were formed in cities and towns. All were organized: students, teachers, workers, professionals, women in the markets. People marched through the streets doing protests, meeting in front of the town hall and speaking by megaphones; but the caravans of armed forces were present everywhere. They came with tanks full of soldiers who oppressed, beat and killed people. Many times they took young people, keep them prisoners, they tortured them and sometimes they just disappeared. Over time, they could no longer make such acts since they became illegal. Participants were considered "subversive" or "communist" and they were executed without further questions. In those same days, state of siege and martial law were ruled in the country.

In the valley we had to be alert, especially on curfews. The Armed Forces convoys made incursions in the stony streets of the valleys, sometimes at night. They carried out massacres and did unspeakable things with women and girls, including rape, which was also a way to terrorize, and then killing. They burned the peasants' houses and stole their belongings, etc. Most people went to sleep near the cliffs where they made a small cave under the rocks to go to and spend the night, and so on.

We, the already organized, were in charge of ensuring a minimum security: we were about eight who kept alert around the clock. While some slept, two hid at the edge of the street, standing guard, and if they saw a troop coming we let go two rockets rod, those which go high. When people of the nearby valleys heard this they knew they had to flee. This kind of announcements were made in chain, each valley that saw the signal of the rockets launched another, so that in turn it notify the remotest valleys, until the warning had been heard in the most distant area.

During the night, shootings and bombs exploding were heard everywhere. We felt extremely nervous when we heard trucks coming. So we had to let go two rockets rod and flee the place because we were only eight young men: six sleeping and two on guard. We had only two handguns, but by that time guerrilla groups were everywhere with weapons to make resistance. Ambushes were already made in the streets against the military and the headquarters of the National Guard and the Police and the harnesses of the Death Squad in the farms were attacked.

The squad set points thereafter the rich gave the farms to ISTA to keep them under control during the war.

Many people left the countryside or went to the farms. There were dozens of homes alone because some had left the country, others to the villages, and many had died. My Valley was completely overwhelmed by the situation. Ladies cried most of the time, grieving for their children. I remember we were on guard where the street was crossed by a stream. There we could hide because there was a groove and only the noise of the stream was heard. It was a quiet, dark, scary place at night. Dogs barked in the distance and the nocturnal birds' singing cooed darkness.

One night, at about one in the morning, we heard one of the rod rockets used to alert. The noise came from the side of the town where it was feared the military would appear. We were scared but not that much because there was no announcement from the village adjacent to the valley. Later, we would get to know that rockets had moistened with the dew and they had to flee toward the abyss without being able to release them. Then we saw several trucks coming down the slope and, indeed, what was coming was a convoy of about eight or nine trucks. The time it took us to awake the sleeping members, trucks were already very close. We retreated a little from the street to give fire to the rockets and start running upwards by the stream to reach a hill where it would be difficult to find us. In a few minutes, the warning had reached the end of that street. People had to get up, leave their homes and hide where they felt safer, because the whole community of the region was involved in the fight, and 'the ears' had already reported that. Then, no one sleep in their homes, but in ravines, caves, old logs or bushes - there beds for the night were made. On many occasions we saved our lives in that way.

Days later, the war intensified. The troops began to appear everywhere and on foot so as not to be surprised with ambushes, and because of that, more furiously. When they came to the valley looking for people, they killed the animals they found on their way: hens, pigs, cows, oxen, even dogs and cats. They also stole some farmers' belongings such as tape recorder, typewriter or sewing machine - which at that time was considered a fortune. When farmers returned to their homes, it was burned especially when they it was made of grass. The houses made of wood and tiles were stoned till the roof was broken, walls were bombarded until they were destroyed. Harvested grains such as corn, beans, rice and other products were also stolen.

In the last days of 1979, they invaded a village in the north of my region, in El Paisnal and killed many rural people. I saw when it was first bombed. I watched it from a hill that was within the land of my father while I left the house and looked a place to hide in the grove, because the armed forces were going to that place. I saw three leak aircrafts flying quite low and suddenly dropped bombs on the village. From there I could see huge flames of several meters high when bombs exploded. They burned huge trees and killed as many people as well as cattle. Detonations were heard in the distance. According to the villagers, they bombed first places where people meets or a communal house and that many were captured, tied up together, piled, doused with gasoline and burned alive. From my place, heart-rending shouts were heard. The helicopter fired with machine guns point-50 and M-60, while troops scoured the area looking for those who fled and hide to the fields and mountains. The armed forces continued their tracks for days; when they found wounded people in the mountains, they finished them off. Many bombs exploded in the paddocks where the stables at and it killed many cattle. After the armed forces moved away, some corpses of people were found in the mountains – no medical care caused them their deaths. But here were some who, although wounded were saved and told their story.

Days after this terrifying event, Father Rutilio Grande was murdered. First he was accused of being responsible for all the people of El Paisnal, in the department of San Salvador, to be "subversive" as the adversaries said, and in November of that year when he was travelling from Aguilares to his hometown, his car was gunned down by unknown group, but certainly were members of the Death Squad. His family was a friend of my father's, who then was told passages of this story. When a prominent person was killed, radio and newspapers released words that the responsible gunmen were "unknown persons or groups". By then, they had already disappeared and killed many members of the Church.

In those days, I met a gentleman farmer. I saw him on the street, grazing his little cow. He was sitting relaxed on a rock under a tree. He took off his hat while breathing mountain pure air and watched his cow eating, which was about to give birth. One day he called me and told me to sit with him. As he held in his hands the cow's rope, he took off his hat and made a cigar with tobacco leaves and told me:

"We are only a cause in this world... We worth nothing... The rich and these powers have everything... And what can we do...? What will you do with your life...? Tell me..."

This farmer had been a coalman in a farm, but due to his old age he had been despised and retired from work, he had no income to live with.

"We must fight for something better" continued saying. I cannot read or write, but you who are young and literate do something to get things better."

There was no doubt that the peasants wanted a change because they were seeing the abuses to which they were subjected. Most people were peasants and uneducated, but still realized that they were experiencing something inhumane.

Immediately afterwards, Monsignor Romero was killed for speaking on behalf of the poor. He was "the voice of the voiceless", as he was consecrated in the country. Monsignor Romero saved many peasants and workers: he took them out of clandestine prisons where they were tortured and disappeared. This happened when someone warned them where their children, spouse or other relatives. The information comes unofficially as prisons were undisclosed around the country.

Only recently Monsignor Romero had written a letter to Washington where he said that the dollars they sent turned the country into a bloodbath. In his homilies and sermons he demanded to cease the repression and told the people themselves, since most of the soldiers were forcibly recruited peasants: "I would like to appeal, especially to the men of the army. Particularly to the bases of the National Guard, police, and barracks... You are brothers of our own people. You kill your own peasant brothers. And in a given order to kill someone the law of God must prevail; it says: 'Do not kill'. No soldier is obliged to obey an order against the law of God. Nobody has to follow an immoral law". In addition, he made a call to the armed forces, saying: "I beg you, I beg you, and I command you in the name of God: Stop the repression!" And this leads him to his death.

Monsignor Romero knew they wanted to kill him: he was told that his name was on the list of the most hated in the country, but said: "If you kill me, I will rise again in the Salvadoran people". Ladies could no longer listen to radios for masses, because if they do so, they were considered communists and then killed. Stations were also burned by military groups. In the villages, there were many *ears* and no one could stop to talk with someone else on the streets because it was dangerous. Buses were stopped by the military, who recorded all peasants who traveled to their homes. The person who carries a gun or a 22 caliber pistol was taken as a guerrilla and then disappeared. They recruited young people they found on their way. They told them that if they were Salvadoran patriots who fought for the cause of the country, money would not be a problem. Many times mothers had to go to the military bases to claim their sons: sometimes he was perhaps the only one she had. The military did not care whether the young man had physical disabilities; all they cared about was teaching them how to kill.

With a group of friends, we started to distribute political propaganda through the valleys and villages of the place: all farmers were enthusiastic about the subject, but had to make an effort to leave their homes so as the government and the military did not take retaliation against their families. The days passed slowly. We could hear gunfire everywhere; bombs explode and planes bombarding and shooting flares at night to see farmers. When night came people cry, especially mothers and the elderly; nights were terrible. It was possible that one did not survive the night. Many peasants no longer worked, they were fleeing or because they had to spend sleepless nights, sometimes in the rain, thinking about what might happen in the next twenty-four hours. A lot of children were already on the lists of the Civil Guard and the Death Squads.

Squads were organized in the villages first, but then squads were put on farms, valleys and small villages. When they caught someone it was to kill him. They had already killed and caused disappearance of many people in the valley. They usually did so in the villages, when the person they were looking for was there, they grabbed him and took him to a river, a lake or a coffee plantation to kill him, or to the molten rock which was also used as a slaughterhouse. On many occasions they simply took someone, especially men, out of his home and in his own yard or half a block, they massacred him. Young women sometimes were raped and killed; and even mothers had the same fate.

In 1980 five bodies appeared one block from my house, with large bullet holes and machete-made remains. They were left covered with a large white robe with the initials E. M., in red. They often did it to spread panic. Days later, they came and killed seventeen people, including a child: it was about seven o'clock and some were working in their fields when the bursts of bullets began firing from the hills to the valley. They killed five members of a family and the lady with the last of her children, aged four, disappeared, never heard from them again.

They surrounded the small village bordering the valley and started shooting from the hills on both sides to terrorize people. Then they captured the young and massacre them in the riverbank. People who were hiding in the ditches and in the brushwood nearby told that when the massacre happened, they heard horrific scream of the victims - their arms and legs were cut with machetes before being gun fired. The bodies remained for three days without burial because a plane was monitoring from the air. If anyone dared to approach the bodies, he risked being killed because the plane was carrying a 50 revolver. According to them, they had executed subversives or communists. Finally, four or five days later we could make a square pit, two meters wide and two meters deep to bury them. The bodies were decomposing; the black vultures had begun to eat them. The memory is kept alive; all those who died were my friends, mostly went to school with me: we had been friends since childhood; we had gone to school together and saw each other often in the river while we swam. A man named José Pineda lost his three children in this slaughter. His life and his wife's life were not the same after that; they found no consolation for the loss of their children.

When the murderers carried out this killing, they had to cross the river to get to the other side and took people by surprise in the valley. On their return, the river was filled, and two guards drowned while crossing it, they were drugged and drunk, besides, they had a rifle and a thousand (or more) cartridges they carried in a team and were quite heavy. Another thing happened, fifty armed militiamen were waiting for them in a strategic place where they had to go back, after a few hours it gun battle between the revolutionary militias and the military were heard: this time, the military and the squad were surprised.

However, at that time, the weapons carried by militants were not fully competent but handguns, automatic rifles; they had short assault weapons such as submachine guns and some other G-3 or M-16, but *the boys* were determined to such acts.

By that time, the guerrillas burned several mayors of the municipalities in the country. Town halls were used to investigate people from the valleys and peasantries, although people were not from the "left", as they called it, they were forced to collaborate and be with them. Days later, the armed forces arrived in the valley on the other side of the river, where they massacred nearly a hundred souls. The activists who were in the militia usually had abandoned their homes, organized, and moved strategically night after night.

On many occasions, they knew the movements of the armed forces, but the soldiers killed without exception. Most of the people they killed were not involved in political affairs; they murdered them because they were family members of a revolutionary militant: it cost the life of the whole family, they exterminated them all. The idea of monitoring to look after our security was dismissed after a few months as it was ineffective, the armed forces implemented new strategies to surprise the inhabitants of all areas, appeared unexpectedly anywhere. Of course, they had guides in the area that helped them, usually belonged to groups of the Death Squad.

In my home town there were two barracks: one was the infantry barracks called "Quarter 64," and the headquarters "St. Nicholas", the artillery one. From there they unfolded the battalions to go against peasantries in the area. Later, groups of soldiers were taken to all the farms, (whether they were in government hands or not, and the valleys of peasantries) they forced people to serve in the Death Squad. Soldiers were commanded by a sergeant or a corporal. They gave instruction to farmers from thirteen years up to the elders: they were taught how to use the weapon and how to protect themselves.

During those days in Nicaragua a great leader of the masses, Cayetano Carpio had been killed. They said, some men followed him to Nicaragua as infiltrators. I do not remember if by that time Section 2 existed, a body advised by the CIA, by the military high and by the Death Squad. The members of this body went to the farms in search of jobs. They came with a backpack where they loaded old tortillas, a canteen or earthenware bowl for water and a curved machete to weed. The most interesting and shameful thing was that they had a great charisma to persuade farmers, who were often entrusted everything. There were times when peasants even gave them a place to sleep for a few days and provided them with food. In return, the army came days after to kill people. Cayetano was a shoemaker in the slums of the capital. When he was killed, people got angrier, with more fighting spirit.

In our place there were several peasant leaders who moved in coordination with the Popular Revolutionary Block (BPR) and were always alert to the enemy. Due to the great convulsion a lot of people joined the revolutionary movements, many others, because of their weaknesses and other factors, ended up betraying their own people and social class.

In our valley, Maximiliano Dueñas's case is the most remembered; we called him Mancho. He was about six years older than I was, at school one could infer his character and see his behavior. He was a "rabble" in our country; we call a person like this who only thinks and does evil. Then, he would become the hit man of the area and had dozens of disciples.

At that time he was about twenty-five years; he was in the ranks of BPR, was coordinator of the area and was working clandestinely with the leaders of the region. He knew all the rural people involved in the movement from almost four villages and various valleys. He was chased many times while riding his horse: he jumped barbed wire fences, very high pine woods and other thorn plants fleeing from the military. He escaped many ambushes from the enemy, but he ended up betraying his people. He was considered as someone really loyal to the cause within the organization, but one day his mind changed and was the first to enter the Death Squad in a town called La Toma de Aguilares in the department of San Salvador during the days when Monsignor Romero was killed. There the first Death Squad was organized in our area.

This man arrived with his command of the squadron to take out peasants who were mutilated and killed in groups. He murdered hundreds of local people with his own hands. He had become the hit man in the area: a hired murderer. First, his family tried to hide him, saying he had gone to the United States, they also said he was already dead, but later on he was no longer hiding. He talked to people face to face.

One day a peasant rally was held at Tacachico farm, owned by the famous Bustamante. The present settlers as well as foreigners wanted to claim mandatory sources that pay twenty-five colons a day with good food for short cane (the "good food" demanded was a portion of fried rice with refried beans and two tortillas). The task supposedly given to the pawn was to create two tons of cane already cut, but the foremen barbarians actually gave tasks that produced up to four tons. It meant double work; the young and elderly sometimes took two full days to complete it. At five in the afternoon there were about 75 farmers agreeing on what they asked.

They were in front of the hull of the farm, where people gathered and lined up at the beginning of the fortnight to count peasants in charge of the work. There was a stone wall around, about a meter and a half tall. There were the military and the Death Squad. Suddenly a first shot was heard –it was an order to start the fire - then there were dozens of simultaneous bursts of G-3 and M-16. Three minutes later, all were silent, as if nothing happened. All the peasants were shot. The leader who was conducting the meeting was a peasant named Aurelio, who had been a fellow leadership of Mancho. Mancho himself was there with the military and the squad; he had done the report and somehow knew about the rally.

Two or three weeks later, my brother and I went to look for work in the short cane in that farm. There were people from the Death Squad with soldiers instructing them: they were about thirty armed men tracking the place; at night, they forced out farmers and kill them. In front of the farm's offices was a small coffee plantation where they made a huge pit to bury their comrades; their hats were on top of the grave, all punched with bullets.

My brother and I also had a terrible time while cutting cane there. He was fourteen or fifteen, but he worked as an adult. At that time, somebody found setting fire to a cane plantation was considered a subversive; when the sugar cane did not burn the bud was stored and used to feed cattle. One morning, we were starting a task with a friend and an unknown man when a fire started in the cairn next to ours. (People made this to finish the job earlier). The bunch leader appeared:

"What's happening here? "He asked. "Who sets fire to the cane plantation?"

"I do not know", I replied.

"Let's see and find out who did it. Woe to him who has done it!" he kept on saying.

The squadron was hanging around, among the cane cutters. They came and searched our bags. We had lunch in ours and in our friend's they found matches. That was enough to take him to a near ditch and kill him. But he was lucky because in the squadron was his nephew and saved his life. Maybe it was not him who did it: sometimes someone who's nearby came and set fire to the task of somebody else to get him in trouble.

At the time, there was also a squad in the Tutultepeque farm. This was the first one organized in farms and valleys from my place. It was the most controlled farm from Aguilares town, the nearest, largest, richest, most populated, and the head of the other farms. The administration of the other farms of landowners who had left the country and the land reform initiated by the government with the ISTA controlled the uprising of people. This place became the hideout of many murderers of the area. They brought squads of troopers that trained those who were part of the squad (advised by others, like Mancho and some even worst) and taught them to torture, mutilate and other unspeakable things. During the six or seven years of war, the farm surroundings became a clandestine cemetery. They buried the dead in coffee plantations, at ground level, and dogs found them. This continued for many years, only slowed a bit with the arrival of representatives of Human Rights to the country.

Mancho was there with his men, among whom were many known. We attended school with most of them and we shared the same poverty working together. Even others from my valley joined, whose names rather not mention. They dedicated themselves to go everywhere, get the peasants out of their houses or farms and kill them. They robbed people their hens. Many of them are still alive, many are dead, and others fled the country, others are in prison sentenced for more than forty years of imprisonment.

Mr. Vicente Escobar's sons, who by then already fled La Loma del Espino and lived in the village in the capital, had satisfied their desire to kill. They joined the Death Squads and started killing people. One morning they went with the squad to get Esteban, "the cat" out, to kill him because of he threatened his father. Halfway down the sidewalk, amid darkness they found four young men from my valley (among whom a brother of Esteban) who were going to a dance nearby, they took the four with them, so they could not tell anyone. When they arrived at Esteban's house, they dragged him off; then they mutilated them with machetes and massacred using machine guns. Esteban received two hundred stab wounds and did not die right away: he crawled two blocks back to his house; he managed to get there after two hours. During that time lag, his wife and their children could not do anything but mourn: they heard the gunshots and she, with all their little children, did not know what to do, whether to go or wait for the body. They wanted to take him to a hospital, but few hours later he died.

I went to see the other dead people. It was awful the way they had been killed: their faces were unrecognizable, their arms and legs had been slashed with machetes, some had ears or fingers cut off. After being massacred with machine guns, they were beheaded, covered with a white blanket with the initials D. S. 'Death Squad' written in red. Their personal belongings such as watches, chains, shoes and jeans were stolen, too.

Usually squads used the German G-3 rifle, the Garand and the Czech. These rifles had a great power; a bullet would flow half of the victim's head. The G-3 caliber is like the M-60. Besides, the militias that already killed about two hundred people of my valley wandered by that time. We could no longer be in the mountains and there were no safe places to protect ourselves. In many places, like ravines and cliffs, there were huge caves where several dozen people could hide. They were called "*tatú*", which is a word of Vietnamese origin.

One day, while my brother and I were working on the land, in the banks of the Sucio River, we saw a thick and steely cable coming down a barrel. The barrel had been filled with dirt and emptied into the river automatically; then went up alone. We did not tell anyone about what we saw, and that helped to defend people.

As the squads and the military always came to kill the relatives of the people who were in the militia and to terrorize, militias were annihilating "ears" and farm foremen who were working directly or indirectly with the oppressive system; so they executed many. In my place was an old man who looked after the land to the mayor of the town. This man whose name I do not remember was commonly called *Camarón* (prawn) because he was a little reddish- was intolerant. He threatened with his gun those he saw crossing the property he's taking care of; he often took away women, boys and girls at gunpoint, protected by the fact that his employer was the mayor of the town. He had been brought from somewhere and nobody liked it. He had no friends in the valley, the only friend he had was my father. My father talked to him and they're comfortable. However, my mother told my dad to be very careful, because the man "not eat it alone," as the saying goes, he was involved in something. A few days later, three hundred militiamen came at night; they broke the door and the roof, and shot him dead in front of his wife and their little children. It is said, they didn't go to kill, they just wanted to talk, to warn and make him aware of the seriousness of certain political issues, but Mr. Camarón fired his gun through a hole and wounded one or two of the militiamen; they got very angry and killed him.

In those days full of terror, a sad stray dog had more chances of living than human. The deaths happened every day, everywhere. There was no one to trust or to tell something concerning ideologies; you could not trust absolutely anyone. When the militia, which at this point were already guerrillas went other ways, people started to stop believing in them. Who stayed in the valley were those who either did not want to leave or could not; and those who left did it for the safety of their families. However, many people changed their way of thinking: the consistency of the militias had failed, militias still were not coordinated with the direction of command, and there were many counter problems for the revolutionary process: this occurred because many had entered to make their own. Some only wanted to rob people, since they had the opportunity to walk in groups and with weapons. Others only sought vengeance for their families. Thus, people began to take care of them. If someone had an enemy and knew that he was in one of the sides, he had to leave his place of origin, otherwise be on the same side to protect his life. For this cause my older brother was killed later.

My brother had four children, which the eldest was only seven years old. Once, he went to the village with his brother-in-law, who had conflict with someone in the militia, they were taken by surprise. As my brother's brother-in-law had his fingers cut in a fight, he wanted revenge. And so it happened. They were grabbed, taken to the river where they were killed and left in a cross on a rock nearby. My brother was killed so for him not to speak: for this reason they killed many.

These days guerrillas removed some people and took away different weapons. Numerous guerrillas executes when they had done illegal things after or on behalf of the revolution. Even individuals that did absolutely nothing went through the valleys extorting peasants. They put a note in the front of their homes that says - in the name of revolution, go to a certain place someday, at a particular hour, and leave some money in a bag. If they did not follow as instructed, the guerrillas would kill them. Of course, people were frightened. This was a delay for movement. Many subordinates and scoundrels were devoted to things like this for a while. Then they began the killing by both sides: by the guerrillas and the army.

The guerrillas, meanwhile, began apprehending and stopping buses in the roads to ask for donations. This was involuntary; people were not obliged to do it. The guerrillas were well uniformed and mounted platforms. There were ladies and girls who also participated in the act with political propaganda, banners and other materials. In addition, in both sides of the road were safety officers with devices to communicate with each other, ready to attack a convoy that comes or flee and if seen they were not prepared for the task. Another guerrilla movement was to kidnap the rich millionaires who were cooperating with the government in killing people. Somehow, one can think that they deserved it: after enslaving the people for decades, now they're massacred. Clearly, they did not kidnap all the millionaires who were against the revolution, only a few of the many traitors who were in the leadership and who had already killed many people.

In my family there was another episode linked to these issues. I had an uncle named Juan Pablo Hércules (I mention his name because I'm very proud of him) who was in his thirties, he lived in La Loma del Espino, had a wife and six children, all less than eight years. It had been, and still was at that time, cantonal-civil commander in the area. For several years he worked in recruitment with thirty men under his command; he kept order in his place and reported all incidents that often occurred in the valley. He and his family lived (thanks to his daily work in the plots he had acquired with much effort). In the past he had problems with a neighbor by land boundaries; this man was bad-hearted, aggressive, and wanted to kill my uncle, but he was smarter with the machete and won the dispute: my uncle wounded him in the hands and arms, and disarmed him. Time passed, but the man still felt humiliated. When the political conflict came, he joined the guerrillas and began to seek ways to kill my uncle; for this, the guerrillas gave false reports against him.

As my uncle Juan was still a cantonal-civil commander, he had to go to report the news in the valley at least once a month. There were many on the list, and Uncle Juan took them off. In those situations he had to face the National Guard lieutenant who was in charge of receiving all cantonal-civilian commanders. My father told him not to submit to the command because it would bring him problems with the militias.

However, if he stop going to the military he would be killed because of being subversive. He was between a rock and a hard place, but my uncle was a friend of the leaders in charge of the guerrillas, he managed twice to erase many names from the lists the Civil Guard had to kill. The first time, he was called by the lieutenant: he told him to report to the command to see a statement. The old man showed a list that included about three hundred individuals, who would be killed; several of them were even relatives such as cousins and others. Many actually were direct or indirectly with the guerrillas, but most have done nothing and had just been put on the list to be killed. My uncle Juan told the leaders of the guerrillas what had happened and they were grateful. About two months later, the commander called him back. This time he almost had the same names; some had already died in the time lag. The guard lieutenant was totally furious with my uncle: he took him by his neck, strangling him while calling him traitor.

"Look, look at this list... Do not you think they are subversive...?" he said angrily and looking forward to ordering the guards to kill him. "You're a traitor to this country, but from now on you have to cooperate with us".

The old man wanted my uncle to be part of the ORDEN or "ear" of the place: a faithful partner to them. My uncle, who carried his gun because he was an agent and had the privilege of carrying a weapon, felt like taking it out and kill him right there, but he restrained himself because he knew he could not leave the place alive. Finally, he managed to remove some from the list. When he returned home, he told the boys what happened. They told him not to go anymore, as that old man wanted him to serve them and that if he did not continue to serve them as commander, he would be accused of subversive and would be killed, as what happened to others.

The situation was not that good to my uncle. On one side was the military and, on the other, the militia. Also, his personal enemy realized he could not kill him neither with an order of the cell nor by using known people to do it secretly. He was being watched because he wanted to kill more than a few apart from my uncle. So, this man deserted this cell and entered a different bordering place. It was at that moment when my uncle decided to leave his home and his children, and joined the guerrilla cell, because at that time this type of cases still occurred.

His family had to leave the place; the children ended up separated, both of them were with my mother (my uncle's sister). His wife went to town to work and earn money for her children. Later they came several times at night to kill him. They probably were his enemies from other groups, the military or the squad.

My uncle told us that life in the guerrilla was not easy. They had to live in the open and as nomads, moving from side to another at all times to avoid being detected by the enemy. They ate when they had something to eat and were always ready to kill and die at any moment.

A few days before my uncle Juan left his home and his position, Mancho's mother was killed by the militias. The lady gave information to his son about the peasants who were not in move. One day when the woman went to buy liquor she was intercepted on the road and killed. Many people were been killed because of what she told. Mancho with his squadron came to pick up her body. Along the way, he passed by my uncle Juan's house to ask him to lift the case and take it to the authorities. The man walked extremely angry and said he would kill all the inhabitants of La Loma del Espino valley. He threatened my uncle:

"Wait, Juancito" he said, "one of these days I'll come for you, your brother, and others".

That same day, while they were carrying the body of his mother in a pickup, they got three persons and took them to the lava close to the village to kill them. Days later he was doing pickups in the town, especially on Sundays. They put in prison those who were caught; held them there a few hours and at night and took them to the nearby molten rocks of the volcano in San Salvador to kill them.

One day, he killed nine from the valley, including our relatives. We discovered it because they did not return to the village; we imagined they were already dead so we went to the molten rocks with some of their brothers. There was equipment (caterpillar) burying the dead: each pile of stone was a sign that a lot of dead people buried below it. The place stank in an indescribable way. The buzzards were so many, had dried some trees where they had their nap after lunch; countless animals were seen standing in piles of stone. A Salvadoran writer wrote in a work that instead of having the *torogoz* as a national bird of the country we should have had the buzzard, because (thanks to these eating resources) they increased in number. The place was sinister, it produced a profound terror; between the lights of the stones you could see the bodies. While the engineer threw stones with the hoe to bury six or seven who had been killed that morning, he saw us, stopped the equipment and stared at us. So we approached him to talk.

"Hey, do you know if last night there were killed or dead people brought here?"

We asked.

The man of about 45 years watched us and then took out a cigar and bit a piece to chew. Then he took a bottle of brandy he had on one side of the seat and took several drinks.

"Without this you cannot work here" he said while covering the bottle, and then added in an apathetic way: "What do you want?"

We repeated what we said first, and he answered:

"Aren't those who I will bury right now?"

We went to see right away, but they were unknown, so we came back to him and answered:

"No, they are not".

"Last night I heard several bursts of shots, on several occasions, by the close to the Cane plantation that is there" he said while pointing with his finger, "Go and see there, maybe they are there", he continued.

We walked down the paved road that passed through there. The bad smell was felt on that stretch of the road. We reached the pantheon of Chanmico Valley; there we found an old man making a pit to bury the dead, and asked him the same. The old man was also drinking his liquor to bear his work, and he told us to go to see inside the cane plants. So we did, and we found about five mutilated bodies. Then we followed a gap made by machete into the cane plantation, and found more bodies, but they were not the ones we were looking for. So, we went back where the old man was.

"I forgot to mention that there is a pit that has about ten killed persons", he said.

The man seemed a little drunk, and told us he had not thrown them land still, waiting for relatives to come and look for them. We went to see and there they were: somebody had stolen their pants and shoes, as well as rings, chains and watches. We wanted to take them out, but they were at the bottom, so we had to get the others out first. Among them was a friend of my mother's relatives. We put them out in case their families went to the place looking for him.

It was days of March 1980 when they killed Monsignor Romero. The pontiff was giving a homily at the Basilica of Divine Providence when he was gunned down. It was committed by the Death Squad, but the mastermind was the founder of the same squad, Major Roberto D'Aubuisson. It was an act that impacts throughout the world: after that they could no longer silence the atrocities they committed and a lot of information passed the country's borders.

A few months earlier, Monsignor Romero had sent the US President Jimmy Carter a letter in which he said that they would no longer send more assistance to the Salvadoran government because it was being used to turn the country into a bloodbath. He said that instead of collaborating with weapons, they would send bread and other food for children who lived in great poverty. At that time they had already killed many priests and other members of the Church, others had disappeared.

Monsignor Romero's funeral was a memorable event: tens of thousands of supporters marched through the streets of San Salvador and in front of the Metropolitan Cathedral. Furthermore, there were many international representatives witnessing the event. When no one expected, suddenly the shooting started. From the roofs of the buildings they massacred people and threw bombs. Many people died that day, and there were many wounded.

José Napoleón Duarte spoke on radio and television, saying that the facts that could be seen were bombs exploding, but no agent of the security forces in sight, and showed the pictures on television. Of course where the bombs exploded there were no security forces: they were on rooftops, throwing them and firing. At first they wanted to make people believe that the people up in arms had murdered Archbishop Romero, but they failed because there was no evidence of such a thing. After that event, if they heard someone saying that the extreme right murdered Monsignor Romero, he's then a dead person. They did not like what people said and wanted to show a clean face to the international arena. Things went from bad to worse.

In the field everybody was amazed with what was happening in the country. People were crying the death of the pontiff as majorities were Catholic. Controls in rural areas were even more frequent. Troops were present at all times, and if they found a person listening to "The Pan-American Voice," he was taken as subversive and killed. "The Pan-American Voice" was a regular religious radio station where Monsignor Romero spoke in the past. He used it to ask men, in the name of God, to cease repression. After his death, they transmitted the masses he held and some messages that were recorded, but it was forbidden to listen to it. A few days later, they bombed the radio station and it was destroyed, it was bombed a few times by government forces. If somebody was found listening to protest music as "Casas de carton" cardboard houses by Los Guaraguao or Nicaraguan Luis Enrique Mejia Godoy, was also killed. When they spoke from the General Staff of the Armed Forces, however, broadcasters transmitted in chain and spoke in the name of "freedom and democracy".

Monsignor Romero was accused of being subversive only because he got into clandestine prisons to rescue people who were about to being murdered or had been tortured. Of course, these prisons were under official secrecy, but sometimes he warned about the existence of some of them. Sometimes, ladies would ask him to take out a son or a husband of that place. He did it with pleasure, and because of that they began to analyze that was contrary to the military and politicians. When they murdered Father Rutilio Grande, Monsignor Romero was very upset, and he started asking them directly to stop the abuses against the people when he spoke during masses or in his homilies. The final point was the famous letter to Washington. The result was his murder; he was executed by an operation of intelligence.

Sometime later, they raped and murdered American nuns. Then it was confirmed that this happened in the volcano molten rocks in San Salvador, a few kilometers from my village. Lava or the molten rocks was a killing field. At that time, the unpleasant smell was unbearable on the road passing through the lava, which lasted for years. Buzzards dried the largest trees that were all around the place. The trees were leafless, black.

People from my place basically divided into three groups. There were those who supported the oppressive system and secretly collaborated with the local squad, which were not many, but many were killed by them. Then, there were those in the guerrillas or secretly supported it, and there were the neutral people who do not participate in anything. At that time you could not open your mouth to talk about anything related to politics, or else you'll be condemned to death almost immediately. My older brother and I wanted to join the guerrillas, but the head of the family hindered us. There, in those countries, one is grown up as a child and obey until he marries or leaves the parental roof, no matter how old you are. Our father told us that he preferred to keep us away but not dead, because after we received training and political classes, it got totally dangerous, he did not want us to continue attending: he was afraid they would kill us.

The killings were even worse. There was gunfire everywhere, trenches and barricades in the streets and roads, planes bombarding the most troubled areas and guerrilla re-concentration. They bombarded towns, hamlets and villages systematically. The Guazapa Mountain few miles from my birthplace became a combat zone during the thirteen years of war, and always being bombed. We heard about several bizarrely huge massacres done in the country, such as the Sumpul River which is on the border with Honduras: while hundreds of people fled from El Salvador to shelter in that country, the planes bombed and massacred hundreds; most of them were ladies, children and elderly people. In those days they had bombed and attacked many under these circumstances, the event remained in history forever as "Sumpul Massacres."

In the area of Chalatenango they almost exterminated all. Many towns were completely empty, looked like ghost towns. Tenancingo, another martyr town, was also mercilessly bombed. There is no doubt that for every living creature of El Salvador it was a very miserable picture. In my area, the foul odor could be detected even in the Sucio River as many bodies passed crumbling into the water.

The river passed near the village where they continuously throw dead bodies, although this also happened along some other valleys. The situation was alike in few lakes in the region: dead bodies floated in the water. The Lempa River is the largest river in the country, this river has two hydroelectric dams, the Cinco de Noviembre, in Chorrera of the Guayabo, and the newest, the Cerrón Grande; they would kill people there and you could see the bodies floating. These dams had been very important resources for fishing for a long time, but we had to stop buying fish because when they cut fish from freshwater, which came mostly from these places, you could smell the foul odor, these fishes had consumed flesh of the dead bodies. People do not buy freshwater fish anymore.

One of my uncles told us he went fishing after a while. He was afraid because dangerous things were often found in the rivers. However, as he wanted to eat fish, he said he did not care even if it was contaminated. So he went and took his boy to wash his clothes while he was fishing. After fishing a while upstream, he began to cast the fishing net in a backwater behind a stone. He threw repeatedly, and always grabbed a fish; but in one of the shots he made the fishing net got caught. The place had a little more than a meter deep. Then, when he plunged to unlock his net he saw that it had hooked up on the arm of a corpse. With the rhythm of the water, the arm (which was already breaking up in the water) -moved. My uncle took the fishing net and as the water stirred, the bad smell appeared. It gave him a sensation of disgust so he let go of the fish he caught. He also saw crabs carrying dead meat on their pincers and mouth. He no longer wanted to eat fish or go fishing in the river.

That end of the year we still went to pick coffee with my brothers (it was the last time I did it). People were no longer chatty and cheerful as before. In some farms there's a Death Squad, had in were other National Guard and soldiers. During the day they walked through the coffee plantations, listening to what coffee pickers were talking about, and in the evening they drew people from the barracks, killed them in the depths of the surroundings. Many were left hanged in coffee trees; it was terrifying. We did not earn much more because wages had not risen and labors sometimes spent more on food consumption although we cooked our own food. We worked only a couple of weeks and returned. It was really dangerous; they could kill us at any time so we returned to our place of origin.

There, in the valley, things were still overwhelming. People could neither find meaning in life nor a course to follow. Only killings and deaths were in sight everywhere. The street leading to the town crosses the valley called Platanillos, close to the Loma del Espino, but closer to the town. There is a school that bears his name there. One afternoon, there were several young people sitting on the rocks in front of the school on the edge of the street. They consumed candies bought in the store; they did not realize that the armed forces and the squad were searching the houses in the valley. When they got there, they found them in the street and massacred them with machine guns, according to a cousin who was there and told us about that situation. Some of them were thirteen or fourteen years old. Also, they took to the streets a lady who had, according to them, her husband and some family in the guerrillas. The woman was in her last days of pregnancy and they likewise mutilated her. It is claimed that when she died, the fetus came out of her uterus. This lady was named María Larios.

At that point, my father told my older brother and me we better move to town, along with my sister who was already married. Perhaps we would be safer there. However, things were alike: shootings and people battings in the streets were heard at midnight.

One night, it was about one in the morning, and in the silence of the night somebody knocked at the door at a neighbor's who lived about half a block from ours. It was the National Guard, and as no one opened the door they began to give kicks with their rifles while yelling: "Go out, son of [...]. Your life will be respected". As they did not open the door, they machine-gunned it.

The next day, the bodies were in a coffee plantation about two blocks away.

I also remembered a lady of about forty years old, a single mother. I cannot remember her name, but she lived in one of the surrounding neighborhoods with her three very beautiful daughters. The young girls would have between sixteen and eighteen years, irresistibly beautiful. I knew them town when we went for coffee picking in small farms around, and this lady was out there with her three daughters, very attentive and communicative with people. Days after finishing the picking of coffee, the National Guard and the Death Squad went to their house: they took her daughters to the coffee plantations; they raped them, then mutilated their bodies with machete and murdered them. It is said that, days later, the lady lost her sanity, she walked the streets of the town, half-naked, or dressed in rags, at times she cried, other times she laughed, and anyone she met she asked, "Where are my girls...?" The poor lady lost her sanity and stayed like that until she died. It is said that this happened only because the girls did not want to be girlfriends of a military, one in the group that attacked, rape and killed them.

By that time my uncle Juan, my mother's brother, took the risk of losing all his children and his wife because he was with the guerrillas. The military could come and kill his whole family, and even kill his grandmother and siblings. For this reason it was necessary to do something; they had to get them out of that place.

This was the guy who for a long time was a cantonal-civil commander in the area, in charge of maintaining order in the cantons. To choose a person for this position, the lieutenant of the National Guard of the town recommends to the lieutenant or to the sergeant who came from the (High commander office in the town) (Military Lieutenant of National Guard). The already appointed commander had to choose, in turn, twenty men from the valley to be in his charge. This commission was mandatory, although they called it voluntary and without any payment. Every Sunday he had to go with one or two of his sheriffs to say whether there was novelty where he lived in the valley or not. When the lieutenant orders recruiting boys, they went to villages and towns, they had to go after the youth of the area. As usual, it was forced recruitment.

At that time, they only had the soldiers in the barracks for twenty months. When the young man had physical disabilities or had no teeth or illiterate they did not admit him, neither in the Civil Guard nor in the police force. But this was at the beginning of this political situation, later on was no problem. However, in the days of the war everything was possible; all that mattered was that the individual had heart to kill and commit war atrocities.

Among other things, they had to report if there were "punches" of liquor or spirits in the area, as its production was illegal. There were bars where commercial drinks were sold, and it was strictly forbidden to take liquor or chicha as alcoholic beverages. If there were civic festivals of the village, the commander had to go to walk around the villages up to a week, with all his men. Of course, if there were lawsuits in which some ended up injured, very common in those days, they should tie them up and bring them to "justice", that is to say, the town National Guard. In the case that someone will be dead, they had to use all means to apprehend the murderer, go to the town and give the part of a dead so a guard wrote a report which was then presented in the court. These were the functions of someone who had to serve "voluntarily" as the government system said. The only privilege that one of this people had was obviously the permission to carry the gun wherever they went.

Because of the pressure he received both from the military and the guerrillas, in a moment he was between a rock and a hard place, he had to take sides. Thus, he became part of the guerrillas. Seeing that the members of his family, including his mother and his brothers were in danger, his other two brothers worried to seek home with other relatives, away from the area and send them where no one knew them. There was an unpleasant surprise: the brothers, who were looking for their house passed among a firefight. The one who was driving was scared, or perhaps was shot and lost control. The car fell in the abyss, and all who were in it were killed. My uncles who helped us in difficult times died there and we never knew where they were buried; we just know they are in a town called Teotepeque, where the great revolutionary man Farabundo Martí was born. The country was so dangerous that no one could go out without worrying matters of life or death.

So only Juan was left, the younger brother of my mother, and we had to do something for him. When the guerrillas gave him permission, he went home to visit his children, his mother and his wife, and we talked. I told him to go to Guatemala, that from there we could be in contact with the family and he had not to worry for the rest of the family because they were going to be fine. The problem was more serious if he stayed in the country, they were going to kill his family in retaliation. My uncle told me to give him two or three days to return to his camp and tell the commander he would quit revolutionary activities, but they could trust him since he would not tell anyone any information about the revolutionary movements. So, he left with his rifle and revolver, and we waited for them to appear in the next three days.

Three days passed, a week passed, and he did not appear. In those days there was the martial law, there was a curfew in the country. My mom told us to go and look for him where we thought he could find him. One of my cousins also his nephew and I were set out on the task of finding him. We grabbed some slings, a backpack, a machete and we left. My mom was crying. First we looked for the river to go down to and pretend that we were chasing iguanas. That night we slept in a cave on a cliff of the river, as we saw it had been used to make illegal liquor in earlier times.

The next day we continued our way until we started hearing gunfire, bombs and helicopters firing machine guns. After a while, we found a man who apparently was a guerrilla. He wore a shoulder injury like the brush of a bullet. While he wiped the blood with a cloth, he said it was not a good idea to get into that area; it was better to go somewhere else. We asked him the camp we were looking for and we mentioned the name of the place. He said he knew it, and pointed us to continue walking along the river and when we got to the bridge we should walk to the right by the stream ditch, and later we would find it there. Then he said "but you have not seen me". We kept on walking in the same direction from where we came.

It was almost noon and shootings were occasionally heard in several directions; bombarding planes, bombs exploding and helicopters firing while flying. We walked a bit and then stopped to pay attention, but we heard anything. At four in the afternoon, we reached the bridge. We walked to the east by a dirt road. We were on one side of the street, which was all trenching. There were large trees cut and put across the road, and gutters of a meter or more deep. Then we started seeing burned grass houses, not only smoldered, cows and pigs killed too, some dead hens and others alive, howling dogs, people who had been killed, some were burned. A number of abandoned houses were burned and their corn cobs, their rice barn, etc. Animals that were alive walked bewildered. The army found that empty valley, the inhabitants were gone, they knew that if they had a family member in the guerrillas they're good as dead, others left because of fear. This was a real terror zone.

Abruptly, a helicopter appeared and took about two turns in the air, then went to a glen to the river bank and threw cans of food. Sooner, we realized that the soldiers were there. The guerrillas were closer and began shooting with rifles as soon as the throwing of food for the soldiers began. When we heard the shots, we hid in some small trees in the middle of a pasture. We trembled from fear and did not know what to do. The street was only a few meters, but we did not dare to cross, we could be seen and shot. We had not realized that there was a small house until we saw that from it they were taking out a man in blindfold, hands tied and shirtless, brought to kneel down under a mango tree.

Those who brought him were soldiers; about twelve of them, pushed him, hit him with rifles, and slapped him.

"Cooperate, then" they said. 'We will not do anything".

"Gentlemen, you are going to kill me anyway!" The man exclaimed as he wept and begged them. "I know nothing; I'm neither on one side nor the other. I just work to support my children and my wife. Please gentlemen, do not kill me...!"

The blows with the guns silenced him for a while. Two of the soldiers, who seemed leaders, walked a few meters to withdraw from the scene and began to speak softly. We came to think they were coming towards us, but they had not seen us. They all had their faces painted black and wore black bandanas covering them. A moment later, the two soldiers returned and spoke to the man who was lying on the floor, barefoot, hands and feet tied, blindfolded and shirtless.

"All right, we're going to let you go, but run, run as fast as you can," said the one who seemed to be the sergeant. Then, he was released and they shouted, "Run!!!"

The man ran, about thirty meters far, a burst of bullets put him on the floor. We trembled with fear; we could not talk to each other. From where we were, we could see the body of the man, who jumped about twice.

For a moment, we saw the wife, who managed to reach the courtyard of the house. She and two children were crying and screaming in a dreadfully in absolute despair.

"Are you sad, my sweet heart?" The sergeant stopped her and added, "Well, I'll make you happy."

The girl, who apparently was pretty, about twenty years old, inconsolably cried.

"My husband... My children... For God's love... No..."

Then, some soldiers grabbed the children while the sergeant raped the woman. After a while, he left tying his belt.

"I do not like this woman, I do not like her because she that cries a lot, he said and turned to another man. "Now it's up to you, my corporal".

The corporal did not answer, but when he got up from where he sat he had already unfastened his belt. The girl begged to be killed, crying loudly. It sounded like she did not want to be raped, they cuffed her. At one moment, we heard what the corporal said:

"If you do not let me in, I'll put the barrel of the gun, daughter of the great [...]."

That was extremely horrible. We cannot even move, because if they saw us, they would kill us. Then the corporal left the place, and spoke to another:

'Today it's up to you, *Antena*."

That was the one in charge if carrying the communication radio on his back.

"After Antena takes her, is there any soldier who wants her? " Asked the sergeant, but no one answered, so he told Antena, "Well, after you rape her, kill her and then kill her children".

The scene continued with children sobbing and the girl crying in anguish, asking them to kill her.

"Kill me, fucking dogs" said the girl in rage and hatred.

Soon, blasts were heard from Antena inside the little house after he did what the others did and there was silence all over the place. The lady and her little angels had passed away. We were astonished; we trembled with fear. At that moment, we somehow reacted, we were eager wanting to leave the hideout and be part of the scene, but we restrained ourselves.

The soldiers withdrew from the place. It was getting dark, and we stayed there all night. We could not sleep because of the helicopters blasted the area, besides a plane came to bomb the place. All the time a plane called push'n'pulls or wagon, threw flares to see 'the boys', as people said the guerrillas who were taking up arms. It was a combat area.

Finally, dawn came. We took off the leaves from our clothes and started walking. At one side of the street there were many houses, peasants' huts burned. When we saw a cart driver we immediately went to meet him.

"Excuse me", I said, "we are messengers of the boys"

"Could you tell me where can I find them? We have a message to the camp."

The man stared at me for a moment. Finally, he answered,

"Are you sure what you're saying, kid?"

"Yes, in that camp were my relatives" I replied, "and we want to talk to one of them"

The old man took a piece of purse from the pocket of his pants to chew and stared at the river.

"Right in front of you there is a path and down to it is the river" he said. "Follow that path until you pass a stream that falls into the river. There, on that cliff, there is a camp."

I thanked him and we kept walking. Soon, we were already in the place. No sooner did we cross the stream than three boys appeared in our way. They were hidden behind some rocks, making well-armed security. They asked us what we were doing in the place. I told them we wanted to see my uncle who was there with them. Then I gave them his name and some other names to prove that I was telling the truth. Then, one of them took us to the camp; there were about a hundred men, all well-armed. Some were eating; others in their hammock, listening to music or sleeping and others were healing gunshot wounds. They also had some uniforms and rifles from soldiers they had probably killed. They even had a uniform from a sergeant who had probably been caught or killed, because the straps did not lie. Also, I think they had a place for private interrogation that we could not reach. After seeing several acquaintances, we found my uncle and told him that the family wanted him in the house. He already knew what was it about, and immediately went and talked to his boss. The boss gave him permission to leave the next day, but not with us, the commander knew that it was dangerous to accompany us. They gave us food, and an hour later we left the place, heading for the house.

The next day we got home. I told my mom that my uncle would come a day later and we would go to Guatemala. At that time, many people left the country every day. Some cousins were going to go on a tour to Mexico City, I had thought to accompany them, but I needed some money and a passport. You had to show money at borders and give some bribes to customs. On the other hand, money was needed for the expenses of the alleged stay in Mexico, as we pretended to visit several places, including the Virgin of Guadalupe in Mexico City. Of course nobody returned from this tour; all disappeared from different corners of the country and the bus returned empty.

I had a thousand colons, which were about four hundred dollars at that time. This money was enough for the trip, but I told my mom that I would wait for my uncle and then we would go to Guatemala to work in different places, so, with a quarter of money it was enough and they would have some left to use in case they need it.

The next day I went to get my passport and give the news that I would no longer travel on that tour. On the way I had to walk to the village, there was a place where some boys

used to be at, it was a remained guerrilla cell. To my surprise, when I was going I thought it I did not see anyone around the small village until suddenly a lot of soldiers appeared with their faces painted black. They emerged from the trees and rocks; they immediately pointed their guns, about ten, at me at the same time. They hit me with their rifle butts and threw me to the ground. They put the gun barrel in my head and cheeks, when I wanted to turn my head to tell them that I was not in something bad, I was told not look at them, and they stepped on my face. I thought it was the end of me. They asked me if I was a guerrilla or if I knew the people of that place. Of course all were negative answers, and after five minutes they let me go. I shook off the dust that covered my face, trembling I continued on my way.

Then, I reached town. It was pretty desolated, but the buses heading to the capital were working, I got on one of them. Later, there was another surprise in Apopa. They were searching buses. They were seeking guerrillas and recruiting young people. They stopped three buses and that was my luck; the bus that I was on was a little empty, and as they were busy, they ordered the driver to leave. I saw some people got off down the buses; they were investigating and tied some young people. Delgado City was the last bus stop before arriving in San Salvador, and there it had to stop because there were a couple of people who wanted to get in. Just a few meters behind where the bus stopped there were several mutilated bloody corpses and few meters ahead, was a murdered couple: a man and probably his wife next to him; both were naked, the man had had his penis cut and had put in the mouth to the woman, and the woman had also had her part cut and had placed in the man's mouth. It was obvious they did all this to terrorize everyone. In those days, it was notable who murdered. I imagine that some received diploma for these military "exploits" for being the "heroes of democracy" in our country.

My uncle and I decided to go to Guatemala to work in the sugar cane, coffee or cotton plantation taking into account that our families stayed in our country and only God was with them. The country was hell and chances to live were rare, so one day we got ready with few cents and started the trip. My uncle had already gone to Guatemala for a few days in the past, but was not accustomed to that quest, he needed his family.

It was a little difficult to leave the country because the whole border line was guarded and the crossing points were full of military, investigating people who wanted to leave. They interrogated all, tried to intimidate them suggesting they were leaving the country because they were guerrillas. On the banks of the Paz River was a soldier on each block, like soldiers from Guatemala hiding in the bushes. If someone tried to swim across the river to avoid customs they were shot and bodies went floating down the river. That was seen daily, often across the border. Many went there without knowing what they were doing, and as the soldiers were hiding, barricaded, people remained there.

If somebody said he was going to the capital of Guatemala, they wanted the address where he was going; if they discovered he was lying, he took the risk of being killed. The country did not want to hear people saying they were leaving because of the war, so they did not let them pass in one post; one had to deal with that and another until the purpose is achieved. We said we were going to visit a relative and used an address somebody had given us, that was very helpful. There were basic things people who wanted to cross did not know and due to that they failed; for example, in Guatemala there are no colonies like in El Salvador, but areas.

At last, we reached the town of Escuintla. We wanted to eat something; so we went where there was a lady selling lunches.

"Excuse me, madam; what do you have to eat?" We asked

"I have some stopped beans, drained beans, chilaquiles... "She said, and mentioned more meals she had.

We did not know what "stopped beans" or "strained beans" were, we asked her to show us the meals. Then we saw that the stopped beans were the beans from the pot, boiled, and the strained beans were fried, mashed beans. After lunch, we asked the lady where we could take a bus to the coast, the port of San José.

"We want to work in cotton short" I said to the lady.

"You are not Guatemalans, aren't you?" She said, "You are like "guanacos...." You are Salvadorians, right?"

We said yes. She was very friendly and gave us more directions for our job search. Then we went to look for the place where the bus was parked. Walking for the first time in an unknown land did not feel so nice... Especially when one walks illegal, we only had permission for three days; then would be left in God's hand.

We reached a place called La Gomera, a small village where only cotton plantations are available. We began asking if they offered any job somewhere but we were told that a farm was looking for people for picking cotton. Because it was the third picking, the cotton had very little weight and there was not that much on the plantation. That afternoon we were already settled, we had gotten two bags each, which would be helpful to sleep in; we would sleep in a stall where they had food for livestock. There, a woman would give us food and payment on Saturday afternoon.

It was a little sad to see those indigenous families descending from the highlands to work. They were suffering because of abuse on behalf of the foremen, the executioners of the farms. Clothes lasted a few days of work, as the husks or corolla of the cotton break it. When dry, the cotton plant is rough and badly hurts the skin. On this coast it is horribly hot and many mosquitoes. The heat was unbearable especially for the indigenous people who came from cold lands of the highest places of the country. They worked with all their children and their wives to earn about a dollar each per day; they were swaddle with typical fabrics and wore their hats. Everything they wore was distinctive; they also spoke different dialects, Guatemala has over twenty dialects and believed to have eighty percent of indigenous people.

After a couple of weeks, we realized we only earned enough to eat. When we carried the bags to the weight, we could hardly handle them, but once weighed, it was like nothing. The weighing was prepared to rob the worker, and we did not earn, just enough to survive; I never managed to make even two quetzals in a day. The stealing of these landowners was hasty; it was a totally slave labor. Within two weeks we got tired and discussed our situation with another Guatemalan laborer whom we felt confident.

"But what are you doing here?" He told us. "If you come from El Salvador, you would better get out of this place, because this is not a place for people who are in transit, here work finishes and not even a hundred quetzals can be saved. It is not worth to say something, because you are killed. They make you disappear as what had happened sometimes before" she continued saying. "You should better get out of here and go to the west of the country, to Quetzaltenango to work in coffee plantations. You can also go to the border of Tecún Umán. You can work in Mexico and live on this side. Here it's getting alike your country, workers have been killed and unknown bodies have appeared in the cotton plantations; they are caught in a village and are killed somewhere else".

So, we got to know that in Guatemala they were doing the same thing in El Salvador. People caught in one place were killed on other places where they're unknown. The lord did not tell all this to two deaf... We just ended up that week, we took our bags where we loaded our belongings, we thanked the lady and the friendships we had done, and left. When we were leaving, the lord called us aside and, in trusted, he advised us that we shouldn't tell we are Salvadorans because they had already killed several, and always because of the same thing; that it would be better if we tried to learn to speak like them, to confuse them.

As we walked, we were a little bewildered, speechless, trying to imagine what another land we would go, not knowing anyone, without warranty to stabilize or even to survive.

"This seems to be an adventure toward the North" I said to my uncle.

"I think you're right", he replied while he lowered his head, very thoughtful, and went on, "I will go farther from my children, my mother and my wife..."

I just answered him that we had to cope with whatever came.

When we were on the bus from Escuintla to the border, I remembered something. Speaking softly so that people would not notice that we were "guanacos", I told him. I remember my uncle Marcos told me that was in Tecún Umán.

This uncle had gone to Northern Mexico, had passed and been in that border town. He had also told me about a friend in that town. I told all this to my uncle Juan, I tried to remember the name of that person and the name of the village. I remembered it later.

"I think I have already remembered" I said then. "The name of this person is Marino López and lives in the village of Tecun Uman".

My uncle was a little delighted, I also felt some relief. We had to find him and, as the saying goes, "by asking you'll get to Rome."

Before Tecún Umán there was a small village that looked more like a small station. In a stall, like customs, the bus had to stop, and they had the right to register looking for illegal people going towards the border and smuggling of firearms. The driver stopped the bus, opened the door, a man got in but only up to the entrance and stared inward while he asked the driver if illegal people were travelling in the bus. He replied, passengers did not seem illegal and only people of Guatemala were there. Only once the journey started again the fear disappeared, then we could concentrate on what we had to do when we reach the village.

Before entering the village, there was another stall check we could sight from the distance. Luckily, the bus stop for other people to get off, we also got off and walked a block. So, we prevented people from the stall to question us. We finally arrived; the town was preparing for its feast and in a few days the fair began, there was a lot of movement. Natives celebrated this big in memory of the prince Tecún Umán, who was the bravest warrior of the Mayans. He was the most who resisted the advance of the Spanish troops. As this is the town that bears his name, the fair lasts almost an entire month.

When we entered the village, it was already getting dark. We took a side street following the description of the village I had heard from my uncle Marcos. We reached a small shop where a lady made tortillas and sold other things like candy, soda or water as they call them and cigars. After a while, we risked to ask the lady about the village Las Delicias. At first, she did not want to say anything. Then she came back and asked us where we were from. We told her we were from El Salvador, but we were honest people and we were looking for Marino López, this man knew about us that we were recommended by someone he did know. The lady told us the last period a lot of new people were coming to town and there had already been several deaths. She informed us that we were in the village Las Delicias and the person we were looking for lived two blocks away. We bought some cigarettes, thanked her and walked to Mr. Marino's house.

When we arrived they were having dinner. We greeted them; we said we were relatives of Marcos and we told them we were in an adventure with the idea of continuing our way heading north. With confidence, he talked to us and gave us food. The man had a very good mood and he found a joke to everything. Later, he gave us only one hammock to sleep apologizing because he had only one and we were two.

"I'm sorry I have no more hammocks, so one of you will have to sleep on the floor", he explained.

"Here are sacks to put on the floor "he said and added, "Tomorrow is another day. Tomorrow, if you want, you both can come with me in my truck to bring freight of yucca, I have to deliver early. Have a good night and rest".

His truck was a cart with two tires pulled by a horse.

Actually, luck was helping us; we had a different perspective of our adventure. Mr. Marino, apart from enjoying telling jokes and cheerful stories he considered fishing as an everyday sport. That way, he also brought food to his family, so the idea to go fishing came swiftly. Once we got to the house to bring the yucca work and sell it in the village, he said,

"Well, we have made a little money. Let's eat and go to the river to fish a while".

My uncle Juan, for his part, also liked fishing; it was his favorite sport. Two fishing lovers had met. In the horse-drawn wagon Mr. Marino asked us about Uncle Marcos,

"When does Mr. Marcos come here?"

"He told me he just wanted to gather a corn harvest and then we would meet here" I replied, since he says he liked go fishing with you.

Don Marino laughed because he has a cheerful personality.

"With Mr. Marcos we always drank a few nips. He is a man that gives everything" he continued while carrying the horse ropes that pulled the wagon in which we traveled on.

"There are some kids from my valley who wanted to come with him" I told him, although he is not so eager to bring them, but they would not leave him alone, so one of these days they will appear here. As the country is getting worse due to the war, everyone wants to leave before it's too late. There is martial law; it is very difficult to survive in such situations.

"Here is already getting dangerous" he answered. "By this river where we're going bodies have appeared and we do not even know where they come from. Some days one comes across soldiers or *kaibiles*, sometimes they capture innocent people. The Meléndez River, the one we're going to, is not so dangerous, but the Suchiate River really is. As there are many people who want to go to Mexico, they are arrested. There were Salvadorans who have been arrested and we have not heard of them anymore; it is not known what they have done with them. So now I warn you to be careful if you walk on the banks of the river" he continued.

A few days later Mr. Marino ran out of yucca. There was no job to do, so we went to the cotton plantation to work. Only indigenous people were there. Entire families picking cotton with their teenage children, even little ones up to four to five years old, on those coasts with the sun's scorching heat. They were almost barefoot, shoeless, wearing their typical clothes of bright colors. Ladies also worked carrying a swaddled baby in their backs. Nobody thought about school or anything of that kind. I felt sorry for Guatemalans indigenous people, poor little guys, they worked so hard...

To weights used to control the amount of cotton had been added some aid, and although one could hardly carry the sack, they weighed nothing. I was used to lift a sack of 150 pounds on my back in the coffee plantations in El Salvador. There, the bags were bigger, but "weighed" only half, although the weight felt like those others.

The goal was to earn a quetzal per head. The pay was daily to avoid mishaps. We did not earn enough for the dinner. I bought tortillas, two boiled eggs and an avocado; that was all I could buy with a day job, and it was already the meal.

As said, there was a festivity in Tecún Umán when we arrived, the famous warrior prince who diverted Pedro de Alvarado. This festivity is attended by indigenous of the entire interior of Guatemala and also from Mexico, the states of Chiapas and Oaxaca. All the Mayan tribes meet there. Tribes coming from the highlands of Guatemala walk a month or more to get there and brought food with them. The crowd is a mix of indigenous people from different cultures speaking different dialects. They all wear typical costumes, each tribe dress differently according to their culture and ritual acts. In the Suchiate River which divides Mexico from Guatemala although they did not have boundaries, the whole family took a bath as a kind of baptism; young girls completely naked together with their parents and siblings. When they went to eliminate waste, they did it all together as well, while they did it, they talked as if they were in a meeting, as something quite familiar. For me, it was a different world. The only thing I understood was when they said "Prince Tecún Umán ', although some of them knew a little Spanish.

I remember a day when they were doing a show with rituals and sacrifices of valuable things in the central street of the village, an indigent dressed all in white asked me, "Are you going to go with us?", to which I replied "yes". There were people who spoke apart from Spanish, from eight to ten dialects and translated to other tribes. What united them was a more natural belief than those religions to which we are accustomed to, the belief in the Gods of Nature - the mountain god, the god of rain, the water god, the sun god, the god of the moon and some other gods. This man also told me of Tlaloc, god of corn. I was astonished; I did not know what to say.

There was no doubt that the indigenous brought a philosophy of thousands of years in their minds. In addition, they told that the

Spaniards had taken their land and proclaimed all Chiapas as Maya land. We talked about Justo Rufino Barrios, who was president of Guatemala who tried to exercise his power over all of Central America; he collaborated with the Spanish domain, he did not care losing part of the Mayan legacy. There are people who still loved him; Ladinos who acquired land through this man loved him a lot, like "Salvadoran national heroes" his Creole and Ladino creoles, Spaniards ranchers, whom he gave large parts of land taken away from the indigenous. Politicians never really want to help people who had problems, but help themselves, among millionaires supported by senior military who had as puppets.

It was really rewarding living such experience of being in contact with the natives, as something else to tell others. I discovered that Guatemalans indigenous were assigned different names than the mestizos, who were put a name in Spanish when they went to register at government offices. Perhaps this was to have statistics of indigenous peoples.

In this place I also met a boy from the Jutiapa department, located on the border with El Salvador. He felt confident enough to tell me many things. He spoke like us. His mother was Salvadoran, and his father, Guatemalan, he had both nationalities. He said he had been in Nicaragua when he it was the takeover and he advised me,

"Here you have to pull your socks up. Say you're from Jutiapa, Guatemala, because if you say you're Salvadoran, they will kill you".

At that time you had to be careful with the *Kaibiles*, which are elite soldiers trained for military operations "against terrorism." This military body was created by Barrios, and it is one of his legacies. This boy was working in the banana plantations of Hidalgo. He picked us up in the park of the city heading to Puerto Madero in the state of Chiapas. There, somebody earned 150 Mexican pesos per day that meant six dollars or six quetzals at that time. As he had Guatemalan papers he only paid thirty cents of quetzal to customs to cross the bridge. I had to cross the Suchiate River illegally and waited for him early in the morning in the park where all laborers met every day.

The work was extremely heavy; cement gutters of three, four and five meters wide by one and a half and three meters deep were made.

The banana plantations were huge. There, the payment was every two weeks, but a week was "on background". The contractors were the ones who benefited from these arrangements made to worker's exploitation. They just had a small engine machine for mixing the sand with cement, so a pawn had to go back and forth all day carrying a bucket of concrete in each hand, as far as the slabs were being formed. At the beginning, many suffered from fever.

In the early days I had nothing to eat and started eating bananas to feed, but after two weeks, I suffered from vomiting, fever and diarrhea, as if it was a kind of cholera or dengue. There were some bacteria or viruses in the bananas I ate. After three days I could no longer walk, felt like I was dying. In the banana plantations there were dangerous things, like flies and bad mosquitoes, whose bites could be filled with worms in a very short time. There were also many vipers and snakes, like tamagas snakes, who usually lives in the water. The ground was muddy; almost everything was covered with water in some parts. In those days I became very weak, I almost could not eat for a week. People had me drink lots of coconut water to hydrate and cleanse my body. Then I realized how good coconut water for these diseases is. I remember they told me that the water of this palm almost replaces the serum that is put in a patient's veins. Had it not been so, perhaps I would have died.

When I was living with Mr. Turito, a very humble, poor gentleman, I helped him since he always liked having his mug of coffee on the fire drink, occasionally he liked to drink a little nip of brandy. This old man, Mr. Marino and his family helped me a lot during the whole week I was very sick and ill. The poor old man only had a grandson who had left him one of his daughters. The kid was about eleven or twelve years old, had no shoes and almost always wore a pair of torn pants. I met his grandson once when he went there and gave them some pennies. The boy was a great dreamer. He said that when grow up, he wanted to be a construction engineer to build his own house. He also wanted to be a pilot. He had dreams of rich professions. With his living condition, it was very difficult to do something like that; he did not go to school due to extreme poverty he and the old man lived. He devoted himself to walk by the river to catch fishes and crabs, sometimes to find fruits or vermin in the forest to bring home. "What a shame...How a mind that can be so valuable in this world is lost..." I thought.

Days later, my uncle Marcos arrived. He came with two boys from the valley and both were going northbound. Of course, these guys would give a sum of money. He told us that the country was hell. From the time we had gone until that moment they had already killed many people in the valley and some others had disappeared. The situation was terrible in the country, and if someone was deported, he risked being killed when he returned. Uncle Marcos brought two fishing nets, he said they would give him something to eat on the way, for he was quite smart to fish and had much experience. He went shrimping; he sold one part and the other was for domestic consumption. So he began to instruct the young boys who were travelling with him so the Mexican immigration police would not arrest them on their way. I also had to pay close attention to avoid mistakes along the way; we did not want to be deported, that meant death (those were the news).

Just in those days when we were ready to go north, another uncle named Antonio, uncle Marcos's brother arrived. He had been deported from Mexico together with ten people he had taken there. He told us they were almost arriving to D. F. when immigration officers surprised them. He tried to negotiate with them, but they wanted a lot of money, so he had no choice but to go to Guatemala, and make a new attempt. In between, he had to bribe the Mexican and Guatemala immigration officers for him not to be sent back to El Salvador.

The thing was that Uncle Marcos and I went fishing on the river, when we returned at night we found a lot of people under the trees of the house of Mr. Marino. Everyone said they would not return to El Salvador and that they still had some money to make another attempt. All had been victims of war; some had lost their parents, and others, their children or brothers. Many cried when they remembered that. A girl said she was the only survivor; her parents and brothers were killed together. She had gone out to do something, when she returned they were all dead. Another girl in the group had deserted the barracks; she was a corporal, she showed us photos of her military life. She said that while serving the Government, the other hand the government itself was killing her family. At that time, a deserter was also an active enemy of the country; therefore, he was assassinated if he were to fall into the hands of the military. All people feared returning to the country; that was a real threat. Nearly all of us were fleeing the war; being innocents.

Uncle Antonio said this time crossing to Mexico was very difficult. For five years he had been taking people to Caborca, Sonora, it was the border of Mexico and beyond, the United States. All just a few hours of distance, for those who decide to continue further north and continue the adventure.

It was known that people who stayed in Chiapas, Veracruz and other southern states were more in danger; the closer one to Central America, the more dangerous it was to be deported. We had to go to places where Salvadorans were not mentioned. Salvadoran groups passing daily through these borders, Guatemala and Mexico were numerous, and the authorities in Guatemala had noticed and asked money to every Salvadoran identified. The immigration officers, preventive police and military squads of Mexico did the same, and Central American did not escape. Mexicans deported them to the borders of Guatemala on buses. Guatemalan customs liked to identify Salvadorans, Hondurans and Nicaraguans because they knew they would collect money. All borders stank of Central American and Mexican thieves and money exchangers, coyotes or smugglers. In all borders in which one need to make a currency exchange, there were offers from coyotes to go toward the North, but most of them were just thieves. It was like war, you could not trust anyone, even young children, who were used to steal money from immigrants.

The guys from my valley, who came with Uncle Marcos, were desperate to challenge Mexico; it was necessary to make decisions, to take risk to achieve the goal, getting to northern Mexico was not an easy task. The journey was long, we had no documents and the area was littered with squads in the roads and in the train stations. Uncle Marcos told them that he was not ready yet, as a stepson who was in Chicago would send him money to Guatemala; but if they wanted, they should make the attempt. In the end, I was told that we try luck; we would go on our own.

HEADING NORTH

Farewell

Farewell is what would happen in summer days,
when the dry countryside, yet in hot months.
And with that farewell, my heart was torn into tears;
that now is so beautiful memory.
The scenery, the countryside and the valley,
those were our nests, our laps,
since that childhood I will never forget,
With a sky so blue, that will never change!
Faith, hope, exist here, inside me,
of seeing again that summit so broken, so blue, and
the green volcano... so splendid!
and a sun in the mountains, blazing.
And then when it moves away there by the setting...
some October winds that come weakly
attracting feelings and something to think about.
Perhaps I not forget that farewell, leaving
my family and all my friends.
With a lump in my throat, I took my way
looking forward, having nothing to talk about,
and leaving behind our nest and memories,
a silence in my mind and a big sigh.
Dear parents, this is all I can tell you,
because I... I'll go and I...
We see you an another day or in a summer afternoon.
Perhaps it is not a distant day... Goodbye.

The next day, the boys of the valley and I headed north. It was about four o'clock in the morning when we crossed the Suchiate River, between Guatemala and Mexico border. As soon as we crossed, we were surprised by federals that were in a pickup waiting to apprehend and incarcerate people; to get money from fines. The prison was covered with piss and filth everywhere, we could not sit anywhere. The smell was sickening. The hole for defecating was full. That noon they told us we had to pay if we wanted to leave. We did not mind, at that moment we gave four hundred pesos each and left the place, at that time it was about $17 dollars = 400 pesos.

Then we went to the city of Tapachula, we passed an inspection without problems, they did not ask us anything, we continued calmly. We arrived late in the city; we only know the railway station. We then looked for a place to eat. Young people from the valley felt very embarrassed; they did not want to ask anything, they were timid and afraid that local people would notice they were outsiders. When local people heard someone with a different accent, they immediately asked him where he was from and some other things that could implicate him. We ate in a small restaurant and we went to rent a room in a modest area trying to save for the trip after the feds had taken some of our money. I told them it was better to look for a job in the port area because we would be far away from the city, we could also get a document that will help us go through the next checkpoint. At that time, they still extended the fourth card (it was a local working document given to those who paid tribute for their work) to anyone; they just wanted to get money.

The next day we went to Puerto Madero, a Mexican port farther south in the Pacific. It was ten o'clock when we arrived. We started looking for work among the people on the coastline. Talking to some fishermen, we learned that there are some construction and fishing work, although we had to wait for several days. We were also told about the possibilities of getting the card; we had to get contacts in the village. They also said that there's work in the banana plantation but the others refused to go because in the previous days I had told them how I almost died. So I told them we had to face the situation, the most important thing was to get the card. I had not tried to get it while working in Hidalgo City, I did not know of its existence until uncle Marcos told me about it.

Seeing the problems that arose we decided to return to Tapachula that same afternoon, to go to the railway station and wait for the train that would take us to Mexico City. It was getting dark when we arrived; the train was there, leaving in a few minutes. We waited until all people got in; we were the last to buy the tickets to avoid interrogation before the train left. We were a bit scattered not to be detected when those boys gathered and started talking. It was noticed they were outsiders; they signaled me to go and buy a ticket. Mexican immigration agents were there looking at everyone on board the train; I beckoned them to realize that the officers were there, but they did not understand and kept calling me. I decided not turn to look at them, it would be more suspicious. A few minutes later, I saw someone who talking to them. I realized they turned me. I ignored them for a while, but quickly I saw two of them coming toward me with a man.

"They have already told me you are heading north" said the stranger.

I asked him who said that, but the others agreed, they took me aside and said,

"He says he can help us, that immigration officers are difficult, but he can help us to reach Veracruz."
"To tell you the truth, if you want do business with him I prefer to return and make the trip with Uncle Marcos" I replied.

The man heard the whole conversation, he was only about three meters away from us; and then he approached us.

"No, look, guys I can get out of here and take you to Veracruz City and from there to Mexico City. There is no problem" he said.

So I started walking toward the exit of the train station. They followed me, the three of them wanted to convince me to accept the proposal. The unknown guy did not stop talking, trying to get us into confidence.

When we reach the end of the station, I was standing on the left of that young man, and my companions, on the right. Suddenly he got from pocket and threw a ball to a place where it could jump, I was the only one who saw and then lunged at it and showed it to us. The ball was the size of a tennis ball; it was clear plastic and filled with newsprint, but a hundred pesos note could be seen by an opening.

"Look! Look what I've found!" He exclaimed pretending joy. "Let's share it down there" and he walked away.

My companions began to follow him, while saying,

"Let's follow him and we get the money he found, and then he will help us to leave."

The young stranger had already walked past about five trains that were standing, and he still invited us to follow him. My companions were walking behind him.

"Come back!" I shouted them. "This man is a sneaky and he wants to steal us our money. Don't be stupid..!"

They were going through trains when I told them that, and they slowed. At the time I looked back where the stranger was and I saw a group of men coming along with him. They had knives and machetes in their hands, they ran toward us. It was dark; there were no other people apart from us, I was terrified.

"Run! Run away; they are thieves!" I shouted to my companions as I turned to start running.

They were trapped between the trains and had to jump back to avoid being trapped by those thieves, but fear made us react very rapidly, we managed to flee to where the crowd was. Although they followed us in the town, we lost them when we ran many blocks.

A little scared, distressed, disappointed and without air, we stopped at a corner. We were thinking about the incident that just happened in unfamiliar lands, where we knew no one, and did not know what to do.

After drinking some soft drinks we bought in a shop and relaxing for a while, I started talking.

"We'd better go back" I said. "The way we are doing things we would not get very far. In these adventures, brothers, do not trust anyone. We have to assume that everyone is our enemy. If someone notices we are not Mexicans, he knows he can beat us, denounce us with local police or the immigration, etc.; he will want to hurt us, either to rob us or anything else. My advice is to go back with Uncle Marcos."

They did not answer me. I continued, "We are on time to return today to Guatemala, at this time there are still means of transportation, there is no problem to cross the Suchiate River, and we are already in Guatemala. But later overnight it can be dangerous, so I'm going back. Whoever wants to follow me follows me; otherwise continue your own way", then I turned around and went to the central bus station.

My companions were eager to continue the journey north, but felt unable to do so. I saw them stopped to argue, but they were behind me, following me until we got to the station. I got on the bus, after a while they did the same; we went back to Tecún Umán, Guatemala. Mr. Marino and all the people who were getting ready to leave for the North made us jokes. My three uncles and others asked what had happened to us, we told them a bit of our adventure lived in Mexico. We knew the situation in Mexico would change, but we had to face reality to get a positive result.

My little homeland

My little homeland, you're so far away I cannot see you.
I remember your beauties as the last day I looked at them.
I miss your landscapes dressed in green and your precious fields
and your beautiful and blue beaches where I'll return some day.

My little homeland, I'm so far away from your heart...
I would give it all to enjoy you and contemplate your beauties.
I've cried and I've suffered walking around distant and strange lands.
After so many years, I want to be with you and my family as well.

You've had waves of pain and uncertainty
where they have watered their blood many of your children.
For centuries have been humiliated, as usual,
waves of exiles who left their precious nest
and only carried your principles that illuminate like a light.

Your land is beautiful; it is so precious and valuable,
your people are called it in the world: "those who never faint."
You're the mole of America, you're tiny and beautiful.
For your feisty history, the world knows you for being great.

We all adore you, your cuzcatlecos children.
Many have done you evil or good with a paradigm shift;
others, deceived; and there are also interested people.
Otherwise they want: they want to deceive your people.

Cuzcatleca land, where the torogoz sings
They left the heart in your land heroes who have already left.
You're the man of the waist of America, surrounded by your sisters,
and behind there is an ancestral history that unites us harder.

My little homeland, with your soil proud of
your people, traditions, culture and customs.
Those who are now in exile irrigate the message
Or your brave history, it was like a bad dream.
But I feel proud to say that I am Salvadoran.

Two days after this incident the whole group was already guided by my uncles Marcos and Antonio who had experience in traveling illegally in Mexican lands. We all had received specific instructions on what to say or what to do if they question us. Uncle Antonio's group would travel separate from us in other train cars. We had to travel by train because it was cheaper, but it was also more risky to get us off it, so we had to be prepared for that situation. Uncle Antonio was with ten or twelve of them told them that they had failed the first time; this second attempt had to work because money was already running out to everyone. In our group we were only five. We had that advantage since smaller groups had greater chances of success. We had to be separated, in pairs, even pretend that we were a couple or parent with daughters or son. At the time of reaching a checkpoint, you had to manage to give answers worth to convince them that we were Mexicans.

After those days of receiving tip offs, the next morning we said goodbye to Mr. Marino, his father and the rest of his family. We thanked them for their help, and he was sad when we drove away. The man already treated us like good friends, we did not know if we would meet again. During the three or four months we were in the place, people had shown sincere friendship. We also said goodbye to Mr. Arturito, whom we called Mr. Turito, the old man with his little grandson full of dreams, the poor little boy.

Knowing that it was a challenge to travel around Mexico as undocumented, most had put our hopes in entering the United States. We were also aware that the path in Mexican lands was not easy. It would be a time of hunger and suffering.

It was about noon when we cross the Suchiate River. At that time many people passed over the bridge, it was easier; Mexicans did not care much in the border because many local people crossed from both sides just for the sake of going for an errand from one village to another. We arrived in Hidalgo and boarded the bus leading to Tapachula, Chiapas, Mexico. When we reached the railway station it was almost five in the afternoon. The train left around six, so we had to sit and wait while. We did exactly as uncle Marcos said - we had to stay calm without showing signs we were outsiders, keep relax, disperse, do not talk out loud, and behave the same way on the train. Immigration officers were there as the train was awaiting its departure time. We bought single tickets when shortly before the departure; we bought them to Mexico City. Finally, the train departed.

In the same car where my Uncle John and I also travelled, in another seat Uncle Marcos with one of the girls who was with Uncle Antonio. The goal was that no stranger sit beside them, my uncle pretended she was his daughter. In another seat were the youth of the valley, and the rest of the people who had come with Uncle Antonio travelled in a different car.

Immigration officers also boarded the train, began asking for documents, starting with the first cars. About an hour later, they were in the car where we were travelling. I could not stop myself getting a little nervous, but I have to keep calm and relax. First, Uncle Marcos talked to them. He was a person with experience in such situations. He was wearing a hat he had bought in northern Mexico, his clothes, his knapsack and even his speech was Mexican. He said the girl was his daughter. He acted with great confidence, and since already was sixteen years they could not suspect that he was an illegal immigrant. Later, they approached us.

"Gentlemen, your documents, please", they requested.

"Well, note that I don't have them" calmly replied my uncle.

"Because I come from work here in Tapachula, but as I'm coming back in couple of days I forgot them. I'm from Arriaga; that's where my family lives and I will see my kids and then I'll return."

The immigration officers all believed him because he showed a little tired rather than nervous and also because my uncle was a tall white man; he never left his northern hat and wore cowboy boots. The man just asked him a new question:

"What is your job in Tapachula?"

My uncle replied he worked on livestock, on the coast of Tapachula. Then they turned to me:

"And your documents, where are they?"

"Well, notice that I don't bring anything with me" I replied.

"Why?"

"Well, this Saturday, that is, four days ago, some thieves assaulted me in the neighborhood and took away my wallet with my money and documents."

"Why do not you get it?" asked the officer.

"Well, I've been out of work and without money for almost two months, I have not had enough to eat, -I replied, and continued talking-: That's why I'm traveling, because I got a work in Mexico city.

As I look young, he was not convinced yet because they knew that illegal traveling to the North was mostly young.

"And where are you from?" he wanted to know.

"I'm from the San Antonio colony, from Puerto Madero" I replied.

At least I remember that of Puerto Madero... I remembered we had been told that in that colony we could find work.

"But you say that today you are coming from Tapachula... "He said.

"Yes, because my family lives there, who lent me the money to travel" I answered.

He just looked at me for a moment, and added:

"Catch you around, young man."

I thanked God when I heard that because I was already getting nervous with so many questions. As I also used many words only a Mexican uses, that helped me a lot. My uncle, meanwhile, had also used lot (caliches) slain of Mexico. That way it was easier to make them believe that we ware Mexican.

They continued, and after several seats they reached the young men of the valley who were together. We saw that they were talking with them, but we could not hear what they were talking about. Soon, they made them stand up and put them the handcuffs, and in the next station, they got them out of the train. The train only stopped for a few minutes, and then continued its journey. We could see the young men were handcuffed by the officers.

Near midnight we felt more relaxed: the train went on his way. At one point came Uncle Marcos to tell us quietly what had happened to the guys in the valley. He also told us that he had already gone to talk to his brother and to find out what had happened to the other car. Uncle Antonio had told him that he had lost two of his group, but he had gone to speak clearly with immigration officers and they let them go for a sum of money.

The trip generated uncertainty: we did not know if they would arrive in Mexico City without further obstacles. That cannot be foretold. La Ventosa, in the state of Oaxaca, is another place where la border patrol used to find undocumented, and it was early in the morning when the train stopped at the station. We waited for the agents to get on and began asking for documents but did not, and we continued on our way towards the city of Veracruz. Of course, the train we had taken was the slowest and cheapest one, and because of that it was called the donkey, and so the agents controlled it most.

Finally, the next night, we arrived early in Veracruz City. As the train would not leave until early in the morning we had to wait several hours at that terminal. We must to sit without moving and without talking among ourselves, and we had to avoid contact with people who would know where we came from. If anyone found out where we were from, he could go with the judiciary right there, with the Preventive Police or even with the border patrol.

Midnight had past when a boy who was in the group of Uncle Antonio and I felt thirsty but there was no water in the station. Sellers had already left so we decided to go out to fetch water outside. But to our surprise, as soon as we left the terminal, three individuals caught us and started beating us, and as if they wanted our money they began putting their hands in our pockets. We shouted them to leave us alone. Anyway, they managed to get us some small bills we brought in the pockets of pants. My Uncle Juan, who was watching us, came quickly and talked to them from afar, and ran toward us. As he was a very big man, they were afraid and fled to the opposite side. We carried large bills in dollars or in Mexican pesos in the waistband: waist had unstitched the wrist around and precisely where one tightened the cinch, there were the bills, folded lengthwise. Thanks to this, the theft was just a small incident.

Finally, after many hours of waiting, the train started to leave heading for Mexico City. We approached it; as always, discreetly, and we continued on our way. I slept during a few hours. When it began to get light we were on the state of Puebla, between Puebla and Mexico City. In the plains of the beautiful state I could see agave plants from where pulque is taken; I had heard about it in soap operas and movies. Such was my curiosity that I bought a jar to taste it, and was really good. At that time a glass of pulque costs five pesos. It was 1981 and the money from Mexico had not yet been undervalued. From the train I also saw how people were plowing with a mule and plow, something I had never seen in my life. I remembered my father when he plowed with the oxen and a wooden plow made by himself. I got wistful for a moment and I felt a lump in my throat, because I knew that I was walking away more of them. The more I walked away, the less chance of see them again. I had never taken me away from my parents and siblings; I had always been a child living under the same roof as my parents, obeying them. But, as it is said, there is always a first time for everything. I also thought about the war: I was afraid of the armed forces and I did not want to be there. Besides, I knew that once I had a stable place I could write to find out about them. And I thought of my brothers, wondering what was going to happen to them. A whirlwind of thoughts and memories seized me for a while. I began to tear up, but I ignored it. I was living an experience that was new to me, in other lands and I had to cope with whatever came. That afternoon, we began to enter Mexico, D. F. When I started looking at that so huge and interesting city, I was asleep and forgot everything I had been thinking of.

At night, we arrived at the central railway. Uncle Antonio and Uncle Marcos began to talk while we waited sitting on some benches. The place was very crowded so it was less dangerous for us to be detected, and we were in Mexico. Soon, my uncles approached us and they told us the next plan on our way toward north. We were told that as Uncle Antonio had to bribe the officers in Chiapas and after the thieves had stolen us some money, there was no money left to keep on travelling. The money had been all spent on food, and only my Uncle Juan and I we had enough to get to Caborca, Sonora, which was the final destination of the trip. So they planned to go towards Michoacán. Uncle Antonio had already been there and had friends; we could work there for a few days, and then follow the path. We shared the money to buy the tickets: all we wanted was to get where it was determined to arrive because in D.F. the situation of the migrants was not the best.

Said and done. We were like thirteen in the group, and we had to share the money to buy tickets and board the bus that led to Uruapan, Michoacán, where would get on another bus that would take us to a small village called Morelos, also known as Antúnez, in Michoacán. We almost spent all night in the central northern bus waiting to leave, but in the next afternoon we were in Morelos. It was a communal center running through cooperatives: holders were poor people who had joined and had acquired these lands as well as agricultural machinery. I think that was a legacy of Lázaro Cárdenas in his state.

There we met the friend of Uncle Antonio. He was a humble gentleman of about 55 year old, who worked selling gasoline to local landowners. He had a home, where he lived with his wife and children, and also a small shop, which was where we would sleep. After they talked for a while and we took a shower, we went to bed to sleep. We were very tired.

The next day, the lord told us that if we wanted to work, he could talk to some rancher's friends who owned agricultural lands. There was work to harvest cucumber, melon, cabbage and other products exported to the United States. There was also work in the packing houses, where the export was made. The state of Michoacán is the leading exporter of avocados in the world, and it also produces lots of lemon, watermelon, melon, cucumber, beans and other products. I remember that in the road traveled a lot of trucks with these products bound for export locations.

Of course, the thing came swiftly: the next day, although late, and we were walking picking cucumber in the work, along with the locals. Those who listened to us talking immediately realized we were not from nearby. When they asked us where we were from, we said that from Chiapas, as we knew it was not often to meet chiapanecos there. Only the friend of my uncle and his family really knew our nationality.

My uncles went fishing at the dam Infiernillo, a hydroelectric dam on the border between the states of Guerrero and Michoacán. This is closed to Acapulco, central Mexico.

Well, as this was the favorite sport of my uncles, and since they did not left their fishing nets yet they went fishing. When they returned, they brought a sack full of fish. They came happy, because they thought they had done well and we would have to eat; however, when the homeowner returned and saw the fish told them they could not eat it because it was poisonous. It was a fish like the tilapia, but a little reddish, and it is said it has many thorns.

Our stay in the place lasted almost a month. There we spent the festivities of the small town. Apparently, Michoacán's people still have in mind the memory of the great ex-president Lázaro Cárdenas. We were told that by 1938, when he was president, he managed to recover oil, mines, trains, etc., that were in the hands of the Americans, and that he was a man with radical ideas. In other words, he was an idealist, and so they remember him a lot. There, right next to where we were, at the peak of a small hill there was a mansion he had left and that today is a museum. From the place, which was quite high, they could see all around.

More or less after a month there, we continued our adventure. We had saved some money and had also made several friends, but it was necessary to continue with our journey and after giving thanks, we said goodbye to the family and we headed to Guadalajara, in the state of Jalisco. In Guadalajara we had to take a train again, heading north of Mexico, up to Caborca, Sonora, where we had to go through two places where the border patrol was, they were El Empalme and Benjamin Gil. We had to become strong and convince ourselves we were Mexicans.

After my uncles told us how it was in those two places, some of the group wanted to give up continuing, for fear of being deported, but the others gave them encouragement to come with us without thinking it too much. We also said we would do everything we could to reach our destination. No one stayed in that city.

We bought our tickets and, as always, separated; we were located in three different cars and we started the battle with the trip. We boarded the train at dusk, crossed the states of Nayarit and Sinaloa, and the next afternoon we passed through El Empalme. The train stayed a lot there because it changed wagons. My uncle, to relax a little, went to buy some tamales; he loved them. He bought some to a woman selling on the train. He was eating just the first, when I saw him stopping chewing; he broke down, and suddenly ran to the end of the wagon and seat at the end of the car, to vomit: the tamale was made of cat meat. My uncle found a cat's paw inside, even with hairs. After he returned to vomit, he said he felt dizzy. Every minute was an eternity to us. The journey lasted over an hour, and nobody had approached to my uncle or me, but later we realized that a couple who came in another car had been gotten off the train as well as the other three travelling in the third car. That made us think because according to what the uncles said, the last place we had to pass was even worse. We were close. We had already passed the city of Hermosillo; it was one o'clock. AM I felt a bit nervous, so I asked Uncle Juan for a cigarette and I went to smoke to the davit train between two wagons. While I was smoking it, the train was going a little slower, perhaps because we were going uphill in the desert. Then a young man approached the end of the wagon and spoke to me, I realized he was also a Salvadoran. About two minutes after he spoke to me, he threw himself off the train. When he felt a horrible dread cry was heard. I did not know if he was dead or not. The night was dark and there was no way he'd seen where he was going to fall. I only remember him telling me that the check booth was just about ten minutes away. I believe the young plan was to surround the house on foot through the desert and board another train once he was on the other side of the check. The train continued its way through the night and, indeed, we were a few minutes from the town of Benjamin Gil.

There, they did the same thing as in El Empalme: unhooked all passenger cars and other cargo back and the locomotive moved by other lines to leave some wagons and engage others.

We remained expectantly, waiting to see what happened. About half an hour, two immigration officers appeared. They were judicial. They asked for our documents, and as we answered that did not get them, they made us to follow them. They took us to the end of the wagon, where the last car was disconnected and they began to ask questions. First they asked me why I was not carrying documents, and I repeated the same story I had told before. That somebody assaulted me and stole my documents.

"So, where are you from?" One of them asked me.

"I'm from Michoacán, but it turns out I was stolen my documents, my birth certificate, and I needed money to get everything, but I didn't have any money and now I'm going to Caborca to work in the grape vines." I replied.

"And this man, what about you? "

"He is my uncle."

"I think that you are not Mexicans" he added. And as they had already asked a couple of questions to my uncle and he almost did not try to talk like Mexicans, they continued to insist that we were strangers and uncle began to get nervous. As a consequence, the officers became even more aggressive.

"No, tell me the truth... Are you Central American?" they said, stating what they suspected.

"No, God's truth, we are from Michoacán."

"Do you have any alcoholic drink?" They asked then.

"No, we do not drink." we answered.

In Mexico they call the alcoholic beverage "pisto", and we call money the same way, so they wanted us to grasp that. Then they continued interrogating:

"If you are from Michoacán, tell me: how is called the governor of that state?"

"He's Coactemoc Cárdenas" I answered.

"What's in the circle of Cuatro Caminos?" he added.

"The Statue of Emiliano Zapata" I replied.

"What is the most widely grown in Michoacán?"

"In Morelos-Antúnez and Nueva Italia we grow much melon, watermelon, cucumber, beans; but there are lots of lemons in the south though in the north there is much avocado", I kept saying.

"Have you marched in Mexico?" he asked us.

We said no. We had no military knowledge. For Mexicans "to march" is to go to the military training, and I had to demonstrate it with a credential. Finally, he made me sing the National Mexican Anthem. I gave thanks that I had learned three stanzas, and with that I left him satisfied. I also told him that my uncle was very ill suffering from headaches and heart aches of the vomiting he had before, and that he had heart problems at that moment; he was delicate and that's why it was me who answered all the questions. In the end, they were asking for money; they wanted dollars:

"Everyone who does not bring documents must report something", said one of them.

I told them that we were going there because we had no money. We were going to look for work to Caborca.

"We do not have dollars" I told them. "We do not come from the United States."

Suddenly, we heard the whistling of the train as it came to hook up the passenger cars. The immigration officers got off and then we could breathe and feel peace after so many questions. Around two in the morning, we arrived in Caborca, Sonora. We stared at each other and realized we were just half of those who had left Guatemala. Uncle Antonio only brought four with him; Uncle Marcos was alone with Dina -the girl who pretended to be his daughter: his brother and Mercedes, the girl who apparently was his girlfriend, had already got captured. And finally were my uncle Juan and me.

Well, Uncle Marcos said, "What can we do...? We're already here and we have to take a taxi to go to the center of town because there is much pickpocket here. It is very lonely, and they can attack us."

There were two taxis around, waiting for the train's arrival. We went towards the big one because we were nine in all and we settled into the car as we could. The taxi took us to the center, where the town park was, but we could not stay there because officers were wandered around the place, so we collected money for a second-rate hotel. We went to one but they did not open to us; then we went to another and the same thing happened. We had no choice but to go to a wasteland. After walking a few blocks, we found one that was full of garbage although there was grass all around. We spent the rest of the night lying on construction waste, and we could not sleep because it was getting too cold.

At dawn, we found the timetable of the bus heading west. We were told that it would leave at two in the afternoon, and it was only eight o'clock and we had to look for food. We were running out of money. Then Uncle Antonio told us that in order to save two others he had to pay more money; we just had money to pay the bus into the West. My uncles knew some people and we could get food and pay later, but they did not know whether these people still cook for pawns on the ranch that we were headed or not. That afternoon, we reached the ranch called "Vineyards of Guadalupe" where Uncle Marcos and Uncle Antonio had already been. Apparently, Uncle Marcos had had an affair with the lady in charge of the kitchen who sold food at the ranch. The lady had lent him money some time ago, but this time she had no money, but she could give us some meals instead; and she did so.

We stayed two nights and a day there, investigating whether there was work, but the response was negative: we could neither get work there nor in neighboring ranches. As my uncles knew other more distant ranches we decided to start walking towards that direction; after walking about fifteen kilometers, we arrived at a West center. Uncle Antonio decided to take another route with those who were with him, because he said that if were many it was more difficult to find jobs, housing or any other benefit, so we said goodbye and they went to another place seeking luck. We agreed to get in touch when we settle in one place.

In the place there was a CONASUPO a grocery store selling everything for the home and even things to eat. We gathered the last pesos we had and went to buy some baguettes, milk, avocados and ham. We spent all the money and there, in front of the store, under some olive trees we sat down to eat. While discussing what was the next step we to take, Dina cried for her brother and her friend. The previous nights she had hardly slept crying and thinking of her people and so her eyes were swollen. We had spent the night in a cellar that that only had packs of wheat grass for cattle and sleeping in the straw really helped since it was quite cold; however, she had not rested. We comforted her amongst ourselves; we told her not to think that much and that she had to go forward with us. She said she wanted to return; she wanted to go to El Salvador. We explained it was too dangerous for her, even more because she had deserted the army, and she was likely to be killed or something bad could happen to her in her way, because there were almost 4,000 kilometers from to our land.

She was young and very pretty, and perhaps that distrusted us because we were all men: three women started the journey with us but she was the only one still in this adventure; only she had been able to reach the destination that we had in mind.

Uncle Marcos had already thought about the place we were going but he had not informed us. Two kilometers from where we were it was located the center of the West. There, at a crossroads, there was a small community consisting of several farms, a church, a school and small shops. That would be the end of our tour, he finally said. My uncle already knew a lady who owns a ranch, and she was very fond on him. So as soon as we finished eating, we started walking toward the center of the famous West.

We reached the ranch at last. The lady, now elderly, walked out of the house, shooing some hens away which apparently put eggs in the mountain, that is, the part that was the farm with fruit trees surrounded by fabric cyclone. She had them in cages where she had special nesting boxes, and although the hens could not leave the little farm because it was enclosed, the lady walked annoyed with her hens. Just then, we appeared in the backyard, where we were received by a daughter in law who lived with her. We greeted her and Uncle Marcos asked about the lady named Maxi. The girl replied that she would go and call her. After two or three minutes, the girl returned with her mother in law. When she saw Uncle Marcos she was surprised.

"I can't believe it! It's you... Why are you coming from so far away?"
"Yes, Mrs. Maxi, it's me, I've come back."

They talked for a while, and then my uncle introduced us to them and began telling them about what was happening in our country and that was the reason why we were walking adventuring. He also said that another niece and her boyfriend had been caught by immigration officers in El Empalme, and although there was very little chance, they could appear there. The lady replied that there was no problem and that she was going to make sure that in the future we had to eat and, of course, a place to sleep. As Uncle Marcos told the lady that Dina was his niece, she offered her one of the rooms of her house, while the three of us were given the pieces where the workers of the ranch slept. They were rooms made of cement blocks and sheets on the ceiling. At that time of year, the weather was quite cold, the air blew through the eaves, between the wall and ceiling, but it was better than sleeping in the open field.

We arrived for the grapes pruning time, so the next morning the overseer came in his truck to bring the workers who were doing the job. At the same time, Mrs. Maxi went out of her house to talk to the man about us. Then she introduced us to him; he seemed to be a pretty nice person.

"Well, if you are looking for work, here's enough for the time being, so get on the truck", he said.

We went with him and started working and after a while and we had it in hand because it was not that difficult. Not even for Dina, who had never done agricultural work, and that helped us feel happier. At lunchtime, the lady's three children arrived: I do not remember the name of the eldest, but he was called Negro; the next was Gustavo, and the third was called Elpidio.

Then The Negro told us that another brother was a politician and when he was about to be mayor of Caborca he was killed in traffic accident travelling from Caborca to the ranch, and his wife was the woman we had met in Mrs. Maxi's house. The Negro also lived in Caborca, with his wife and family, and he was also a politician there, that is why he rarely visited the ranch since he was frequently busy in things related to the municipal government.

After three days of being in the ranch Juan, Dina's brother, and Mercedes, his girlfriend appeared in the ranch. When they met they cried with happiness. At the ranch in the desert it was a rain of blessing. Mr. Juan joined our group to work, and Ms. Mercedes went to live at Mrs. Maxi's home. We only were with girls only during working hours, then Mrs. Maxi took care of them and we only saw them again when they gave us maize stew, soups and other foods Mrs. Maxi sent us. We were grateful to her: was our axis in that adventure.

We had told our bosses we wanted people to believe that we were from the state of Chiapas, but they could not because they had many trusted workers and ended by telling them the truth. But the foreigners, those who went to work at the ranch, we told them we were from Chiapas. That worked for all that time we were there; and Southerners who go to work in Caborca and northern Mexico were mostly from the states of central and northern of the country, and a chiapaneco in rarely seen or someone from the southern states. Instead, some are seen in Oaxaca, Veracruz, venturing through the region. For all this, it was a bit easy to lie to them: they did not know anything there or the ways of speaking in the area.

One day, some boys from my valley who had been on the road also appeared. One day, when we had returned from work and were talking three, we saw them arriving. They were very happy to find us. They felt. They told us all the adventure they had lived in that time: they said the border patrol that caught them did not want money; they arrested and sent them to Guatemala. There they did accept money and no longer sent them to El Salvador: they left them in Tecún Umán. Then, they went to Mr. Marino's place until they receive money from Los Angeles, California, because they had brothers there. With the money left, they had had to give some as bribery, they had managed to get to where we were and avoid being sent back to our country. They only rested three days, and then went to Tijuana, where they would meet a coyote. They had secured work in Los Angeles and his brothers were funding around, especially because as some of his brothers had been killed in El Salvador, the brothers who were in California did not want them to come back; they knew they were going to die there.

At that time, many of those in the governments of Central American countries became rich with the war. They took advantage of the political situation and the support of the United States. They trafficked in drugs and weapons, and used all kinds of political and military maneuvers in the region. Central senior military were linked also with the CIA. They were eating both of a cake divided among few.

At the ranch of Mrs. Maxi there were vines, olive and orange trees, so pruning and tied guide grapes only lasted about six weeks after we arrived, as employers wanted to do it fast to proceed with olive and orange trees. We continue, then, with olive pruning, which lasted about four weeks. Then after the picking of olive work that was paid for boxes; therefore, many of us earned more than others. Then we continued with orange trees, which were also paid for boxes picked and loaded onto trucks coming to pick them up.

We were in the orange pruning when one day El Negro came and said he wanted to talk to us, all Salvadorans, privately. We meet the four of us with the two girls and walked away from the others. He told us that two Salvadorans had killed a Mexican there in the region. The federal and the judicial police would check all the ranches, and the Salvadorans found would be deported to their homeland. He also said that we should not worry because he would know, in Caborca, when they reached the area and he would come to distract them. Many of these agents were acquaintances.

After three days, he returned in his car. He parked near the oranges and secretly he told each of us the officers would come at any time. Then he talked to some girls and other workers; we were about thirty women and men. Shortly afterwards, two cars arrived and parked on one side of two trucks that were carrying oranges in bulk: we had to climb a ladder and empty the boxes onto the trucks. In each cart came two agents; they were in civilian clothes, but brought arms openly and stood around the truck. When he saw them, El Negro came out to greet them. As soon as he approached them, they laughed. I could hear when they asked him what he was doing there, and he replied that was his ranch. They knew El Negro had a ranch, and they laughed even more because he was the owner, and he was the one who pays. Judicial officers talked to El Negro during 45 minutes. Then when we got closer to the truck to put the boxes of oranges, they stared at us and said:

"Well, if you know something, please warn us, you hear..?"
El Negro replied yes, and they added:
"We'll go because we have to keep working."
Finally, they left and El Negro once again told them, "Yes, rest assured that I warn you if I know something."

After they left, El Negro remained smiling and stared at us shaking his head. We cared especially from some workers from other ranch who would not hesitate to announce us.

Two weeks later, the day of payment, El Negro told us that there was no more work for about two or three weeks and that would be work only for two watering men, two tractor drivers and a mechanical ranch. However, he assured us he would find out where we could find work.

Likewise, he suggested us to ask everyone we knew to help us too. Thus, in three weeks we would return to the ranch for the grape cleanse. We thought that the olive and orange would take us more time, but there was less work than we had estimated. That same weekend, then, we started looking for work through friends and acquaintances here.

Two days later, we had already found work on a ranch which was about four kilometers away. The ranch was called "El Bonito": actually, it was not so nice but it was called that way... That Monday morning we arrived in the place. There were only workers from Guanajuato state, since the boss was from the same state, and the overseer, too. They invited us to stay, but we did not consider it a good idea and preferred to walk every day to Mrs. Maxi's the ranch. The job was to weed the vineyard because there was much grass under the seeding furrow. We found the local in that place weird: as they did not know how to treat people, and it seemed that all who were venturing out there had been fleeing from their land. They were not very sociable.

After two weeks of working at that place, a Friday, the employer told my uncle Marcos:

"Hey, I'm taking your nieces to Caborca. I have to go and bring the money to pay all the people of the ranch, and they say they want to make some purchased with that, so we'll come later, and the girls would get the full day paid.

My uncle told him that was fine, and the man left that afternoon in his truck, which was double cabin, with Dina, Mercedes and the overseer. Upon return, the news was not good. The girls told us that halfway both men were a little drunk; they stopped in lowland where there was a dry creek and both struggled and tried to rape them. They had to run across the sand stream up. When the men realized they did not want, the managed to convince them to get into the pickup, and thus reached the ranch. We were a little anxious waiting for them and the payment, too. We did not like those gentlemen's attitude and decided not to go to work at the ranch anymore.

When we returned, we told that to Mrs. Maxi and she shared our idea and told us that soon there would be work on the ranch. However, during the next week there was nothing to do there. Watering men told us they no longer wanted to work and would go to the North. Dina and Mercedes were very lucky because Mrs. Maxi's brother was the owner of the big grocery store and the man loved them working in his store. Although Mrs. Maxi's husband was dead, she kept a good relationship with the family that respected her. So the man employed the two Salvadoran girls, especially after they told him what happened at the ranch "El Bonito".

Meanwhile, the watering men convinced me to go to try luck with them. Both said they had contacts on the other side, so I made the bags and I took a few days to send money to my mom and my dad to El Salvador. For the first time in my life, I was sending dollars: I sent two hundred dollars, and I was satisfied, really happy. There were so many Salvadorans in the area that never sent anything to their parents... I cost almost five thousand Mexican pesos. Ronald Reagan was president in the United States and Miguel de la Madrid in Mexico, and the dollar rose every day. Finally, I went with those men from the ranch, and the others stayed doing their work.

In Caborca we took the freight train coming from Guadalajara to Mexicali. Thanks to Mario Moreno, "Cantinflas".(comidian movie star) He paid to the Mexican president 2 million dollars who encouraged that people could travel without paying, or trap, in freight trains throughout Mexico. So we left, and that afternoon we were in Mexicali making plans. They had told me they knew people at the borders, but after walking around Mexicali, Algodones, San Luis Rio Colorado, Tecate and Tijuana, we neither find contacts nor work for the other side. They devoted themselves drinking in bars, dance clubs, etc., and soon the money ran out. I slept in parks or squares where police or borders did not bother me seeking money. I slept in places where there were trees to hide, and in the morning I went to search for them and I found them very drunk. In about four days, the money was finished and began asking me for money. As we had agreed that if one of us needed money and the other had it he would have to share it, I ran out of money too. However, one morning when they were half drunk, reacted and wanted to look for work. They did not want to return to the ranch in Caborca, and we had to look for work in the area. We were told in the Cincuenta y Siete, a small town between Mexicali and Puerto Peñasco, there was work in cotton. This place is so named because it is 57 kilometers south of the border between the United States and Mexico; moreover, by the middle of the town is the border between Baja California and Sonora. We took the train and reached the place. We met the rancher who told us we could work but he did not have a place where we could sleep. We went, then, to a large water canal for irrigation and, under a tree, we made a "house" where we lived about three weeks. We slept in the outdoors. We also got a metal backet to cook, and I got in the canal to take clams to eat. The canal was made of concrete and was about five meters wide and three meters deep. They could not swim and were afraid to get in it.

After the first week of work, the employer paid us and asked us if we wanted to go with him to a horse racing in Puerto Peñasco. Without having more to do, we said yes and went into his truck. He had some Budweiser's in his truck, and gave us one each. We travelled at back because her daughter was forward; she was in charge of controlling the business of the ranch. They told us that they wanted to go to the United States, and they already had the documents. We arrived at the horse races and there were many people. There were bets everywhere and money arose. I bet once and I lost. I did not want to, but the man was quite persuasive, or rather, he liked to convince others to join him in the betting. Then another race came; a pony would run against a horse. The boss was advised by another man who told him that the pony would win, so we were persuaded to bet: the race after started after the sound of the shot and the pony was winning, but a few meters later, another horse took the lead and ended up winning the race. Then, we returned home. We all had lost, but the lord invited us to have dinner and drink some other Budweiser's beers. It was Saturday, and by Monday we were at work and living under the tree that was "our house."

Within two weeks, we decided to return Mrs. Maxi's ranch. We said goodbye to the Lord, and he took us to the station. There awaited the train from Mexicali to the south, bound for Caborca. The freight train coming from the South arrived first: wagons carrying no cargo were full of people; many went to the other side. In a wagon there were about ten or twelve Mexican hanging from the staircase and a gringo who had been pulled out. The car stopped right in front of the station, and some Mexicans who jumped the train shouted at him to get off, that they were going to hit him. The gringo, who spoke Spanish, replied that he was not in favor of any political ideology and that was out there because he liked Mexico. Mexicans were outraged and brought him down hitting him, saying:

"You come whenever you want…Why can't we go to your country?"

The gringo replied that he did not even vote and did not care who the president in his country was, and he only wanted to be respected. Mexicans hit him. He said he was not to blame for the problems between both countries; he also was a labor. Finally, Mexicans told him he did not deserve to be in those trains, because it was a freight train and it was only for Mexicans. There were other Mexicans at the station, and if they had not been present, they would have killed the man. Finally, he could not continue his trip to Tijuana, where he said he was going because they did not let him board the train again. The scene was, in a sense, interesting. I felt sorry for the American, but I could do nothing because if I spoke, they could realize that I was not Mexican. After that, we stayed there waiting for the freight train heading south.

When we reached the ranch, several who worked there told us they wanted to try their luck to the north. One of them was Mr. Pedro, a man of Durango, friend of my uncle Juan and mine. Thus, the three decided to make the attempt. Overall, we were about eleven men; later we discovered that there were two men from the ranch "El Bonito".

We took the freight train again that went to Mexicali and then went to Algodones. There, we bought many gallons of water, three each, and took a bus on a road that runs to the edge of the border. Later, we got off the bus and started walking down this desert where only threatening birds of prey sang. It was the evening of that day: we were eleven in the group and each one had the three gallons of water. Also, my uncle Juan and Mr. Pedro had a few bottles of tequila to avoid taking excess water, they said. Two days later, at dawn, tired of walking we decided to sleep. We left the gallons opposite side where the wind came and went to rest, but, to our surprise, when we went to fetch the water we discovered they were surrounded by tepelcubas (snakes) and rattlesnakes. They had smelled the water and were seeking it. They wandered around our water, but we could move them and grab the gallons to keep walking.

At noon we feel tired so we got to sleep until something unexpected happened: a small plane had found us and shortly afterwards the border patrol arrived and captured us. When we checked us, an officer said one was missing and he asked where he was. They had checked the tracks on the road and our shoes, and they had discovered that one was missing. The officer made a double check, and saw that person was still missing. Finally, from the small plane he was told by megaphone that was one that was hidden among the trees, climbed. Then, the plane flew near him, taking the buds of the tree, and said by the megaphone:

"Get out or we're going to take you out by force."

Finally, he came down and saw that he was the Caborca.
After that, checked our shoes again and took us to the Office of Yuma, Arizona. Everyone knew that my uncle and I were from El Salvador, and before going on to give information, the Caborca told my Uncle Juan in very cold tone:

"I'll say that you are Salvadorans."
"Do it, son of a [...] –For my mother I swear- answered my uncle, - but I'm going to come back and you will have no time to regret it, so do it..."

The Caborca boy did not have the courage to do it, and we said we were Mexicans. We gave our names and said we were from Michoacán when they asked our place of origin, and there were no problems with that. We always said that when it came to the law.

The next day, in the evening, we were back at the ranch of Mrs. Maxi. Once we arrived, they returned our positions. There everyone was accustomed to see people passing by with illusions heading north, so it was not unusual to see them returning in a short time. I got the same job I was doing before.

After this episode, my uncle Juan decided he wanted to go to El Salvador to bring his wife. I could not stand being without her, he had not learned even to fry an egg using firewood for cooking. So, one day he told me he would go for her, and if my brother Francisco wanted to come, this was his chance. So, I took the last money I had saved and

151

gave it to him to fetch my brother. A couple of days later, he took the road to El Salvador. Also, my uncle had left a saved there money in our country. He was though on the news we only heard unpleasant things; he did not care.

We were visiting El Salvador in the year of 2000
when he died of heart attack.
The man who was, my uncle, my friend and
more through this journey of life.

Almost a month later my uncle Juan, his wife and my brother were back. He told me that the situation was very bad. On the border between Mexico and Guatemala, the Mexican border patrol had betrayed him to the Guatemalan customs, and those had taken him to the border with El Salvador to betray him to the Salvadorans. Then he was at the office of El Salvador for almost a week. There, he was beaten and tortured with electric shocks: they wanted him to say that he had left the country for subversive or communist. My uncle and others he knew who were in the same adventure were also caught, and he believes that perhaps they killed them. My Uncle Juan arrived covered in scars and bruises in all body; they had also given him electric shocks in his private parts. However, he was lucky, because a lieutenant in the National Guard spoke by phone from the head office of the country, and thus he saved, but the ones he knew in his adventure did not have the same fate: they made them disappeared there, in the border.

My brother told me that he had been in the village and that was why he had not lived so many adventures with the military. He told it was very dangerous. They had already killed a lot of innocent people, a lot of neighbors and relatives, and in some places they had hilled children, elderly and women because men fled the security forces. The military, the National Guard, the Treasury Police, the National Police and Death Squads crossed and intimidated and killed people. People from the squad of Tutultepeque farm and a town called La Toma de Aguilares, who were the real killers of the area, they also made the bodies disappear as they had clandestine cemeteries in the valleys and in the farms they control. They had done that in many other towns in my region, and that also happened nationwide. In our place, my valley, they had formed a Death Squad to do the same thing. My two younger brothers had been placed there in the squad. The youngest was about thirteen, and the other was around sixteen. The commander, an ex-former soldier of an artillery barracks in the region called "San Nicolás" sent an officer with a group of soldiers to instruct people, according to my brother. This commander already hated my father and wanted to kill him when I was still in the valley; he thought that we, the elderly, were in the guerrillas. Because of this man they had killed my older brother. Due to this, since he was training, my younger brother decided to leave the valley: he got into the artillery barracks and from there began to mobilize to see if he could defend the family of this unscrupulous villain. There was no longer a fight against or in favor of the United States, but part of the same people who just wanted to satisfy their desire to deprive the poor even their minimum belongings and kill them, while others tried to survive amid so much oppression. Many people ignored the intervention, but most people ignored the reasons for it.

Summer came to the wilderness of Caborca: in the room where we lived there were thousands of mosquitoes entering by the eaves, and thousands of flies. When we were eating, the time when we brought the food to the mouth, fell three or four flies on the bite we were about to eat. Those who already lived there had air conditioning and their houses closed; therefore, they did not suffer that problem. The weather was extremely oppressive: the heat was horrible, and food such as meat and vegetables uncooked spoiled. In just three or four hours, everything was rotten and stinking. Then, there were sandstorms: we had to stop working and go home. We closed everything to keep the sand out, and when we wanted to open there were sand hills on the outside.

My brother and I decided to go to the North. Coincidentally, an individual from Querétaro arrived and assured us that his cousin could give us work there. We made plans to leave immediately. Before we left we place, Mr. Antonio Rubio, who was the mechanic ranch, called us and said,

"Before you leave, I want to talk to you. I'm from Sinaloa. My country is very beautiful, and I also had to leave because they were killing my people and sooner or later they will kill me because my family was in politics; they always liked politics. This country is beautiful, but it is not our, is the Yankees and they had bought us: my land exports all for Americans. Besides, there are many mines that are not ours although they are in our land. Corruption is the main issue. Mexico is ruined" he wailed, and then continued, "it turns out that there was a world competition where they were going to pick the most corrupt countries in the world. They named China, Brazil, the Philippines, the United States and other countries that had a lot of corruption, but Mexico did not appear. Then, one who was on the board of lawyers asked, 'Where is Mexico?' Moments later, a very well dressed and very diplomatic guy said, "Mexico had already paid in order not being included."

Finally, we could undertake the journey. A man from Michoacán who was in the ranch had married a girl from Texas would return to the United States: she was going to pick him up in Nogales, Arizona. They had a van, and my brother and I were going to move with another man from Querétaro. The situation was hard because when the lady was coming across the border, the Border Patrol seized the van. She could not pass, and we were stuck, unable to cross to Arizona. After this, the man from Querétaro talked to a friend, apparently needed money to make it for us to Nogales. This friend knew the movements of the patrol: we passed through an underground tunnel, and then we paid a taxi that took us to a hotel, where this individual would arrive.

After crossing to Arizona, the boy from Querétaro went to work to another place and we got a job with ranchers from Glendale, in the grapefruits pruning. However, when we went to get our pay for the worked week, they called the border patrol and it came immediately. We fled through the orange plantation so that they would not catch us: right there we spent the night and even slept a little. With my brother we started thinking it was Easter, and instead of paying us, we were thrown over the patrol: we were all full of thorns due to working between those orange trees. For illegal people, considered worthless, things were not the same as for the other: the world was not fair to all human beings.

Fortunately, three days after we found another job picking oranges, and days later came the boy from Querétaro to tell us that he had already gotten a trip to Wyoming to go to work with the sugar beet fields: a man would come to pick us up in Glendale. Of course, we said we were ready to go to work there, because the patrol bothered much in those areas of Arizona.

Two days later, Mr. Mike, the master, came. He was a retired old man, very nice people. Three of us went out with him the next day, because he said he needed to rest for one night, as the trip was about twenty hours or more. So we traveled toward Powell, Wyoming, leaving behind all those incomprehensible things, but the pain remained in our hearts. We had written a letter to our family from Sonora, and a month and a half later we had received a reply. Our older sister, who was the one who wrote the letters, said that our mother was crying continuously for our dead relatives, for the children who were in the country taking risks, and for us who we were in distant lands. The war continued, and it was more intense than ever.

While the old man was driving, he told us a lot about his life, his youth, how he had become a military and when he walked by some Eastern countries that were also in revolutionary wars at the time, and told us the suffering was terrible. The trip lasted almost a day, but finally got to Powell, Wyoming, without any problem.

Already there, the lord told us in confidence that if we did not have money, we should not worry about food, we could cook what we wanted as the time for work arrived, it would be in a couple of weeks, so we could only rest in the house for several days. Sometimes the man took us for a walk and even introduced us to some of his relatives and friends. He made us feel as if we were members of the family and he always treated us that way.

He also took us to meet some of the Americans owners of ranches where we could possibly work in the future. Mr. Mike and the ranchers were waiting for a cousin of Guillermo, the boy from Querétaro, called Serafín and would bring a good group of people from that state to work as he did every year. That man, his brother and Guillermo were the people who supposedly got the agreements with the ranchers. Beet plantations occupied many acres and the job consisted to remove the access of the little plants and leaving only one every 30 centimeters, or every foot in the rows of sugar beet and remove the weed when the plant was only two inches in size.

After almost two weeks there Serafín came from Mexico. He brought twenty men who would work with him, along with his brother, his cousin and us; we were going to add to the group because Guillermo had spoken to him by phone. The same afternoon when we arrived, they went to talk to two ranchers' brothers named Jimmison. Immediately they said we could go to the ranch house of these men which was about a kilometer from the house in which they lived, in the vicinity of the fields and surrounded by several trees. In the group brought by Serafín there was a Honduran man named Miguel who had come with Uncle Antonio from Guatemala. It was the second time that Uncle Antonio had brought him from Central America to the north of Mexico. I met him in Tecún Umán while waiting for my uncle, and I went with him for short walks around the village when it was the civic holiday, and we shared some food and water.

From these agreements Serafin and his brother benefited from. Mr. Mike had gotten those contracts as ranchers knew him. As he told us, he was born in Texas, but after leaving the army moved to Wyoming and always worked on ranches, in agricultural tasks, with machinery. Ranchers appreciated him very much after so many years working for them. One of the first Mexicans he met was Serafín, so he presented him to the ranchers, and as Serafín was a coyote, he took advantage of that agreement to bring people from the South and make money thanks to them.

As we reached the rancher's house, one of the Jimmisons', we made a general cleaning, as it had been uninhabited for almost a year. Mr.

Jimmison assured that everything was working well in the house: they vacated the septic tank and did other errands so that the house was fit for all men who would live in it as we were twenty-five. Serafín had come with people in two pickups, and Serafín's brother, named Juventino, arrived in a car from Billings, Montana, accompanied by a black girl of that city. That same day we had a meeting in which Serafín said that he would pay per acre, and that he would keep with ten dollars per acre. In addition, food costs were to be divided equally, that is to say that when food was needed Serafín would buy it and then he would collect money from each one of us. We all agreed with that. Finally, he told us it was already the first crop of sugar beets, about 220 acres, where we had to remove the grass and the bud. Then, the boss brought another refrigerator for the house because he said that one was not enough, then hoes, which had to be prepared and ready to work. More than half of those who were with Serafín had already come with him before doing the same job and they said it was not very difficult.

On Monday of the following week we started working. My brother and I took us a couple of days to go hand in hand with other workers who had already done the job before. Serafín told us they were paying fifty dollars per acre. We were doing a little more than two acres each a day; all workers were quick to work. In addition, many Texan families who came to do the same work could be seen. Parents came with their wives and children, males and females, to earn for food in plantation of beets, and although it was not so profitable for them because they did not work from sunup to sundown, as we did, they like that kind of life.

Sometime later, Mexicans began to hate us and did not know why. We were treated with discrimination and contempt. They began to say that we spoke in Spanish because, they said, those who spoke Spanish better they were, but it was not true, because much of what they were saying only they understood. They were from a range in Queretaro and almost had no school. Things were complicated because they drank every evening, and Serafín included beer in the expenses for everyone to pay equally. My brother and I did not drink and we had to collaborate in the cost of drinks. That was not fair. And the worst thing was that when they got drunk, it was more dangerous to have problems with them. Finally, one evening one of them struggled with my brother who was cooking, and the thing turned into a big scandal because they were all drunk. The friendship that Miguel, the boy from Honduras, had offered me in Guatemala had disappeared: he had turned to the Mexicans side and he felt he was the right hand of Serafín. Everything happened after he had told me that he felt more Salvadoran than Honduras because his mother was from El Salvador.

That weekend Mr. Jimmison came, he had heard the scandal, and wondered what had happened to us. My brother and I told him that we were not Mexicans and we had had a problem with them. Then he told us that his brother had a house where we could go to live in. Serafín did not agree with the change but he accepted it when the rancher told him we left for the house of his brother. Then he told us to get our bags ready because he would take us to the ranch of his brother, which would also have much work to do days later. We had already known his brother walking with Mr. Mike, and as soon as we got to his home they began talking about the problem in the other house. Mr. Jimmison explained that we did not drink and everyone else did, and that was already a detail of the problem.

My brother and I did not understand much English, but since we came to the United States began asking the meanings of some words in English; Mr. Mike taught us, and we wrote sentences used to ask questions. Moreover, in northern Mexico I had bought a bilingual dictionary and a book of conversations, and Mrs. Maxi had many visitors coming from the United States and did not speak Spanish, so I had the opportunity to practice with them, because I always thought I would travel someday.

The agreement between the two brothers was that we would begin to work there, and Mexicans would arrive later to help. On the other hand, we had no idea about payment agreement they had with Serafín Landaverde. Live there, just us, was very relaxing. It was very quiet, nobody made scandals; there was not music that kept awake us until late at night and we rested. About two weeks later, the rest came to help with the work of the ranch. We already knew they would arrive any day, and we worked from dawn until the sun went down: in a week, the job was finished. Serafín said there were other ranchers nearby who were friends of the Jimmison and needed people to work because workers had not arrived yet. However, while we were occupying the houses, the

Jimmison were going to charge money for the stay. No one objected, and everything went smoothly.

As two of the boys from Querétaro were apparently angry to live with so many people and the conditions in which they lived, they decided to move in with us, because the house in which we were living had five rooms and it was newer, prettier and more modern. They told us that they had already been previous years with Serafín and had always done work for Jimmison and other ranchers, and they had never had to pay for being at home even if they had stayed all summer. They also told us that they had already paid them for the trip from Mexico up there, and that they had charged them more and without telling them: they had only taken the money from the payment without consulting them. In addition, we were asked if we had not noticed that the more we worked, the lower the payment, that, in the end, they gave us what they wanted. And they also asked if they had already told us that after working in Wyoming we would go to the state of Nebraska, for the harvest of beans.

We answer we had not been informed by anything at all. So they told us they thought of taking people for about four hundred dollars to work in that state, as they did every year. One of these boys said he had worked with Serafín this way for about three years, and there was always more money, but this time the situation was worse. This young man had learned with other friends who were already living in the area that the ranchers were paying better salaries but we were getting less money than in those other occasions. My brother and I had already paid Mr. Mike for having gone to Arizona for us, and the old man was happy. Likewise, we had agreed a payment with the guy who took us to the border of Nogales, but when we arrived in Wyoming Guillermo told us it was as much for each, and as payments came from his cousin, we had been cheated as well. The thing was that these subjects were already used to swindle people. On the other hand, we were a little satisfied, since we had sent a little money to our parents and some letters in which we told them we were good and wanting to know about them and other people.

The work only lasted a few weeks. We had already met other Mexican boys who asked us why we worked for Serafín if this man was known for being a swindler, and there were some who wanted to kill him, his brother and his cousin. They assured they could get us a job where they worked, and there everyone received his payment. So we got their phone numbers and did not tell anyone. Finally, Serafín's group telling us that we were going to Nebraska to the bean harvest. We answered them that no one had told us about that, and so we would not travel to anywhere. The three Landaverde were angry with us and said that, by hook or by crook, we would take us with them. Miguel, the man from Honduras, even pulled out his gun. The four of them were armed; they had 9 mm and .357. The others stayed in the two pickups and a car they also had. They wanted to take everyone so they did more money swindling people anyone discovered those scams. The other boys who were with us told us we better left to a stream to spend the time while they left, but we did not want and decided to stay at home that afternoon. They became very demanding and wanted to take us by force, but luck helped us. Mr. Jimmison, who perhaps saw the arrival of the carsappeared with his dogs; he arrived when they were with their guns in their hands, although he did not see them because we were in, and this lowered the tension in the air. As we could, we told the lord they were going to Nebraska, but two of us and the others who were in the house preferred to stay. Soon, they moved away while threatened us saying we would see again, and we should told those to the others. As Mr. Jimmison was still there, we did not answer them, and then walked away.

The rancher was still there, with us, practicing her little Spanish when they the other boys arrived, who probably were hiding watching the situation. The lord clearly told us that he had never received money for housing and did not believe that his brother had done it neither.

"When it is winter, it is expensive due to heating; but today, at this season, you can stay here and there in any problem" he said.

And he added that at that time in the area where the house was situated he would not have cattle because the fence needed to be repaired. Besides, he asked us if we saw cattle out we could tell him or lead the animals to another pasture since livestock would go to the road. Of course, we replied there was no problem. After that, he called his two dogs and said goodbye. For our part, we were happy these people had left and also so gentle manner in which Mr. Jimmison had behaved.

The following Monday we went to work in the big ranch of Mr. Pablo Rodríguez, a man from Texas of both, Mexican and American ancestry. He was a very right man, spoke very good Spanish treated the workers with respect and honesty. He was the richest rancher in the area, and everyone knew him. In his ranch he had more machinery than anywhere else: there were up to ten machines cutting wheat and others taking beans which was planted on thousands of hectares. There worked many watering men, tractor drivers, truck drivers and keepers of livestock, the sheep —since he had a lot of sheep-and even horses. The man had a great staff at his ranch, all well-organized. His wife was a white, American woman, and worked as a tractor and trailer driver: she spoke Spanish well and she loved working on the ranch. Sometimes they invited us to eat something in the garden of his house; they enjoyed listening to us and the talked about their lives together.

They only had one daughter who was studying at a university that was far; I do not remember the name of the place, but apparently it was a very expensive university.

Four days after, two of the Mexican boys who had gone with Serafín returned. They came all injured. They told us they were travelling in two pickup trucks with canvas and a car, and in a rest area, heading to Nebraska, they stopped to rest. The bosses were drinking and insinuated that the money had been spent or stolen in Wyoming and some quarreled. Then, the bosses, including Miguel from Honduras, took out their guns, humiliated the boys, but then followed their way. Later, the front tire of the pickup blew; it was carrying more people than the other; it ended in a gutter and became unusable. People had to hide in a cornfield. The others waited until the police arrived to lift the car and then returned to look for them, but they no longer were found. Some of the hidden people went one way, and others to another direction. Serafín did not care about them: he had already cashed the money of the trip. These guys told us that if this man returned to Querétaro, he would be killed there because he was a bad person.

Those who came back got work with Mr. Pablo. He offered us a home to live and there we went. Then, my brother and I bought a car: it was a Chrysler model 1979 and in very good condition.

We had already worked for Mr. Pablo for two months when the border patrol appeared and arrested us: they took us to the county jail.

Two days later they brought our other friends to the jail. They told us that almost fight against the officers: all took out their pistols and were on the verge of making a firefight. We spoke with Mr. Mike, who brought us some clothes and other things of value we had, and we asked him to communicate with Mr. Pablo to ask him for the payment of the last days worked, and he did. The lord received the check; he went to cash it and took us the money to jail. A few days later, we went handcuffed on a plane to Denver, Colorado, and from there we were sent by bus to Ciudad Juárez, Chihuahua, Mexico. We were sent to Mexico handcuffed, all of us. There were some Texans who did not like us because they thought we were stealing their work and they reported us to immigration office from Billings, Montana.

And there we were left, in Ciudad Juárez, Chihuahua, although it was not really our country: we had to adapt to the system and see what could be done to continue to survive in life. My brother decided to go to Querétaro since then began making friendship with us. I decided to go with those returning to the North. So we separated: we divide the clothes and I took my way, heading to Nogales on the border, with the other three comrades who had also been deported. We stayed for a couple of days in a friend's house who was going to travel back with us, and there I met his brothers and the rest of his family. Then we went by bus to Nogales, Sonora, to seek the crossing. We had to wait almost another week while the trip was organized. A few days later, we were in Powell, Wyoming.

When we met Mr. Mike, he showed us the local newspaper in which we appeared on the front page on the plane. There was also an article on the border patrol where it was said that the Government would fine the rancher who employed illegal people. On another page appeared Mr. Pablo Rodríguez in a meeting he had with investors in the area. The photo showed Mr. Pablo with his hand raised and with his index finger extended, and the article quoted him: "I, whenever I have work to an illegal immigrant on my ranch, I will always employ him. Furthermore, the best workers are from Mexico, and I do not know what the mistake is of giving work to a person who wants to survive." People said that Mr. Pablo was the man who had more money in banks in the area and had great influence in the agricultural sector of that place. We liked what this man said in the newspaper and it encouraged us to ask him for work again.

That afternoon, we went to look for him, and as it was already quite late, we find him at his home. When he saw us, he rejoiced and amazed that within two weeks we were back in place. He said there was still work collecting irrigation pipes and fixing fences for sheep and cattle, and other things, like picking stone with the tractor and other tasks. We started to work, and everything was fine, but the third week while we were doing our tasks, Mr. Pablo arrived to warn us he had heard the border patrol had been in a nearby ranch and they would probably come to Mr. Pablo's ranch at any time. So, we immediately got into a pickup, carried some of our stuff and went to a town called Thermopolis, in the state of Wyoming. We stayed for three days with a friend who lived there. When we knew the police had already gone away, we returned to Mr. Pablo's farm, but we were no longer safe there. We only worked a few more days to finish the most urgent tasks, and then we took the car we had bought with my brother -which all this time had been parked at Mr. Mike's house- and went to West Virginia, where there was a contact to work in the picking of apple.

The journey was long, but we found the place where supposedly we would find this comrade. However, when we arrived there, we were told that he had been there but had gone elsewhere; they did not know where. We looked for him during several days but did not find him, so we decided to return to the west of the country since we had another contact in Las Vegas, Nevada, who had also promised to get us work in construction. As we were tired from travelling, this friend of Las Vegas told us to rest a few days, while he got work for us.

We had been working during a week when our comrade ruined his car. Since it was Saturday, we did not work, so we all went to help him fix it. While we helped him and we talked about life events, suddenly immigrations officers came and asked for our documents. The four of us had no papers at all, and we were handcuffed and taken on their van. A fellow said the car was mine, and he was also taken prisoner. In addition, we lost the money we had earned for that week.

In front of the place where we were, there was a building in which lived almost all Cubans and they did not like Mexicans that much; and as at that time the government supported them they kept collaborating with it. At that time, when they came to the United States all they did was discredit their country, Cuba, and its system. They did not work, they lived on welfare and subsidies they were granted, and hated Mexicans. For them, on the other hand, all the other Hispanics who were in the United States were Mexican and deserved their hatred.

We were three days in the jail in Las Vegas. They just gave us a frozen sandwich per day. I remembered there was another Mexican who did not seem to be quite right in his head, saying, "We are nothing, we are nothing..." and "These damned men do not like us, they are racists, but Mexico one day they will lose it, for God they will "and kissed the fingers in cross shape and while he walked inside the cell where we slept, from side to side, as if he wanted to say they did with us what they wanted and we could not do anything about it.

There I also realized, by the way of speaking, that there was another Salvadoran. When I asked him where he was from, I confirmed it. He told me about his birthplace, his hometown. Then he wanted to know if I had said I was from El Salvador. I said no, I had said I was Mexican, because I did not want to take the risk of being deported. He said that it would have been better if I had said it was Salvadoran, because they were giving temporary permit for legal stay in the country because of the war. He also said he had that permission, but he had missed a hearing which he had to attend, and because of that he was there, but in a few hours he would leave the cell, and all he had to do was not miss any other hearing. It is worth saying that Salvadorans who were registered under that program were at risk, mostly, of being sent back to their country, deported, and this way they kept them under control. Next day they came and released him. At first, they did not charge bail to get out, but after a year and a half things had changed and now we had to pay a considerable amount. It was to be paid to the Government or the Immigration and Naturalization Service (INS). I was thinking of my immediate destination.

My comrades and I were sent to Mexico, and we went again to Nogales, Sonora, where their families were living, and stayed for a week and half. Then we got a connection in Tijuana, and we went there. The border crossing was like a war. It was very difficult. Our comrade in Las Vegas, a very hardworking man, spoke with a coyote. His wife financially supported him and he would go to Los Angeles: in that way, we all ensure our way to Los Angeles, and then she would come with money and take us to Las Vegas. Under these circumstances the coyotes let us cross.

It took us three days to cross the most difficult points; they took us to a place in Chula Vista and then to San Diego. There, we descended for drainage tube about twenty meters and then crawled inside another that was about one meter in diameter, and crossed a highway connections as half a kilometer. The pipe was very dark and dirty, and when we left we were very tired of squatting, crawling the tube drains. That looked like the war. After about five or six days, we were in Los Angeles. We were taken in about six cars, all filled with people, and then we were put in a room. We were hungry: we had not eaten for days, we were almost starving. They said, "Well, if they come for you and bring in the money, I will let you go, but I want the money for the four of you so you can go!"

The four of us agreed that we would not get money for these thugs, we asked to borrow the phone and called to Las Vegas and from there they said they were going for us, and they trusted us. Only were the four of us. At least forty individuals had been released. We said they were going to pick us out there, in a corner, and they would take the money. So when they went to make a routine operation, we escaped: we had to jump from a second floor. I hurt both hands. It was one o'clock; in the morning we ran for those lonely streets and hid in some trees as soon as we saw that they were armed looking for us. After they left, we paid a taxi to take us to the bus station and then called my friend's relatives to come and pick us to the terminal. They soon arrived and we went to his home.

We stayed at my friend's house for a few days. Then I met a woman who helped me with the food. I asked if she could give me a job at her small restaurant, but she said no because she already had the few people needed to work with her. A few days later, she told me she would help me so I could travel and go to pick up my car. Finally, I traveled to Las Vegas with the ticket she bought me and left the other comrades in Los Angeles. As soon as I got to the bus station, the border police was waiting for me. They grabbed me, interrogated me and took me to the research department, and there I told them that I was Salvadoran. They already knew me because they had caught before. So they gave me a beating: they wanted me to sign the deportation. They beat me all; I was locked in a room and they gave me blows. They badly hurt me that day, trying to make me sign the papers to return deported to El Salvador, but I did not sign anything. I was beaten in military style, and then they put me in a room and did not give me any food; when I begged them, they said that if I wanted food I had to sign the document; anyway, they would not. Finally, three days later I was sent to another place. During all that time I almost had not eaten, because they had not given me anything to eat, and also I had bruises all over my body.

I was transferred to the place where were all prisoners, either political or not, from Central America, from the rest of the Americas and from the rest of the world. As they took me there, they stripped me to see if I had weapons and made me a pretty thorough examination. When I entered, I found myself in an unknown world. There were about 1,200 Salvadorans, about 800 Guatemalans, Nicaraguans, Hondurans, South Americans, Asians, Africans and a few Europeans. There were about 3,000 prisoners there. There were several barracks and each was occupied by many who slept there. The cooks were about twenty, and they were paid a dollar a day to work there. We were driven to the church to convert us to Christianity, and every two weeks we had to go to a judge to see if we signed deportation. They called it "voluntary deportation".

Salvadorans who were there were mostly supporters of the Farabundo Martí National Liberation Front (FMLN), the revolutionary front, and talks of this nature could be heard, although there were many former national and former military guards who often caused clashes because of the political ideals of everyone. Among Guatemalans, most of them supported revolutionary ideas, and the Hondurans alike. On the contrary, Nicaraguans were different; they were mostly reactionary, spoke only evil of the revolution and for that reason many lawsuits were generated within the prison. Many sought the support to get residence permit in the country.

There we did several things: he played dice, the Salvadoran style, and officers let us do it. The dice were manufactured right there. The got plastic bags; melted them and when plastic was a stick it was cut and then they did the little holes. Many were able to pierce a bone they took from meal, and made them more special, but not all the time they were lucky enough to get them pass because it was illegal. Chefs also made their moves: they took some sandwiches and during the break time sold them for a dollar, so with that many they could buy many other things. Salvadorans ran the prison, since the group was very large and some had been political leaders in our country.

There was a lot of racism among immigrant officers: some of them were white, others were black and there were even some Americans who had Mexican family origins who also were racists. Once a Salvadoran guy was badly hit and they almost break him an arm and the thin leg, so they had to send him to hospital. A great number of Salvadorans then jumped the chain link fences with barbed wire above, and they were also beaten by the officers. I remember pieces of radios flying everywhere as well as their truncheons until they were ordered to leave the place, and as there could not take any weapon they could not shoot at anyone. This time Salvadorans manage to get the moving of those officers to another place, because if they stay there, they risked being killed during the night shift when they cared the barracks while prisoners were sleeping. They were obliged to do so because, as I knew then, there had already been situations where agents had been killed. Very complicated conflicts in which hundreds were sometimes involved had occurred.

At that time, in the United States there were three places where political prisoners and illegal from Central America and the Caribbean were. There was one in California, another in El Paso and another one in Matamoros. Most prisoners were Salvadorans and Central Americans fleeing the war generated precisely by the United States. There were times when some prisoners managed to escape, and only once one of them was grabbed. Generally, this happened when there were big fights in prison. Jail was for undocumented immigrants: most came from El Salvador, and some others were Guatemalans, and we joined when there was a rallying cry or a revolutionary cry.

The thing was that there they played goat and other types of games, of course, for money. When there was a struggle, the game had to be suspended because generally officers entered the place where he were played and watched television. Once, one player owed money to another from a bet, and he threatened him saying that at night he would retaliate. I slept beside the one owing the money, and when the sun rose, I saw the guy who slept under this covered in the blood coming from the one who was sleeping up... Someone had gone and had given him stab wounds, and the guard who cared for night did not notice that: they slept during their guards thought they were supposed to be on duty all night.

All this made me see that my problem was harder than I thought at first. Then, I began to read the Bible and learned to play chess with my teammates. Then, we started a small company with two of my friends: we bought old socks, undid them to have thread and with them we manufactured bags and sold them. We made them very beautiful and in different colors. In El Salvador we call them nosebag. There were three partners, and I made up to three a day. In addition, we played a lot of chess. We organized a competition of about two hundred participants that lasted about three or four days. I was taught by one of the best players, and it turned out in the end I won him the final: I was the winner of the chess championship. I was happy, because he had used tricks, and they worked. The friends I made in prison, that had already been there more time than I had, respected me more because of these things, and because we were making money to survive there, to buy cigarettes and for other expenses.

Meanwhile, there was an institution, 'Simpson Mazzoli Immigration Bill', who was helping me and trying to lower my bond through someone who was supposedly a lawyer. They also were trying to get my car to sell it and use that money to get me out of jail, but they found out that it was me who had to go, take it out and sell it, personally. Lawyers could not do much about it. It was a funded institution ran by churches and humanitarian coordination centers, and did not have much political force, even less when dealing with the immigration office of the United States. Every two weeks, I had to go and see a judge in charge of deportation: all that was said in those hearings were related to the signal the deportation and that in our country nothing would happen to us upon arrival.

In those days there was a group of about sixty Salvadorans who had already signed, but did not want to be sent to El Salvador, but for Nicaragua, Costa Rica or Panama. However, they planned to go together, deported, and once the plane took off, they would force the pilot to go to Montreal, Canada: most feared reach El Salvador and die there. We made a strike for nearly two weeks to send them deported all together. But the border patrol could also imagine what they might do all Salvadorans together, and thus only sent small groups of five to ten on the same plane. I remembered a Sunday; we were about three hundred Salvadorans supporting these boys: we had already spent almost two weeks on strike. Some were impatient, made more scandal and destroyed some things, like telephones, televisions and other service items. La patrol paid attention to the whole event. It was required the same immigration officer in the country to negotiate the case with the agent. A few hours later, he arrived. He came in a helicopter from San Diego, California, with two others who were with him. He was a little drunk because, as we got to know, he was at a party. He was very upset with what was going on.

In prison there was a Salvadoran boy whom everyone respected as a leader. I never knew his name, but everyone called him the Pelón. He was tall, dark, arrogant and studious. This guy was the one who started talking to the head of the Border Patrol who had just arrived with his bodyguards. His helicopter landed in the field where we played soccer, where they had taken out benches to sit and make arrangements or decisions. At one point, this man grabbed Pelón's neck with fury, strangling him. The man was from the Government of the United States and the boy had to take that into account; however, the boy was young and strong, and was very relaxed, so he just told him to let him go, while the rest of the people present there told him the same thing. The man reacted and after a few moments released him, after more than three hundred people present there shouted at him to do so. Outside, the jail was surrounded by the Border Patrol, the Police and perhaps another Body Law. After a while talking, the old man went to the offices: an hour later he came out, boarded the helicopter and left. Soon, they said by megaphones that those who were supporting the claim, we could leave if we wanted to, and that the patrol would make everyone a fair process, but we should come back to the barracks to sleep, and who did not do so would be punished.

Of all the people who were supporting our peers, a group of two hundred fifty to three hundred began going out: in fact, it meant a throwback to the support. Each had to say his name and a surname; as a secret key, we mentioned the second surname as personal identification. That way, about a hundred of them could go, and everyone who left the closure was shouting that he was a traitor to the cause and the crowd took gravel and threw it to them. At night, they began to call us one by one, in alphabetical order. When it was my turn, they took me in front of an immigration psychologist, specialist in political issues, to interrogate me. He asked me some questions; he wanted to know why we were doing that. I answered what I had to say, and he sent me to another department where they stripped me and searched me up even under the tongue. After that, we were taken to the dungeons, where it was dark and we were without food for three days.

When we left that place, some colleagues had the newspaper and the incident of what had happened the day the old man arrived in the helicopter. There also were photos taken from the air, where it could be seen the jail surrounded by security and police patrols. The press and local TV had been present thanks to the contacts of some colleagues. And so, in that way, we had to wait for the promises from the patrol towards the Salvadorans who did not want to return to their homeland either for political reasons or the risk of die.

Life in prison continued its pace as if nothing had happened. The comments were that many Salvadorans were deciding which country to ask for deportation. Only talks and rumors were heard, because most cases were related to political conflicts and other hometowns issues. The fights among Hispanics, African, Middle Eastern and other group occurred all the time. Moreover, there were quarrels within civilians because of political differences: Nicaraguans, Guatemalans, Hondurans and Salvadorans were fighting. I remembered several former National Guardsmen who were there all the time and had fights with Salvadorans who had other ideals.

I remember a Salvadoran fellow who told me that, like many others, he had changed his name in prison: his name was, Rolando La Feria. That means (Rollin the coins), But it's still a name. He told me he had taken part in the seizure of power in Nicaragua, when they brought out Somoza, and that the revolution had taught him a lot. He also told me that he had to go to make political activity to another Central American country, and that this had caused him an illness that forced him to abandon the revolutionary ranks of Nicaragua and El Salvador. He was asking being deported to Nicaragua and they did not want to give it to him. He said that if sent him to El Salvador, he would not come out alive from the airport. This man smoked a lot. There was another countryman who sold cigarettes; as cigarettes came only once a week, this man took advantage to sell them very expensive, especially when they were scarce, and then he charged a dollar. The seller had been an officer of the National Guard, and both men insulted each other. The ex-guard said:

-I'll go deported to my land, I will enter the National Guard again and you I'll put you in the line of fire, and with my gun in hand I'll shoot you. Be careful, because there, in La Union, we have the best snipers in the country and you will not get out alive when you come to my land.

"You know how we consider power in Nicaragua: gripping and fighting with guns, and we finished those of the National Guard who had Somoza" replied the other.

"Those who gave themselves up gave us their rifle; they cried bitterly when they surrendered. And that you tell about the line of fire, I have heard it several times, so I'd like you to do it when we see there on the front line."

The revolutionary man also told the ex-guard that had a mind of an imperialist tyrant when in fact he was a poor. They hated each other; it was a huge hatred of political roots. The man told me that nobody knew his real name since he had left his land, since he already had many years of fighting and of political guerrilla experience; he had commanded forty-five men in combat and also, when they took a village, he was the one who gave talks to people. He said he would give his life for that cause.

Finally, it came the day when I decided to sign the deportation: there were no longer opportunities to stay in the country. I sent a letter to El Salvador, where I told my family that would soon be arriving there. The lawyers wanted to help me, but the situation was tough for immigrants. The bond I had to pay was 3,000 (US dollars), and lawyers only managed to lower it to 2,500 dollars. I had no one to lend me the money, because I had no relatives in the country or friends with whom we were in contact. The car was lost; it was a car that was worth about $ 1,500, but according to the lawyer and the people of the church, it had been sold at auction of the police. I had been almost six months in jail. There I spent one Christmas, New Year and even my birthday in the jail. People from the humanitarian organization did not want me to sign deportation, but I told them I preferred to leave, even die out of that place; I wanted to see my parents. They understood me, gave me strength and courage, and motivated me to think about the days of my adventure.

I talked to the best friends I had in prison, the two with whom I was associated to sell knapsacks. They both wore one year and three months there, and neither wanted to stay any longer. Both had parents and younger siblings in El Salvador. When I told them about the decision I had made, they said they would also do the same, and together we went to ask for a hearing to the office to speak with the judge who handled the deportations. I had received a letter from my older sister, in which she told me that our parents were sick and very overwhelmed by the situation, and to be careful when arriving at the airport.

After three days of having gone to make the request, they called us through the megaphone to see the judge. We were about fifteen young men. They sat us on chairs and told us we were signing a document voluntarily and that it was a very particular decision. The judge even smiled with happiness when the Central Americans came to sign the deportation. We were informed that for three years we could not re-enter the country as we had violated the immigration laws of the United States. They also said that some would be deported in two or three weeks from that moment.

Churches could not provide much in the things linked to the situation of refugees due to their economic difficulties to pay lawyers who prosecute those cases to the INS. They did not guarantee the life of the deportees, and the Government of the United States provided any defense for such individuals neither and less to litigate for their civil rights or diplomatic nature problems. All these difficulties were discussed at a summit meeting of the church that was in Medellin, Colombia, where all great religious, including Pope attended. They dealt with Latin American political issues, matters of the Church and the deportation of people from the United States to their home countries, where there were political conflicts because of the risks of being killed. There was a member who said: "Immigration: do not desecrate the house of God."

Since the announcement that we would be sent to El Salvador, our minds changed. We talked less and just thought what we would do on reaching our homeland. We closed the small company to make backpacks and we dedicated to plan the return after a couple of months, because we knew that in our country it was very difficult to survive. We also talk about whether we had contacts in the government, in case somebody wanted to kill us. They had better. I only kept correspondence with my friends and family so they would be alert when I arrived to the country. My contact came through my brother in law, who worked at the Central National Police in the capital, and my younger brother, who was in the Army. I already had the names of their leaders and all information of the places where I could locate them on the phone. As time passed, we were getting ready: at any time we could be called to leave for El Salvador.

The afternoon least expected, almost three weeks after signing the document, they began to name by the megaphone the ones would return to their country. After calling three or four, they mentioned my name. We were only seven, my friends were not called. On the other side of the pen, I started talking to them through the fence. We mentioned that we would not go together and I did not know the others who were in my group. Anyway, I would have way to communicate with my colleagues, and they with me.

A few minutes later, they took us out and put us in a truck bound for Los Angeles, California. Three hours later, we arrived, handcuffed, to Los Angeles and got us into a Mexican airline. That night we arrived in Mexico, D.F., where the Mexican immigration office grabbed us, always handcuffed, and took us to a hotel. We were told we would sleep there and the next day, in the morning, we would get up early to get on another plane bound for El Salvador. One of the three officers said we would better do not try to escape, because the entrance would be watched.

The next day, the Mexican immigration office came to take us. We thought we were going to take the plane, but the officer told us:

-Bad luck; you're not leaving yet because the airport of El Salvador is closed. They have bombed an aircraft of the LANICA airline, of

Nicaragua, and no one can reach the airport until this problem is resolved.

International flights were canceled. They said that this airline was owned by Nicaraguan president Anastasio Somoza, but as the Sandinistas had seized power and the airline had become the property of the Sandinista state, perhaps because of that the attack had happened. For that reason, we were there for four days. During that time we were to eat at a restaurant, always the same, and though we were always handcuffed, it was clear that it was safe for them as the place had good gates so that no one would escape, and the place was prepared to feed the deportees who were from the United States to the south of the continent.

The day when we would fly finally came. The comrades who were with me were very thoughtful and talked very little during the flight; the concern could be seen on our faces. Only one was from the capital; the other six were from villages and were further away from our families. Between six and seven o'clock in the afternoon not a soul could be seen on the streets because of the curfew and in the streets only military, members of Death Squads and national police were visible. Furthermore, there were planes that bombed and in the evenings threw flares in areas of the country; they said that was done in order to see the enemies, but in that way they killed innocent people. In many cases even they murdered people of the Church who were exercising religious acts.

When we landed, we were taken off the plane and then taken to an empty room. Those who went to get us walked in civilian clothes, with Ray-Ban sun glasses, mustache and longish hair, and I think they were from the Section 2, the body created by d'Aubuisson as a part of the Death Squads. It was a body that did tasks of an intellectual nature and dealt with special investigations and torture in clandestine prisons. I was told later, these men were from the artillery barracks, where military engineers were. They were dangerous because they went to the valleys and there deceived and persuaded farmers. They used to wear work clothes and tools of peasants, but when they realized how the valley was political and military organized they arrived to make killings invasions.

Many even worked several days or weeks, living with peasants while getting the trust of the people of the valleys.

These detectives separated us all and they investigated one by one in separate rooms. They asked me if I knew the others who came with me. I told the guy who was interrogating me that I had known them during deportation, before that I had never seen them in my life.

-Come here... I want to ask you some questions, -the man said. He took me to an empty room where there were only two chairs; he ordered me to sit down, and went on: -So, have you been deported?

-Yes, -I replied.

"Did you know that those who come as you came here are hit?" He said then. "We kill them quickly. To begin with, your hair is long, you do not carry documents. You say you've been out of the country for two years. What if you walked by Cuba or the Soviet Union and return here from Mexico? I'm sure you left the country because you were guerrilla"...

That man really grieves me with what he was saying, but I replied, "Please listen to me, I left the country because I could no longer find work and I was in Guatemala and more than a year in Northern Mexico, in Sonora; but then, I went to the United States; I was grabbed by the border patrol when I was crossing the border and I was in jail for almost six months because I did not want to sign my deportation. My brother-in-law, who is married to my older sister, belongs to the police, and he is the type of police that cares for Napoleon Duarte."

I mentioned this because that police dealt with the security of the president and was very well seen in the police headquarters in the capital and the country's customs; then I continued saying, "I also have a brother who is an officer in the military artillery "San Nicolás".

And then I gave him the name of my brother and the names of the colonels and generals with whom my brother was related to and those who knew him, because my brother had already sent letters telling me not to be afraid when I came to the country.

"That's my headquarters..." He interrupted then. "Wait for me, I want to see if everything you told me is true." He left me there for about thirty or forty minutes, then he returned.

"I've already phoned to see if what you said was true: you convinced me that everything you told me is true. But some of your friends will not have the same fate. You can go, but you have to be very careful because here the situation is still bad."

I left the airport a little scared. It was already becoming dark. I just got off the bleachers where I was, I looked for the last pickup that was heading to the capital, since there would not be another because of the curfew. After seven in the evening, there was no transportation in the country, and if there was any, I was risking life taking it. At that time only three of the seven who had arrived could leave; the other four stayed there. If they did not have any contact in the military, perhaps they died there. We could take the last transport. Almost every block, across the road, there were soldiers on both sides of the highway. We finally came to the capital, which was devastated. Fortunately, I managed to take a bus headed to where my people were, although it would leave me halfway, in Apopa. There I found the artillery militaries had cannons on the road, firing bombs towards the Guazapa Mountains. Traffic was stopped. I got off that bus and took another going to my town. It was a Saturday night, and I was very lucky they did not kill me: I came at last to my sister's house, where the next day I would see my dear old lady, my mother.

My sister was surprised when she saw me although she knew I would be deported at any time. She embraced me tightly. She was very happy to have me there, and some tears were dropped. Then we talked about what was happening in the country: her husband and my brother were military of the Government and could not do anything about it. In those days, life in El Salvador was very difficult, very hard.

"Do not worry," said my sister, "mom is coming tomorrow, and we'll give her a surprise because you are here, she knows you we're coming, but she does not know that you are already here."

My sister's husband just went once a month for twenty four hours; he took care of José Napoleón Duarte, who had been brought from Venezuela to fix political and internal problems of the country. Duarte won elections in 1972 but the military had dismissed him because the rich and the United States did not suit them he was in power: they took him out of the presidency; he was taken to secret prisons and tortured. If I'm not mistaken, there made him blind in one eye and cut him some fingers. Then he was expatriated. However, they made him return by a political strategy especially planned by the Americans with the idea that he took over the control of the country, as President of the Republic. His people did not support him any longer: they had changed their ideology and they had come to ARENA side, the Republican Party. But Duarte ended up winning the presidential elections with the goal that he would defuse the problem in the country. He had been brought to solve the political problem that was in the country that, according to the Americans, it was easy to solve. Of course Duarte was the puppet, because behind this man was the military leadership and in the same country there were members of the CIA making decisions. Mr. Duarte was run by his people and by the United States, and could not solve any internal problems of El Salvador.

Just as Dr. Guillermo Ungo kept his political ideals to death, Duarte was upset, and after what they did to him, they still could change his mind and bring him to the country as a puppet, because the military of El Salvador and the United States did what they wanted with his government. Central America was not being threatened by communism, as said the White House but rather by hunger and exploitation. Major Roberto D'Aubuisson, meanwhile, had said that if the entire leadership was in his power, he could exterminate all those subversives and insurgents in less than six months. (A wipe out in the country). He told this to the United States: the White House and the Pentagon. Among those involved, there were also Chileans and Argentines of Nazi ideology that supported and advised them on the basis of their experience: they learned to create terror.

When I arrived, I realized that many things were not going well in the country. When were the ballots, according to information gathered, who won the elections was the Major Roberto D'Aubuisson. Conservatives supported him, the military had not to give their vote because they were automatically from the ARENA, and on the other hand, the neutral people were afraid of reprisals and they did not know certain things that happened and could happen. They all went to vote, it was valid to put a blank vote, only to avoid problems with the military and the right-wing extremists since then it was necessary to show in the identity card the stamp had proved attended the vote. The person who did not have that stamp could be killed: he was taken and put to death as a communist subversive. Thus, the president Mr. d'Aubuisson won. However, as those who ran the game did not want this man won, they returned to call elections until Duarte "won" the presidency through corrupt maneuvers. At that point, the man was already a puppet; neither the military, nor the neutral people or the FMLN liked him. Everyone said he was a traitor, no matter who he was.

The day after my arrival, my mother came to my sister's house in the town. She was very happy to come back to meet us, and me too. She told me that she was the only one traveling down the street that was very close to our valley, and that other people crossed the river to catch the street that was on the other side and walked toward the town along the Riviera. Thus, people avoided problems with the "Civil Defense".

I have to add that in those days, the one who said Death Squad was killed, so we had to call them that way: Civil Defense. That had been decreed by government representatives, including Mr. Napoleón Duarte, who supposedly was with the people and was very democratic...

I returned to our house with my mom, who told me that if I went alone they could kill me before I arrived. We went down the other road. On leaving the village, we found the command of the Civil Defense in my valley. They came to give the weekly report in the artillery military base, and there came my brother: uniformed and with a large machine gun. My mother entered the bus and my brother invited me up to us to travel on the grid, as was usual there. All wore uniforms and had their rifles, as wishing that something would go along the way. Soon, my brother told me how was the thing at home and told me about my other brother, who was in the artillery barracks, where they came from them.

Then I learned that the commander wanted to kill my mother, accusing her of guerrilla just because she was the only one who was on the other street, but she did it because she had to go and see her mother, who lived two kilometers away. In the area there were many guerrillas, and my mother was friendly with them and sometimes brought them things for the town, but that was all. Because of this, the commander wanted to kill her and always said that my mother was a communist guerrilla.

On the other hand, my father was threatened. The commander of the "Civil Defense" did not like him and had sent some sergeants and lieutenants to intimidate him, just to get money from him: as this man knew that we were out of the country, he thought we were making money. When they formed the now called Civil Defense they pressured my father to sell part of the land and give this body which he obtained from the selling. The commander knew that our family had no money, but he thought we were in the United States, and he wanted dollars.

My brother also told me that during the days of break they had the opportunity and people to take revenge: they said they could go to remove that man over the family. They made such maneuvers. Many members of the Death Squads robbed the people and said they were doing it on behalf of the revolution: they went to the houses with rifles in hand, with masks and speaking of FMLN only to steal. My uncle, my father's brother, had been blackmailed twice that way, pretending to be guerrillas.

For those reasons, my younger brother got into the armed force, and then took a position in the artillery barracks called "San Nicolás". From that moment onwards, our family was more respected.

DEPORTED TO EL SALVADOR AND BACK

I got home. My father was very happy to see me: he gave me a hug and felt happy with tears on his eyes that again we were together. He told me many things that were happening in the valley and in our country. While he was doing the housework, he told me that he no longer felt flavor to life.

You could no longer say Death Squad, and the person who called them that way they could kill him at that precise time; it was called Civil Defense now. A person who said that Monsignor Romero was killed by the military would also be killed: at that time, we had to say that the guerrilla had killed him. The same happened with the murdered American nuns; they had been raped, tortured and murdered by paramilitary groups such as the National Guard but it was important that people remain quiet. They always bombed and burnt the radio stations where Masses of Monsignor Romero were transmitted. Subversive took peasant women who listened to these stations, such as La Voz Panamericana. Programs in which they talked about the truth of what was going on could not be heard; they were forbidden. Many people from the valley had disappeared: many had been killed, others had left the place. The squad from that place called Tutultepeque was looting the people of all these valleys. Later, clandestine cemeteries were found in coffee plantations, where they buried the people they had murdered.

My father and mother had some neighbours nearby (*They were God fathers with my parents*). A son of them got into the guerrilla because Mr. Vicente Escobar was seeking him with the Death Squad and the National Guard. Sometime ago, the old man was riding and as he had sent to prison the young man's uncle and had threatened the valley, this boy grabbed his neck and wanted to strangle him. The old man then looked for him to kill him with his children or with the Death Squad. Finally, they did not kill him, but they came to his parents' house and the man was strangled. They gave the woman a more painful death: there was a kind of coffee plant called *pacar* there, so they cut a coffee plant of about three feet tall, they sharpened the top of the trunk and they sat her at the stake until it reached her neck. It is said that nobody wanted to see Mr. Vicente Flores and Mrs. María Cabrera that way, as they had been at the scene.

I saw my parents quite depressed about the situation of the country. They went to sleep in the caves they had already done and they told me that the situation was going to last for many years. In other words, my father told me that he no longer felt the taste of life as before. My old father was no longer a happy man.

I also knew that some weeks before I was deported and arrived to the country, my cousin, Oscar Flamenco, had been deported from Mexico; I had planned to travel with him two years earlier. This cousin was imprisoned in clandestine and torture jails that were in the capital, and his family had not been able to take him out; though they could not see him, they knew he was alive. Thanks God, they were in contact with him through Peace Corps members and people of high military leadership of the Government, friends of the family for his father's side. At that time, only high ranking military officers formed the government structure ministries. My cousin's paternal family hobnobbed with some of these extremely arrogant characters. About a month after he had been imprisoned, his family managed to release him. He was emaciated; he did not look like the same person. He had changed physically and mentally; they had taken him in the dark, under physical and psychological torture.

My cousin told me that he was captured in Tampico, Tamaulipas, Mexico. First, he was imprisoned for almost a month in the Federal District. While he was a prisoner in that city, his older brother had an accident while he was working as an assistant to a truck driver in the state of Nuevo León, Mexico. When he told me that, I already knew that my other cousin had died and then buried in the capital of Mexico. Then he went on saying that he was sent to El Salvador overland, imprisoned, and politically investigated in Guatemala when he was handed over to the authorities of the country with about three dozens of Salvadorans deportees. Then, he was taken to the customs of El Salvador, on the border. Anyone had travel personal documents or anything that identified them as Salvadorans. As soon as they were in Salvadoran land, they were thrown face down on a truck. He told me that he had long hair, like almost everyone, because of their hair they were accused of being guerrillas, and when they tried to speak to the guards, they were given a rifle butt in order to do not turn around, since the guards did not want them to see their faces. They were trampled and beaten while they were taken to the capital prisons for torture. In those jails, they did not give them food, and when members of Human Rights arrived to give them something to eat or coffee, the police who were there threw it. The torture came to three times a day, and it is told they said: "Just tell the truth, we'll let you go. Is it true that you went to Mexico to study communism or to go to the Soviet Union or Cuba? ". Obviously, it was a farce. Most people left the country because of the situation in which the country was. There were about six in each underground, and were blindfolded. My cousin said that sometimes he could see when they were about to hit him and he could prepare his body and muscles; but when they realized he could see they tortured him more. They put them electric shocks in the genitals or tied a bucket to the testicles and they started pouring water until they fainted or lied to be killed and stopped suffering. Many disappeared every night, because they would kill them overnight; but when they took someone, they did it during the day for people from Human Rights and the inhabitants to see.

People from the Human Rights could not do much because they also were threatened; and they could only bring the prisoners a little food or coffee and find a way to give the relatives some news of the detainees. They also made small reports of each of them and took them to churches and other sources in order to be heard. My cousin told us that some would tell him: "You might have people who can help you, but many of us do not. If they torture me as hard as they did the last time, I am going to say I'm guerrilla so as not to continue suffering". My cousin also said that at night heartbreaking cries were heard when the cruelest persecutors arrived to torture. At night, they drew some prisoners to kill them, and when members of the Human Rights asked about them, they said they had let them free.

Days later, when my mother and I went to visit my sister, I could see my brother-in-law, my sister's husband, who had been given permission to return home. My brother-in-law was at his house for a couple of days; he was drunk, and told me, "With the butt of my riffle I hit those bastards of the Human Rights and I made them dropped what they were carrying for the guerrillas who were locked up. I wish they all were killed and could no longer reproduce. Those people, belonging to the Human Rights, are guerrillas too, and come from Europe, Canada and the United States. Here they say they are nuns or members of peace. In fact, they are communists."

"But look how was Oscar, my cousin, there that they almost killed him" I said. "Do not you think that all those deported and the other people who are there are innocent...?"

"I believe your cousin is not a guerrilla, because I know him" he answered and went saying, "And look, I usually go to these prisons and I never see him when he was in prison."

"How could he know him or say he knew him" I replied, as it was not advisable for him and my cousin was bandaged the whole time?

My brother-in-law had already been absorbed by the system with his ways of thinking. He and his father were imprisoned and tortured in prisons alike when he worked for a shoe factory, the ADOC, in 1973. When there was an uprising because of the loss of Duarte in 1972, they were tortured in clandestine jails they had in San Salvador, and as they were missing, they were presumed dead. My brother-in-law, his father and other family members were followers of Duarte. It was at the time when people in their demonstrations said, in their banners, and loudly: "Duarte, though I do not get annoyed." My brother-in-law also mobilized together with the workers of the factory where they worked: they rebelled against the government system, and for that reason, he was about three weeks in cells, being tortured daily; but he had already forgotten that.

After two days of being at home, the escort of the Death Squad of the valley came. They were uniformed; they ordered me to go to serve "the homeland" and told me that if I refused, there was the firing line waiting for me. My brother came with them, and said, "Listen, brother, you have to do it, there is no way out; we must do it just to survive."

The commander gave the order to look for me to replace one who was ill and sent other units to charge the ill man who was missing his turn. I went with them. When we arrived at the camp, they dressed me in green and taught me how to use rifles, M-16 and G-3, which is a far-reaching German rifle with a potential shot. I was also taught how to use the Garand rifle and Czech. They are sniper rifles, effective at the target, but only grab five shots in the load apart from the one in the chamber. I learned to disarm the most important rifle; the G-3: it had fourteen pieces and it had to be disarmed in less than thirty seconds. That rifle weighs about fifteen pounds, plus the chargers, which have twenty cartridges, and you always have to carry a pair of chargers filled and ready. The following day they took me to a search down the mountain, to the riverbank. Then, the second commander told me to give turns rolling on the floor while shooting in bursts of one, three and five, and finally, all the cartridges in charger, which were twenty. In burst of three, one has to hit the bulls-eye even one shot. For me it was not very difficult to learn to shoot: never before had I shot with this type of rifles, but I had already done it with other smaller caliber rifles. When we got to the camp, I was told what days I had to be on call, and that it would be at night. They called it "do security". There were six stone trenches; in each one, there was a gunman twenty-four hours a day and between the trenches, there were some canals or barricades where another person could hide in case of attack.

In that cell, we were about fifty, and during the time I was there, it was said that a guerrilla infiltrated and studied the place to attack it. In those days, the guerrillas wiped out a Civil Defense much stronger than ours in a village called El Jocote: there were many bad people there -including some army officers- who went out to kill people at night. We heard the shooting at about two in the morning, and it was said they did not leave anyone alive. Then, we knew they did not annihilate us because they felt sorry for us. They knew that all we were in the trenches were against our will and that many were evangelistic and they said that if the guerrillas came they would surrender and handed over the gun. The commander was in the cell on his own initiative, but he did not care much about politics, but money: when someone could not go because of illness or any other thing, the commander sent uniformed men to collect money, and if the person had no money they took grains such as corn, beans, rice, etc. This man was getting rich at the expense of the whole valley. In addition, he extorted people together with some of the Civil Defense and they wore masks and went to rob people at midnight. They did all of that in the name of the revolution.

My uncle was threatened through a statement. This type of announcement said things like this: "On behalf of the FMLN, I inform you have to go to leave [amount of money] in [any place] at [time]. If you do not do it, you are a dead man". He was extorted twice in that way. For things like this, many do not sympathize with the revolution, since because of their ignorance and naivety, they were deceived, and others died in the same way.

The place where I lived was in dispute by both sides; therefore, it was more dangerous. The guerrillas had regions under their control and the military had others: as our area was under control of the guerrillas, there was more danger. Helicopters flew in groups of six or more, ready to strafe the valleys and peasantries.

Days after I had been recruited, we were sent to Guazapa mountain as part of the artillery barracks of San Nicolás. A squad of soldiers arrived with the order that all Civil Defenses who were in charge of the barracks had to leave immediately for Guazapa, a hill where there are several towns and many peasantries under guerrilla control from the beginning and combat zone during the war years. In that place there were planes bombing, helicopters strafing and ground military operations.

This headquarters had under its command tens of Civil Defenses in the area, and all had to go to that place to support the Army. In about two hours, we were ready and went out there, supposedly to fight. The quarters provided us with weapons, ammunition, uniforms, shoes jungle, etc. Of course, they brought us the remnants of the team: shoes and uniforms of soldiers who had died in battle, and often had blood. The weapons also were of the lower: carbines, Czech, Garangs, M-16 and some G-3, but the older ones.

The battalions of immediate reaction such as Atlácatl Atonal and Belloso went there. These three had been trained by the United States, by the CIA. We were about eighty men who belonged to the Civil Defenses of three valleys or farms. The rest were about eighty soldiers from some quarters. We went as alternate members of the military operation; they do not like to say where they are from, and they all had their faces painted black. Among the foot of the hill, we got together to receive attack and defense instructions. Four to six helicopters flew together, very low. One could see the man stroking his guns in the air. The Fuga planes flew in groups of two, three and four. The soldiers were launching in the area a "bottle operation."

A guerrilla friend told me that when it came to invasions, the two most dangerous military strategies were the "bottle operation" and "the ring". In the bottle, they first form two or three rows of soldiers in a bottle shaped figure, with a single end (which would be the mouth of the bottle). Then, they disconcerted the enemy with planes and artillery. Many people who support the revolution die because they cannot defend from napalm bombs; most are children, elderly and women. Around that mouth, there are three lines of soldiers fighting, but the mouth is open: thus, when a person wants to leave, is murdered. The guerrilla strategy was to break out and look after the release of all the people at the mouth of the bottle at pure combat, to take innocent local people from that place.

The cell was ready to take orders from military displacement. They were going to launch an invasion of those features with 5,000 soldiers. Civil Defenses were going to the rearguard of the combat, but finally it did not happen. It appears that we had a gunnery sergeant commander of the unit and a sub-sergeant, who was "the antenna", that is to say, the one with the radio for communication; the sergeant had to be on a par with him to receive orders from their elders. At that time, we knew that the guerrillas were very close to us and we preferred to keep quiet. The sergeant sneezed three times, but no one said, "Bless you" as we are accustomed to say in our culture. Then he told," What dammed and hard is sneezing in a pasture". Like insinuating he was surrounded by uneducated people.

"Well, why were you a cow then?" A soldier answered.

"Miserable recruit, son of a bitch, you are going to pay for this when we return to the barracks...!" replied the sergeant.

The sergeant had wanted to insinuate he was sneezing in a place where there were only cows because no one had told him "bless you" and he encountered the answer of that soldier. As far as I knew, the military could not punish a soldier while he was in an operation. The soldier was not a recruit, but this sergeant called that way all soldiers, although they were "*chucas*", that is to say, soldiers who were in the armed forces over time. The soldier thought what would be expected when returning to the barracks.

I also remember that the sergeant danced with his German G-3 rifle in his hands and said with a full heart,

"I wish some guerrillas fell. I like to catch them alive to have fun with them."

Later, it would be the displacement and what was waiting for us in combat. There were seventeen planes flying and strafing and helicopters with machine gun point 50,s M-60,s to exterminate the towns and villages. Anywhere, peasantries, villages and towns, helicopters could be seen flying barely above the trees in groups of six, eight, ten or more, strafing. They were green helicopters, those that are believed to have been brought back from Vietnam helicopters. Although many of these areas were already controlled by the Death Squads and, of course, by barracks from the area of that place, they did it anyway. The places that remained neutral or politically neutral were considered subversive and, therefore, were continuously attacked by helicopters and planes.

The Fuga planes that bombed peasantries in conflict zones were the B-37. El Salvador had bought those planes to Israel some time ago. The push'n'pulls -Salvadorans called them "wagons" and the military named them "little birds" in radio communications- fired flares to see the enemies: set the target for bombers or Fuga planes. The cart also carried point 50 and put the target for bombers planes with smoke bombs. With artillery and air force, military disarmed the positions and guerrilla combat lines. Later, a guerrilla veteran who was during six years on the frontlines told me that there were times when one wanted to become an ant in order to not be seen from the air. The military threw napalm bombs of 250, 500 and 750 pounds- whose use in a war of this kind was, as I learned, illegal- that burned trees where they fell. These bombs were already well known by the guerrillas. The shockwaves killed generally civilians, since almost all the guerrillas could defend themselves: they had to carry a dry stick in the shirt pocket and when they saw a bomb coming, they had to bite the dry stick so when the waves came the mouth was open and did explode neither the brain nor the lungs. Just being well barricaded behind a good rock was enough to survive, the waves did not kill them, and they only remained deaf for a few weeks.

In eastern El Salvador, there are uranium mines that at that time the United States was exploiting to build more bombs to destroy the population, because farmers did not know how to defend from this type of bombs. However, where they had no control and could not take it with the military, enemy forces or the guerrillas, they were too close to the front lines. There, they had to make a ground combat, rifle to rifle and artillery, and aircraft moved away because they could not bomb the opposing lines. Then, there were many casualties in the guerrillas because their strategies were better than those of the military were. The soldiers could not stand being without food and in a combat environment for long hours, so in that moment they withdrew from the lines asking planes bombing, when sometimes it was not possible.

I prayed to God that they find nothing. The forces of the people were very intelligent in that operation: to avoid the artillery and the aircraft they got close to the enemy. In that case, the enemy cannot shoot with guns or shell with planes, and begins a ground combat. There were bursts of rifles, mortars and rocket launchers. The fighting calmed down after midnight. We were posted behind the rocks, waiting for the command voices. The guerrillas started shooting with snipers; they killed some soldiers going forward. The push'n'pull planes were throwing flares to see their enemies. We slept there among the rocks and behind very thick trees. From time to time, the combat calmed down, but suddenly the shooting started again. We spent three days in that operation. The military did not get anything because the soldiers are very comfortable and want everything served. When the helicopter came to throw them food, guerrillas attacked it with burst of rifle FAL G-3 and 50, which was strong enough to shoot down a helicopter or hit the vulnerable point, and attacked the positions. Then the helicopters, which were those left over from Vietnam, had to get away. Soldiers did not eat and thus exasperated. Many died because they went out from where they were hidden to shoot, and then bursts of lead fell on hem.

I remember a fellow who was near me, hidden in another rock, at about five meters: the fire had calmed down and he told me that he wanted to defecate, but did not want to do that where he was because he could not bear it later, breathing bad air. It was about two o'clock. I advised him to do it right there, to make a hole and then buried it. As he hesitated, I told him to try lifting his cap with a stick: as soon as he did it, a burst of bullets pierced the cap.

Every year, the military set fire to the whole hill to burn it so they could see their adversaries, and they did it at that time. Besides, the hill was mined in both sides: the mines were everywhere, on sidewalks, slopes, cliffs and narrow streets. It was dangerous to fall in mines or ambushes; there were many who fell into such places. Likewise, the guerrillas made holes and put bamboo on them -called "booby traps"-, and when soldiers fell on them they were stuck on stakes.

We bore hunger during three days. Finally, when we arrived we found nothing. We only found blankets of our mates in their provisional or non-regulatory camps, which were built for meetings, military training or lectures. It was possible that they already were in the shelters called "*tatús*" that were everywhere. The military did not realize until the war ended the existence of these shelters where civil people hid underground. Especially children were hidden in those places while the military invasion was taking place. They also had hospitals for wounded from the guerrillas and arms garrisons.

Finally, we return without any results from the military maneuver ordered by the military leadership of the country and the United States. The military battalions had several casualties. We saw some being carried in hammocks or on their shoulders, being taken out of combat. Some were dead and others wounded.

At that time, planes threw reactionary propaganda through the peasants' valleys to persuade people. This was done everywhere, but it was more frequent where they knew there were people from the opposite part. Furthermore, at that time it was said on the radio and the newspapers that the guerrillas who surrendered and handed their rifles their lives would be respected. On television, some cases were shown by the Government to deceive militants who were holding a gun. They made a lot of propaganda of that kind, false, to mislead the country people. This type of strategy was often used in the media.

Then more military arrived at our camp and taught us new political strategies of combat or war, but they were still learning, since the guerrilla militants knew more. Most of us who were there in that Civil Defense, secretly supported the other side, but we had been pressured by that military government system that kept this war with the support of the Americans. Military instructors told the soldiers it was a shame that each guerrilla has the ability to fight with three to five soldiers in the front lines: this really angered politicians and military instructors of the area. The fighters had already learned to survive in the midst of a war, and when there were invasions, they only killed civilian peasants who knew nothing about the war. The media said they were guerrillas or rebels, although they were children, women or old people the ones they murdered with their attack artillery, because they did not know how to defend themselves from napalm bombs and most were not involved in anything.

In addition to "the bottle", military used an operation called "the ring", which consisted of enclosing a zone – it could sometimes covered three, four and up to ten villages- with three lines of troops and then attacking the center with aircrafts and artillery to destroy the inhabitants. In most cases, in the area there were both civilians and guerrillas, and for the guerrillas it was difficult to break those strategies. When the guerrillas break the invasion ring and take innocent people out, the fight becomes a fight between soldiers and guerrillas. Sometimes those invasions lasted up to a week. The shootings were brutal between the two sides.

In those days, Colonel Monterrosa lost his life: his helicopter exploded. At that time, he flew with a Father and a CIA consultant. Monterrosa worked for the CIA; he had been trained by the Americans and was a commander of the Atlácatl Battalion.

This man had done many "cleansing" with his military and political strategies. Shortly before his death, with his battalion, he carried out the massacre of more than 2,000 peasants in the Mozote in the Department of Morazán, in less than three days, and the killing of Jocoaitique, Morazán. They murdered people through horrendous mutilating ways; they raped teenagers, killed old people and women. This was even harder after the guerrillas destroyed the entire headquarters of the Union. Many peasants were considered missing; and it is said that many children were taken to be instructed and recruited when they were grown up using them to kill their own people.

Colonel Monterrosa did all this in the name of the country, as he told his Atlácatl Battalion -which had immediate reaction and trained in the United States: "In the name of the country, because it is the most beautiful thing we had on Earth. And in the name of God, because it is the most sacred thing for us in El Salvador". Moreover, he told them that communism hated God, but he never mentioned anything about the hunger that the people were suffering. The Salvadoran people did not need to hear sermons neither about communism nor about God; they needed more justice and rights to survive in the great crisis of extreme poverty in which they were immersed.

A cousin named Genaro, whom I went to school with and lived with during our childhood, was sent by the Atlácatl Battalion to North Carolina to be trained by the Americans. When he returned, he already wore epaulets of military grade and his political ideology had changed. I no longer met him, but we wrote because I was in the United States while he was training, and thus I could realize his political and military position.

The attack to Monterrosa was planned in detail. The FMLN raised public awareness of the news that the Autonomous University of Guadalajara had given them new radio equipment and installed it as evidence in my village. The radio worked extremely well. Secretly, they put explosives to the old team and let the infiltrators knew where it was located.

The military knew where they would find it and wanted to confiscate it with the Army. It was then that Monterrosa made the mistake of going and search the equipment the radio "*Venceremos*" did not need and was in Guacamaya, in the department of Morazán, practically abandoned but under the control of those who fought for the people. He was very happy because through some infiltrated in the guerrillas he had managed to take possession of the radio, which was found alone, without anyone watching it: the equipment was alone. After that, he considered taking it to some American advisers who were waiting for him, but the bomb exploded in the helicopter and Monterrosa did not reach his destination.

The armed forces, guerrillas and people in general knew that Monterrosa had been the victim of an attack; however, the Army said they had killed Monterrosa, because he was a right-wing extremist and he had killed many innocent peasants in Morazán. That was not true, but as the man was already dead, they were making firewood from the fallen tree, to clean the military footprint of the injustices which news had spread all over the world. It could not be said that Monterrosa had been a victim of FMLN: they wanted it to be said that the military leadership itself had murdered him. Thus, they expected that the abuses in the country would already end with the death of this man.

In those days, United Nations Peace Corps and other bodies began to intervene. Therefore, they started to discover clandestine cemeteries that had some of the so-called Civil Defenses. Some corpses were no longer buried, they were put face down and they threw ground on them, but the dogs found them and satisfied their hunger.

Meanwhile, I was in the Civil Defense. There, I was told that if I wanted, they could take me to another Civil Defense where I would have the chance to kill people. I not even answered the commander not the sub commander. The only thing that came to me was: "If they knew that one of these days I will go and I am not the least interested in walking in this life and less killing people..."

Some days later, my other brother arrived. They had given him permission for about two days. I had not seen him since he had left the country. He was in the same artillery quarter and was one of those who fired the cannons in war. He knew a lot of topography and knew how to hit the target with cannons and mortars. He told me he had shown up at the barracks because he felt bad seeing how the commander and the officers humiliated and threatened with death our father just because they wanted money. In earlier times, he had been forced to sell part of the land to give them money; but our father was capricious and courageous, and when said one thing did not change his mind. My brother told me he was in the military artillery barracks where the Civil Defenses were reported every week: he had gone there to gain more respect for our family.

"And I'll do my best to be better than this commander and deputy commander were", he said.

He told me four young men also wanted to take part in the barracks, but only he succeeded because the others did not pass the theoretical, physical and practical examination. That usually happened; when there was a young man who appeared, the examination was very delicate and hard since they feared he was a member of the guerrilla who did that to infiltrate. When recruiting, however, they did not care at all. They drew up to five hundred grams of blood to who did not remain in the barracks.

"This commander wants to kill our mother" continued my brother.

Just because she walks along this street and no one else travels on that street. The commander knows that in that street there are guerrillas and my mom stares at them every time she passes but she has to go in that direction to see her mother. He wants to kill my dad because he dislikes him and wants to get money and intimidate him. I think he is a thief like all the other and our father does not want to participate in the Civil defense.

"Do you know why?" My brother kept saying.

"I already have some good friends of confidence in the barracks that are from Section 2 and they told me that if I want to kill him, they come to do it for me in one night."

However, my brother never had a bad heart to hurt him. Instead, he visited him in his home, which was situated where was the Civil Defense post. My other brother told me when they went to track in the mountains he liked to go with the commander, in order to be near him in case of a confrontation with the guerrillas.

As there had been an attack against the Civil Defense of the place called The Jocote a little while ago, we were all alert and nervous; and uncertainty and silence in the darkness got on our nerves. Bombs and gunfire were heard in the distance everywhere. Planes bombed and helicopters would strafe every day. Helicopters fired with .50 and M-60 in the foothills of Guazapa, and from our place, we could see the flares thrown by planes to see their enemies. The chief passed more often to check the trenches so nobody falls asleep at night.

One day, at about two o'clock, I was moved to a trench facing a cane field. The wind was blowing. The reedbeds make much noise when there is strong wind. In the darkness, I stayed watching the edge of the cane field and saw something moving. It was something between black and white, and gradually began to approach me: I got a little nervous and placed the G-3 rifle in burst of five in rest on the trench. I only had my eyes above the stone trench. At one point, I could no longer bear it: the target was getting closer, and if I let him coming even closer, I would be at a distance enough to be reached by a grenade. Without thinking any more, I fired what I saw. With the shoot, the others who were sleeping suddenly wake up, and fell into gutters between the stone trenches. I saw that the target collapsed and made a loud noise, and then I realized it was not a human being. Then we all met and became aware that I had killed a poor cow that was eating around the cane field. Supposedly, there should not be cattle there, but that cow went out of his paddock and only came to find its death.

The following day, the foreman and the commander went to the village to talk on the phone with the owner of the farm and communicate him what had happened. The owner, a Spanish man, told us to eat the cow, since he was -above all- afraid to get to the place. Therefore, that afternoon, there was meat for the whole valley.

Some days later, two young men went to rob some houses where they thought they could find money. One of the thieves was the brother-in-law of the commander and the other was a good friend of confidence of them. They had done that before on many occasions. They disguised well, they put masks on their faces and went to gunpoint other boys who lived alone to accompany them on the mission so as to a crowd of fighters could be heard. In that way, they went to intimidate the family who lived in both houses. While they were gun pointing in the head at master of the last house robbed, a daughter recognized one of them. Although he was well disguised and he had put rags in his mouth to change the way of speaking, she mentioned his name. They almost murdered her and got money from the man. The community was then convinced and began to believe that even the commander was on the side of those thieves and bandits who pretended to be FMLN guerrillas. Partly, such people ruined the revolutionary process because they manipulated the naive people and vilely deceived them.

The following day, those men of the valley went to the barracks to present a report of what had happened. Then, the commander got a statement from the barracks. He did not feel very well, as his brother-in-law was involved in the problem. One day later, the Civil Defense arrived to hand them over to the barracks, and then, a dozen of soldiers came to do the same. With the soldiers, they were no longer loose as they were with the commander; instead, they went handcuffed to the barracks. There, they were imprisoned and then investigated and they told them that they could be killed and disappeared because of what they had done. After a few days of imprisonment and torture, they were given a choice: they could enter the barracks and everything ended there. The two agreed, but did not hold "physical "*chicharron*" they put on them, and they preferred to return to serve the Civil Defense. They took a lot of blood from them to use it in the military hospital. It is said that one of them fainted when getting up from the chair where he was sat. When they left, they were warned that if they were caught in another problem they would die.

In those days, the SEMFA headquarters was attacked; it was the headquarters of military engineering of the country. Likewise, the guerrillas took the headquarters of Chalatenango when they pleased to take weapons and ammunition, and kill people.

Sometime afterwards, in the United States, I met an individual who was from San Luis Potosí, Mexico, and he told me he had been in California and he had had the chance to get the American papers by entering the United States military corps. These soldiers were first sent to train in Honduras and then to El Salvador, to fight against the Salvadoran people. This friend had entered in a battalion for Honduras. After three months of training, they had sent him to the Chalatenango barracks called Paradise. He told me that the guerrillas came soon and destroyed all the barracks, and only a few escaped and fled to Honduras in the mountains, because that place is near the border between the two countries. He said that when he finally returned to the United States, they gave him what he deserved for his sacrifice: the Green Card.

My younger brother told me that they had recently ended the headquarters of La Union, where there were many from the American and Salvadoran intelligence supposedly. That quarter was strengthened, as the US intelligence passed weapons and other support resources to the guerrillas from Nicaragua by the Fonseca Gulf. There were buzzards that were enriching themselves with money from the United States. The barracks was burned, destroyed. It should be noted that these casualties were not reported in full to the United States; senior military reported that, in contrast, they had occurred in the battlefield.

My brother also told me that he had been out of the Army during a year and that he had managed to work in the Kimberly-Clark factory, an American multinational that is close to my town. After a year, he lost his job and was forced to enter the barracks again, since in the country there were no jobs. When he came and talked to the lieutenant, he said he wanted to return to the battle line in the same guard and the same position he had. The lieutenant told him he had never been retired. In other words, he had always been working: that is that the lieutenant had not reported the abandonment of my brother and, therefore, the lieutenant had kept his income. Much of the money that the United States sent was for thousands of addressees who were already dead or had deserted the army, because they still collected the money for the opposing ranks. Therefore, this money was split up among few who were alive and were high military.

I want to add that my brother had done that because of the letters I wrote to him with much entreaty: his stay in that place may have saved our parents and other relatives from death. When my brother came out, my parents already lived in the house they had built with the money that my other brother, Manuel, and I had sent them while working in the United States. However, the Death Squads always threatened them as they constantly traveled to the countryside, their area, and the gossips ran through the valleys of the place.

Likewise, my brother told me that while he was in the National Guard, had been a few days in the military hospital, and had seen hundreds of soldiers totally ruined. Most were war wounded with amputated legs or arms, etc. He told me that on one occasion he started talking to one of those who were there: a young man of about twenty years. The young man, who asked him to take him to the toilet, was in a wheelchair, blind, partially deaf, with both legs cut to the thigh and both arms cut between the shoulder and elbow. However, he had no trouble speaking, and said, "Look, buddy, I no longer wanted to live that way. Those bastards have ruined me. I was still conscious and I knew the treatment and I knew I did not have to have my legs and arms cut but I was put to sleep and when I woke up, I was already just as I am now". The high commanders saved much as they doing this type of maneuvers. When someone died, some men only took the corpse to the family in a box and gave the mom or any family member a little money to make a small family gathering or a wake, and to bury him.

He also told me he had to go through a training called "escape and flee". He said they put them in a pit and threw them teargas. After they supported that, they put them out and made them jog without clothes, completely naked, and hit them in their backs with a branch with thorns, while they carried a completely naked man on their shoulders. They did it to train them to run away with a wounded and under those conditions. During that same training, they also brought a bitch: everyone had to give the dog sex; then they killed it, and everyone had to eat her raw head. The aim was that the soldier who was in this type of specialty should be courageous and by doing this, they created hatred in his heart as well as desire to kill: that was what they were told.

In those days, my mother constantly cried and was very concerned especially for the two of us that were in the Civil Defense. She said: "Children, it is better to have you away, but alive. I wish you were away from here. You can write and send us cents if you can; do it. But being here, jobless, with the risk of being killed..." She was right: it was better to leave the country again. It was hell being in that life without a future and full of uncertainties. My brother and I talked to our parents and planned the trip. They saved some money I had sent them from the United States, and at that time, I needed for the two of us to travel, so they gave it to me, with sorrow and tears for our trip.

At that time, the commander did not let me go alone to the town because he thought I could leave the country. Therefore, we made up a plan: that afternoon we went to the camp of the Civil Defense and told the commander that my brother had to come with me to the village to get my identity card because my previous card had been abandoned in Guatemala and I had returned to the country without documents. My brother had to come with me because I had to go through other Civil

Defenses. They did not know me, and they could kill me, but they knew him and so he could speak for me if they stop and investigate us.

The next day, in the morning, we said goodbye to our parents. My mother began to cry. We left as soon as we could in order to avoid those moments of pain. As supposed, in our way we had to go through two Civil Defenses; they stopped and investigated us. We said we were to town because I had no documents, and there were not too many questions because they already knew my brother. When we reached the village, we saw that the commander's brother-in-law was also there: the Civil Defense of the town had captured him and he was handcuffed.

I went to do what I had to do with my documents in order to leave the country. Then I phoned the two comrades I had met in the prison in California- that supposedly were going to be sent back to El Salvador after me-, to know if they were in the country and if they were ready to travel again. I spoke to both of them and, thank God, they had arrived safely to their homes. They had returned deported just three weeks ago. We agreed then that we would meet in the house of one of them immediately. Thus, we travelled with my brother by bus to meet them.

When we were about to reach Apopa, we saw that the traffic was stopped at the intersection of the detour to Apopa and the road leading to Poy, the border with Honduras. There were cannons and mortar launchers in the middle of the road, firing into the hill of Guazapa. After an hour, we got permission to pass. Finally, we reached San Salvador, reeking of military and police everywhere. In those situations you cannot stop at any time; you always have to keep walking, because if you stop, they think it is to do something against them and they can even kill you. Therefore, we just caught another urban bus and went to where we would meet friends, in Santa Lucia colony, Ilopango.

We were happy to still be alive and meet again. Then, we talked about the trip. William told me he was ready to return at any cost; he only needed a couple of days to ask for money to his relatives. The other young man was thoughtful and could not find how to begin; finally, after murmuring a few unintelligible words, he told us that we would not accompany and gave us his reasons.

-Listen to me, I would like to travel but I have no money. Then, by chance, one of my friends told José Napoleón Duarte I was here in the country, and he sent somebody to tell me he had a job for me in the government. He knows that I can write and speak English, and that is why he needs me; so, tomorrow I have an appointment with him personally, and I will not miss this opportunity. The travel interests me, but I have to lose one to achieve the other- said my comrade.

We told him that if it was what he really wanted, it was fine, and he should be very careful with his life because although Duarte was the president, the military hated him to death, and it was a risk to work in his government. As we did not have time, we quickly said goodbye and agreed with William that we would be at his home in two days to leave the country.

We returned to the village, to a colony where my sister lived. We could no longer return to my parents' house if we wanted to make the trip. The next day, in the morning, my mother came to visit her daughter and to see if we had already left the country. She told us that the commander's brother-in-law had been found dead at dawn on the outskirts of the village and that the commander had said that we were to blame for his death. My mom was even more worried. In addition, there were people who saw us there, in that place, and that we witnessed the moment of his capture. Some told that to the commander, and they said they had seen us entering the hall. Although the man already knew we were going to get documents, he thought we had gone to give a report. This gave us more impulse to travel and we had to leave the country at any cost. My mother said goodbye to us after a while, and we were sad and talking about the trip, since the passage through Mexico was not easy. The following day, we said goodbye to my sister and headed to San Salvador to meet our other companion. We slept that night at his home so the next day we could leave for the border with Guatemala. William also said goodbye to his family. All had given us their blessings and asked God to accompany us on our path full of dangers where we could even find death.

We travelled in the first buses to Santa Ana and then went to the border of the Chinamas. We arrived at the border and asked permission almost at noon. William and I got it -of course, the permission was only for three days in Guatemala- and we paid. Then a problem arose regarding my brother who was nineteen.

"But this person cannot pass because he is under age" the agent said, and continued, "Unless he is traveling with a family member who is twenty-one and signs a document in which it is stated he responsible for him."

I told him I was his older brother, and he continued doing, then, the process of leaving the country.

Then he asked us where we were going, and I said to Guatemala City. He asked me the address, but I could not give it properly since I had not it ready in my mind. In Guatemala, there are no colonies, but the areas are listed. The man did not believe my story, and told us that the permission was only given to those travelling to the capital city of Guatemala, only for three days, so beyond the capital, it was illegal and any person could be captured because it was assumed he was heading north. From Salvadoran and Guatemalan customs, they tried to stop the flow of people gathering on the borders with the idea of leaving the country.

A few hours later, we tried another attempt, but it was useless: they knew we were going only for the city of Guatemala. Finally, we set out to go to another border, and in the city of Sonsonate, it was already dark.

When we arrived in that city, it was getting dark and there was a curfew. Not a soul was seen on the streets; it looked like a ghost town, and only the National Guard was wandering around. In the distance, came a group of them. Before they saw us, we lost sight of and seek the home of some relatives of William living nearby to spend the night.

The next morning we woke up early and left for the border of La Hachadura: we had everything ready in case the made us some questions. We went through all the coastal cities of Guatemala country and arrived at the border where my friend Marino Alvarez lived. When we got home, we were greeted with great joy. My friend told us that Mexican heavily guarded the border and that if we wanted to move toward Mexico, it was better if we went to another border at a place called Las Mesías. That night we arranged the trip. The following day we went to cross the border and take the means of transport heading north.

We went to Las Mesías, we crossed the bridge over, and as soon as we were on the other side, we merged into the crowd, bought other clothes, and headed for Tapachula. Once there, we looked for the bus station and finally bought the ticket to Mexico City. That night we boarded the bus that would take us to the Mexican capital. After a couple of hours traveling on the bus, we got to an immigration house. An immigration agent got in and started asking for documents. We were in the last seats, and I noticed that William was very nervous. He told my brother to calm down and do not show nerves; however, our friend could not hide what he felt. The officer first came close to me and asked for my documents. I told him that we had been robbed and we had lost everything. Then he asked me who was traveling with me. I replied that the young man next to me was my younger brother. Then he asked where we were from, and I said we were from Puerto Madero, from a colony called San Antonio. After that, he left us alone and started asking questions to William, who could not answer. I had already taught him what he had to answer, but nerves and shyness made the officer suspect he was a foreigner, so he asked him to get off the bus. Therefore, I explained to immigration officer that it was not possible because he was my cousin. As soon as I said that, he ordered the three of us to get off the bus. It was a hut in the middle of the mountains of Chiapas. It was almost one o'clock in the morning. In the house, there was only a uniformed officer, the one who had gotten on the bus: He was a disabled person; he was crippled in a shin and in an arm, and could hardly walk, but he had a dozen partners or executioners civilian around, and I am sure none of them was from the immigration officer. Otherwise, they were there to help intimidate and hit all the multitude of people coming from Central America because of the war.

The bus continued on its way and we stayed in that place, asking God to help us getting out of the quagmire in which we were. William was taken away for interrogation separately. My brother and I were taken into the house and they started to threaten us. When they checked us, they found me all the money I had in my pockets. Then they told us to confess the truth and they assured us that the following day we could be dead in a ditch next to the house. We were completely naked; they threw cold water with a hose and beat us for a while. Then, two of the four men who had taken William appeared and said, "That guy told the truth...! They are from El Salvador; the other dude has already told us."

Right there, at that time, they gave us another beating because we were lying. Later, they allowed us to get dressed and took us out to the street. A half block away, they had William. Then, they brought him near us, and he told us in front of some of them,

"Now what...? Anyway, we have to tell them the truth. What can we do?"

So, the immigration officer turned to me.

"Look, here I have your money... How much money will you give to us?"

I knew we had already lost all the money, and we had to negotiate with them to let us go.

"You know that is all the money we have and we do not have more" I answered.

"And we are heading north. We need some money to reach the borders of the United States."

"We want 50,000 pesos each" he answered. "If you want to go, I send you in a shipment bus to Mexico City in the morning."

The money they had been taken from me was the amount they were asking me for the three of them. William had not been registered, therefore, they did not know if he had money, and not to make the problem bigger, I told them to take that money.

"You did well" he added, "because if you had been deported, they would not have given you that money anyway."

For a moment, we got upset with William because he spoke when they were about to let us go without giving them anything, but everything had already happened and there was nothing we could do. We sat in some steps, cold, waiting for the dawn and the bus that the licensed thief had promised. In the morning, at about seven o'clock, a bus arrived: they stopped the motorist and called us. Soon, he came out and told us to get on the bus. We did it immediately.

The bus had no seats except from both on the front and we had to travel lying on the floor all the way. At one point, the driver went down to eat and asked us if we were hungry, and we said yes. He went to a restaurant and then returned with food and told us, "I work this way with these men..."

I still had the rest of the money they had not found me in my pants, as I had some in the waistband, where the girdle is, and some in the hem. The thing was that they did not find all the money I had: if they had found it, they would have stolen it and the beating would have been even harder, because Mexicans immigration officers behaved in that way in order to make one feel more humiliated and to thank God we were alive.

The man left us at the north bus station, where we had to go towards Querétaro to see if we could find my other brother and if he had a better idea to move to the United States. I had promised my mother's sister, -who apart from being my aunt was my godmother- that when I was in Mexico City would visit the grave of my cousin and spiritual brother. However, given the circumstances and the little money we had, we could not stay a few days in that city and it was better to move to achieve our purpose. We went then to the city of Querétaro, and slept in a hotel. The following day we would go to a village called Ahuacatlan of Guadalupe, where we would see my brother in a ranch that was under that jurisdiction.

The bus went into the mountains, and then we arrived at the village at noon. Then we looked for the little trucks traveling to the ranch called Santa Águeda. The trip down those hills lasted about two hours. People stared at us, wondering where we were from and why we were going to the ranch. At last, a man decided to speak to us. First, he asked us where we were going, and I said that for the Santa Águeda ranch. Then, he wanted to know if we knew someone there, and told him I had a brother named Francisco, or Paco. The man quickly knew who he was. He also realized that we were coming from far away, from another country, because everyone knew my brother. Everyone got to know what we talking about, and there were no more questions during the journey.

Finally, we reached the ranch in a valley. The street did not continue. There were only cliffs. People had four, five or six donkeys to carry their wares on the sidewalks where they had to walk to get to their homes. Where the bus came, they had just broken the street with a machine, and as it was the last stop of the transportation, there was selling of food, soft drinks and beer. It was so high that the clouds passed below, in the lowland canyons. The man I spoke before approached us and told us, "We have arrived to Santa Águeda. My son is already therewith six donkeys to transport the goods because I have a shop up there, and now he will take it. Meanwhile, I want to invite you a beer and talk about Pancho, your brother."

The man told me that my brother had a small carpentry workshop and he had done some work for him, and everyone loved him because he was right, a good person. Then, the man had an idea.

"Do you know what?" He told us.

"As you are a surprise to Paco, I will dedicate a song on your name. I am sure he will not believe it."

At the ranch, there were two types of radio stations heard even in the most hidden corner of the area. They were like radio hams that communicated through megaphones of high power the shops had. The man went to the house and dedicated some songs on our behalf.

As soon as we finished the third beer, my brother appeared at the inn where we were with his friend. We hugged. Paco saw that our younger brother, who was traveling with me, as a fully formed man. Immediately, we introduced our companion, William, and we walked down the sidewalk along with the man who had given us his friendship and trust. My brother took us to the house where he lived with a woman who loved him like her own son and looked after us very nicely. She told us to stay the weekend there: it would be her niece's birthday and there would be a little party. She had about twenty maguey plants and a large pot filled with good tasty *pulque* she got every day. The man sold it because he got a lot and prepared it very well this natural drink.

The day of the party came. The family made a hole of about a meter deep in the ground, and then they put firewood in it and made a fire. When it was all burned and there was only the fire pit red hot, they threw maguey leaves freshly cut over the coals and then the meat of a whole sheep. Then they covered it with maguey leaves again and finally plugged the hole with soil. They called this barbecue. Meanwhile, we started drinking glasses of *pulque* and making music for the birthday girl, who was already a young woman and enjoyed dancing. People treated us very well, even though we were foreigners. We talked a lot about the situation in our country and that was the reason we were there. It was lunchtime: the barbecue was fascinating, very tasty, and that natural homemade pulque was very rich in flavor. In that second trip in Mexican lands, I could try those two things that are very traditional and typical throughout Mexico.

After four days, we were still in the house where my brother lived with the woman. Then, I told him what had happened to us during the journey.

"Note that we are running out of money" I said, "And we will have to leave."

My brother did not want us to leave, but I told him that the Santa Águeda ranch was not my destiny, and I wanted to reach the United States. Well, as I said, our parents were involved in poverty, and in the North, there could be better opportunities to give them financial support. My brother took two notes, one of five and the other of two, gave both to me, and told me, "Here you are; it is all I have."

That same night, we left the Santa Águeda ranch and went to Tampico, where William's father was. The man worked in PEMEX, Mexico's oil company, and we wanted to know if he could help us with some money.

We arrived at Tampico hungry and with no money, but we paid a taxi to take us to his home. The man gave us a place to spend the night, but he had no money to give us because he was very skirt chaser. In addition, he recommended that we go to Cuencamé, Durango, and the next day we went there. We arrived at a house of a family who owned a small restaurant and we gave the man a letter that William's father had given us for him. The man made shipments of packages and documents for the railroad workers of Mexico from Cuencamé, Durango, to the city of Chihuahua. He said that in a few days he would go to the city of Chihuahua and gave us something to eat while we were there. During that time, we helped the lady who was there to ship to customers, mostly truckers traveling away, as the small restaurant was on the edge of the road leading to Chihuahua and Ciudad Juárez, the boundary of the United States, which borders with El Paso, Texas.

While we were traveling, the man told us how he had befriended William's father and told us that his wife had died very young. Therefore, he had a house in the city of Chihuahua, where his two daughters lives and studied in the college of that city. After several hours, we reached Chihuahua. It was early morning. His daughters were awake because they had gone to a party, as it was the weekend. The man introduced us to them: one was twenty and the other eighteen. Both were very nice, smart and very attentive.

The man was only three days doing his business rounds, and then returned to Cuencamé. We had not gone because the girls insisted on us to rest a few days, so we lived in their home during that time. The Young women did not want us to leave the city: they always told us that in the United States we could no longer get papers, that we would not leave and instead we could find a job there. They had a car, and they took us out for a ride in the evenings through the city to impress and convince us to stay there. The lowest had fallen in love with me and said that in the future, after she finished her university, we could marry. The other girl liked William and said the same to him. However, after a week, while they were attending their classes we decided to start our journey to Ciudad Juárez. When they returned from school, we talked about our plans. They did not feel too happy with what we announced, and they said they wanted to finish school, because his father was sacrificing himself for it. However, they could no longer count on his father because he had a new woman with two small children and the restaurant we already knew. The mother of the girls had died many years ago and they lived alone in that house. Though the house was very nice, they felt abandoned and lacked of affection and family care. Finally, we agreed that we would write each other and keep in touch by phone, and the plans between them and us would be still on.

The following day, in the morning, we said goodbye to the girls before they went to school and we went off the road to ask for a ride to Ciudad Juárez. We spent the whole day trying to get truckers to give us a lift, but we did not succeed, and when it was the time, we assumed the girls could be back, we returned to the house. They were surprised when they saw us coming and made us a joke. The next day, the same thing happened, and we could not leave. I wanted to do it through a ride because in that way we got off on the road, without reaching the dugout where immigration was before Ciudad Juárez. I thought to take a detour towards Allende, on the road leading to the border of Agua Prieta. Although they saw us getting off a freight truck, they would think we were local from the surroundings.

On the third day, the girls decided to join us and be late at school. Since they were there and were very beautiful and young, a truck quickly stopped and it had cabins behind. We said goodbye to the girls, and we never saw them again. Without turning on, we continued on our way. We told the driver to let us get off just before the house: we thanked him and he went on his way. That house was called "the 28" and there they robbed the undocumented immigrants who came from Central and South America, and tourists traveling from the US to Mexico.

Hitching rides and walking along the side of the road, we went forward until we reached the village called Allende. There we spent the last pesos we had: we bought two baguettes, milk and some avocados, and after that, we had no money left. Later, we slept under a small bridge about a meter high, under the road. It was so cold that we made a fire to keep warm and to sleep. The next day, we continued our way: first, we got a few short rides, but then we hit another truck and took us farther. This man was a contractor: he devoted himself to make concrete irrigation waterways, and offered us a job, but we said we were going to the North. Finally, we arrived at Agua Prieta. We thanked him, he gave us some money, and we immediately spent it in a store where illegals that walked through the desert used to be there.

Other colleagues from Allende, Chihuahua state joined us and told us that they knew the shortest way to reach the nearest town, in Arizona, although the entrance still belonged to the state of New Mexico. That Sunday afternoon, at about three o'clock, we started the walk through the desert. After a while of walking, we found the obelisks of the border between the two countries. It was late, but we kept walking. After two days, our friend of Allende had neither coffee nor food and we got lost; we deviated from the path we should have taken. Big birds and birds of prey were heard around, threatening. We kept walking, always erasing our tracks when we crossed the streets. We slept in cannons so we could not be seen. However, one day, an immigration plane detected us and shortly after, they were looking for us with cars suitable for the desert. In the distance, we saw a cloud of dust and we thought it could be a kennel coming in our direction, and it was indeed true: people are paid per reported head.

We were walking apart, a block of distance between each other. When I could see the plane coming, I shouted to my comrades to hide. I was right: it was the American immigration police, the U.S. Border Patrol, looking for us. We hid into cannon. It had many thorns, and when we went down the cliff, we saw the officers seeking us down there in the street they had, next to a stream. We laugh at what we had done and continued walking down the cliff. Then, we slept under some mesquite trees. We did not have any food and we warmed ourselves with a fire we did for the night: hungry coyotes howled and the fire warmed us ahead, but our backs were very cold. That night, there was a heavy snowfall, and we had no clothes for that.

The next day, we arrived at an abandoned hut in the desert. The wind lashed everywhere. It was Thursday, and we had not eaten for almost five days. We were starving; we just wanted food. We were too weak to walk. The cabin looked abandoned for several years. In the dark, I looked for something that would help us: I found the kitchen and a barrel lid that could be useful to make tortillas since I had already found a –that used to roast chickens. As soon as I prepared the first tortillas, the others began to eat them and immediately began to vomit. That was not good to eat. The wind was strong and it was cold, but we slept there and the following day we left for the nearest town.

We got into a canyon where a small river ran to avoid the detection from the aircrafts, and after walking a few meters, we saw a family camping on the shore. After realizing they were just tourists with tents, we decided to go. When they saw us, they noted we were immigrants; they called us and greeted us. The woman and the man spoke little Spanish. They gave us a can of beans with meat and a loaf of bread. We thanked them; they wished us good luck on our way, and then we kept walking. We lost sight of them; eagerly we sat to eat what they had given us. I had run out of shoes: they had no sole. In the desert there is much cactus barely visible on the ground; I had hurt my feet and they were bleeding everywhere, not just because of the thorns, but also by the sand that in the shoes. The skin of the feet had come out. When we were walking along a path, I found some old shoes that were big for me, but I put paper on the tips and wore them.

We entered the United States through the lands of New Mexico, but after so much walking; we were already in the state of Arizona. The small village we saw in the distance was called Wilcox. It was Friday, and we decided to sleep on the train line running between east and west, in the south of the country. With the Mexican compatriot who accompanied us, we went to the small town with seven dollars my brother had given to me in Querétaro. We wanted to see if we got something to eat, risking the border patrol could take us. We bought two cans of food and some bread. The others were in the small bridge where the train passed. We had not eaten anything for a week, except for what the family had given to us two days ago when we crossed the canyon.

Later, we fought against death and we held on those trees to walk. There, my brother and I remembered the tortillas my mother made. We had not defecated from three days since our bodies were empty. The gringos were connected with the immigration police and people from almost all the farms reported us. However, as we were passing by and we were not going anywhere in particular, it was difficult to seize us. They only found traces and stories about us along the path. During a few hours, we walked in a place that had some big trees. Then we took a rest in the shade of a tree and we immediately fell asleep. After about three hours, when the sun rose, I woke up and turned to see all sides: I heard a plane flying near us. I looked back, and then I saw a row of dust rising in the heights. I thought it was a car approaching us, but soon I managed to distinguish the border patrol unit that had found us through the plane, which had already found the footprints. Immediately, I shouted to others to hide. The immigration car passed, as well as the small plane, flying in zigzag checking the plain between two mountain chains. After that, they no longer kept looking for us, perhaps because they lost faith in doing so.

We continued. By then, we could only walk holding on the trees. Our faces had been transfigured, partly because we had been in front of the fire, warming up. Facial skin came out; we tore off the pieces of skin. We were too weak to walk and we had not eaten for almost eight days. We always had water because we found windmills and they were always with water for wild animals to drink. That afternoon, we were in a place where passes the freeway number ten on one side, and the train, on the other. There, under a small bridge, we settled down and slept, very cold.

The following day, it was already Sunday; we arrived at the outskirts of the city of Safford, Arizona. We walked in a few settlements where there were no illegals, only gringos, American Indians and Chicanos in the area. Then we reached another ranch, where we spoke to the manager of all tractors and other machinery, and he told us that there was no work for anyone, neither for illegals. Therefore, he gave us some bread, milk and a bottle of soda, and asked us to leave because if we did not leave, he would have trouble with the law. The atmosphere was very hot as far as illegals was concerned, and although it was necessary to have Mexican people, there were no government conditions for that people to work there. At that point, people from Allende, Chihuahua, decided to take another way. They said it was better for all of us to take separate paths, to see if anyone could help us, either with work or with food in order to survive in the day. We were five and we had to split into a group of three and another two. We said goodbye. William followed them, because he felt bad about what he had done in Chiapas. However, when they were away, we saw that William was coming back. Perhaps they told him that he could no longer continue with them and he should come with us that we were looking at him. After an hour, he returned, and then the three of us started looking for luck in the surrounding ranches.

That evening we found a trailer that was an empty house and was open, and there we slept. In the morning, we left for those ranches looking for work and food. We arrived at one ranch and looked for a man- descendant of Chicanos and Indians, who spoke Spanish-responsible for tractors and other machinery, and we found him in the garage where they had the tractors. They were just starting to plow the land, as the Mexicans say, and he was alone. We said we were illegal and were looking for work for food. He stared at us and then told us that at the ranch, there was only work for tractor drivers, but they had to be legal, and they were ready for the work coming. Two irrigators were also needed, but as he already said, they had to be documented. Finally, he told us to wait for him that he would return soon. A few minutes later, he came with two bags with food and gave them to us. He wished us good luck and that God accompanied us on our way. Before we left, we went to the house to ask his wife for water. The woman gave us a bottle of soda and a carton of milk for the road, and we left the place to cause them any trouble with the law.

We went down to a close river and started eating. We ate and ate, and we could not satisfy our hunger. We had left on a Sunday and it was Sunday afternoon again: we had just eaten two bites throughout the week and we had walked more than two hundred kilometers through the desert and ditches to avoid being caught by la border patrol. Then, we continued walking.

After walking along the riverbank for not being discovered, we saw a rancher who was in his pick-up watching his wheat field, and we decided to get on his way to talk to him. We climbed the cliff and when we arrived on the shores of seed, the man saw us and waited until we got where he was. We asked what we were doing there. We replied that we were illegal and were looking for work, just to survive, because we were very hungry. The gentleman was very white, but he was from Spain, and he told us he wanted to take the weeds from the wheat. The *pamita* was a weed that was in the middle of the wheat field and threw a yellow flower. He also said that he soon had to get it cut. I told him that if he wanted, we could do that work. Then he asked me how much we wanted to earn the hour, and I said that, at the beginning, we wanted food, and then he could give whatever he wanted, whatever we deserved for the work. I told him our aim was reaching Phoenix, Arizona, or -better-, Glendale, Arizona. He replied he could pay us about two dollars per hour after each meal. Without thinking it much, we accepted.

The white man took us to his home, gave us some refried beans, and fried eggs with bread. The food was good, but we could not satisfy our hunger. The place to sleep was an old barn in which cold air entered, though it was better than being out in the open. Dust and icy wind battered everywhere. In addition, there was only one canvas to cover ourselves, one of those used in tracks, full of dust and grease, and we would wake dirtier than when we went to sleep. However, the man also gave us a place to have a bath. We worked for a week and a half, and then he told us that his nephew had to go to Phoenix to find food for their dogs. We paid him for the ride -after that we only had about twenty dollars each- and we got in the back on the canvas of his truck, heading to Glendale, Arizona.

When we arrived at the orange-growing area of Glendale, where I had been before, I could not orient myself because it was almost two o'clock and the night was dark. I felt lost, but I told the driver to leave us there, near an orange plantation. He left us there, and we slept among the orange trees until dawn. We walked on one side of a railway line until I could recognize the place where we were. We arrived where the tractor driver was; he was a Papago Indian and a good person. We knocked on his door, which was locked. We listened to music and his car was there, so he had to be in. Soon he answered, opened the door and invited us in. He said he had been drinking for over a week and had not worked on the tractor. Until that time, he did not recognize me. After talking for a while, I told him who I was. I had passed and been with him a year earlier. He felt more confident and gave us their friendship. Then he told us he was hungry and had neither food nor money, and we offered to go to the store to buy something to eat. We immediately went there and bought some food and beers. He was happy that we had come to his house. While drinking a beer, he told us that on the same ranch where I had always been before, there was work, and he suggested us to go and see if we could work for a few days.

The man took us to the ranch the following day. Orange trees surrounded the place, and while he waited for us in his car, we went to look for the man we had to talk with to work in that place. Sometimes in the adventure, we met with ordinary Mexicans who discriminated people from other Latin American countries, but as I mimicked the Mexican accent, they thought I was one of them. For that reason, I had to speak to avoid letting them know we were from another country. I spoke with the subcontractor, and he told me it was the time of the cut of onions, broccoli, beet, lemon, grapefruit and orange. Work started at eleven o'clock, because the immigration police bothered earlier, and the worker was daily paid. I immediately went to talk to the Papago friend to tell him that we would stay there to work the next day. At the ranch, there were at least forty workers and there was no place to sleep, but the man showed us the attic, alfalfa and bundles of wheat were stored there, where we could sleep. We had no blankets to cover, but we lay in the dry grass and had a stove to cook.

First, we went to work in the onion plantation. They were only seven or eight hours of work, but the payment was very low: just we won seventeen to nineteen dollars per day. Meanwhile, I was investigating how we could travel to the north of the country, as the immigration police was present all the time and arrested people in their work places. We were afraid: the return trip was not easy. Mexicans got drunk and caused a scandal, and the police often came, especially on weekends. Those who were captured were sent to Mexico. Then, came prostitutes seeking their business, and that was another problem: they fought over women, drinks and music. We stayed in the attic, isolated from them, to avoid problems.

After a few days of being there, we met a person who wanted to travel to Idaho: he had a car for six people and he was taking his brother and a friend who was a tractor driver, and told me that with the three of us he completed the trip. We talked, and he then informed me he just needed seventy dollars each for gasoline, and that was all to make the trip. I told him that in about three days we were ready to travel. Therefore, we agreed that in three days he would come for us. He also told us not to worry about work because the ranch manager where we were going was his friend. The ranch was around the city of Pocatello, Idaho, and the work was in the potatoes fields.

One day, we decided to walk with my brother and William for the orange field. Meanwhile, we talked about the trip and about what was waiting for us. We got in the field when suddenly we found an extremely large prickly pear plant: its trunk was about three feet in diameter and one could walk on its branches. The plant had oval leaves and they were almost two feet long and a foot wide. There had been many people around the plant: its leaves had dozens of names printed with a knife. They were people from different states of Mexico and from other Latin American countries. The large plant could have had five hundred leaves, but most were written with the names and origin of many adventurers who had passed by there. We climbed the tree and with a knife, we wrote our names and place of origin in an artistic way, and they remained there, in that anonymous plant. In the end, on another leave, I wrote: "Ever onward to victory!" It is the largest prickly pear plant I have ever seen in my life. Then, we went to sleep for the last time to the labyrinth of illegal laborers. Two days after, we started our journey to Idaho.

Catarino took us; he was a tough driver. He kept us lying because he feared getting into trouble, as we were six in his station wagon. After twenty-four hours drive, we reached the villages of Pocatello, Idaho, and then went to a small village where we were supposed to work. At the ranch there were the butler and another worker; both were Catarino's friends and acquaintances. The worker slept in a trailer, and there was another trailer for us. When there were crises, in that place only potato was eaten; you only had to buy oil, and every day you ate either fried or boiled potatoes while you waited for work and money.

Two weeks later, I started working with other Mexicans, but there was no work for my brother or for William yet. I had to ride a tractor and pick up stones from the field that would be plowed to plant potatoes. The owner, who was a rancher gringo, realized he needed more workers, and three days after, my brother and William were working. We were happy because we would soon have money since our parents probably needed it: my mother had two sons of Uncle John, who also ventured into these northern countries and had left his children in El Salvador.

The owner paid every two weeks, but we had a surprise the day of payment: Catarino had already talked to the butler, who was his friend and came from Guanajuato, Mexico, as well as him. The butler had spoken with the gringo rancher about the money we owed to Catarino, so the boss made the checks in Catarino's name. Then, he went to change them but only gave us twenty-five dollars each. I was outraged, so I talked to him. The cynical man told me that we owed him much more money and that he would take away from each paycheck he got. I replayed he had told us that we only owed him seventy dollars, and we had already given them to him before leaving Glendale, Arizona, and he had not mentioned any debt. In a sarcastic way, he replied mocking, he had not imagined how far it was Idaho from Arizona, and that gasoline was more expensive and it was a problem for him to travel with six people in his car. Finally, he added that if we did not like it, bad for us, because he could keep as much money as he could, whenever he wanted. He was with all his people and families from their own land that supported him. We were not even from Mexico, and he knew it, so we had nothing to gain in the ranch.

That day was Friday, and all the people from the ranch went to the village in their cars to get drunk at the dances in Mexican clubs. I stayed with my two companions, thinking and feeling a little depressed and sad, but suddenly I had an idea: I told my brother and William I would go to find a phone that was about five miles from the ranch in a small fuel station. After a while, I van stopped and gave me a ride to that intersection, and I called Mr. Mike, the retired old man with whom we had been with my older brother in Powell, Wyoming. He accepted my call and I explained to him everything was happening to us. He was glad to hear from us again; because I had written to him while I was imprisoned in California and I had told him I was deported to my country. He already knew the situation of my country, so he was not surprised that I was back in the United States. After talking for a while, he told me he could not go and look for us because he was invited as the oldest person at his grandson's wedding in Billings, Montana, that weekend. However, he assured me he had a nephew who could come, and we just had to pay him for his journey when we had money. I accepted immediately, and he asked me to call back in ten minutes. I waited, and after ten minutes, clock in hand, I phoned him again: he told me that his nephew would start his journey on Sunday and he would arrive on Monday at noon. I gave him all the necessary directions to find the place where we were located. I returned pleased to the ranch, hoping that everything came out as planned. I told my brother and William the maneuver we had to do: we could not say a single word about our plan in front of other people.

At midnight, Mexicans arrived; drunk and mentioned that one of them was missing because he had been caught stealing: he had been taken prisoner and was going to be deported. Then; they awakened us and insulted us for nothing. They treated us very badly just because we were Salvadorans. Thank God, nothing happened, because we did not react, and they felt too drunk and went to sleep.

The weekend ended, there were no further comments about work. It was Monday and we had to work. Suddenly, Catarino appeared and told us to go to work. I said we were not going to go, and when he asked me why, I replied we did not feel well. "After they pay me, you will feel better," he said, and left in his car heading to work. At about eleven o'clock, I saw a car coming to the ranch: I recognized the nephew of Mr. Mike, who was just as he had described him by phone. There was no one at the ranch, because everyone was working, so it was the best time to leave the place. I did not know the boy, but he already knew what he was doing and who we were. We took the few things we had, and after five minutes, we were travelling to Powell, Wyoming. The journey was a little long. As we passed Yellowstone, he told me he had to repair his house: he had to change lines, plywood and tiles. I told him that I could do that job, and so he felt more confident.

We arrived at Powell, Wyoming. Mr. Mike was waiting for us with open arms and told us we were welcome in his house; yet, there was no work in agriculture, but we could rest because soon there would be. However, his nephew told him he had a job for us at his home. The boy worked at the oil wells Wyoming, his salary was good and he wanted to fix his home. The next day, we got all kinds of tools and I put me in charge of the project. After two weeks, we had finished the job. My brother and William helped me to do the job right. Finally, he ended up owing us money for the work we had done.

By then, we had received three letters from Catarino Uribe, in which he told us that if we did not send him the money we owed, about a thousand dollars each, he would come with his brother and he would kill us. I had made the mistake of giving him Mr. Mike's address while we were traveling with him to Idaho, and I had told him we would go there if we could not find a job in Idaho. We had to solve that problem, and surprisingly I had a good idea. I asked William if he had friends in Los Angeles, California, and he said he had a lot. I told him to call his most trusted friend. He did it immediately, and then I spoke with him and told him that he would soon receive a letter in an envelope. The letter inside would have the address of his home in Los Angeles and destination in Pocatello, Idaho: all he had to do was to put it in a mailbox and tell us if there was any correspondence later. The letter had already its stamp; it only needed to be put in a mailbox in California to have a seal from Los Angeles. As Catarino knew my handwriting, I had to write this letter personally. I wrote in the letter: "Look Catarino that back in Powell, Wyoming, an immigration office has been settled. The immigration police had captured us when we arrived, and we have been sent to Ciudad Juárez, Mexico. We came back and went through Tijuana by means of Salvadoran friends. We have come to Los Angeles, and here we are. Mr. Mike has read your letters over the phone, and today I am writing from here, from Los Angeles, California. I write to tell you that you do not have lost your money. Come here, to Los Angeles, and I will receive you with lots of Salvadoran friends you want to know you because you are a very good person". Obviously, after a few days, Catarino received this letter in Idaho because since then, I had not gotten any threatening letter from this man and everything went better.

After three days of being at Mr. Mike's home, Fernando, the man from Chihuahua, came. We had ventured together and the Border Patrol had caught us the last year. He was glad to see me and told me he was still living with the American girl of Mexican origin. He also said that he traveled to New Mexico to bring two cousins who wanted to go to Wyoming. At the same time, he came to talk with Mr. Mike, to see if the man could give them a place to stay to sleep a few days, while he found a job for them. Don Mike quickly assured him that there was no problem; the three of us and Fernando and his cousins could be there for a few days. For my part, I spoke with Fernando and suggested him to form a group among the six of us and take contracts with ranchers to work in the sugar beet. He liked the idea and said we would do it, because if the group is not of five or six workers, ranchers do not give contracts. He said that although he had been living for several years in the United States, his English was not very good to do business. I said to leave it to me, and I told him that during the months I was in jail, I met a good friend who taught me English, and I could manage the business.

Fernando went to Albuquerque, New Mexico, and three days later, he brought his cousins to Mr. Mike's house. We met and talked about the group we wanted to form to make more money. We were relieved to know that the traitor Serafin Landaverde would no longer appear there, because the government was looking for him due to the taxes he owed, and he even risked being put in prison. A week later, we started walking in the villages talking to ranchers to propose them to work in the beet crops. Fernando had a car and a truck to use as transportation for the group. Indeed, a few days later, we were working under contracts with ranchers, and we were earning well.

My brother and I started to save and send money to our parents, for them and for us to save a little in the bank. William also sent money to his family, because he had lots of younger sisters and no father support them. Mexicans did the same. Of course, between us there was nothing hidden: the check was always divided into six equal parts, and on weekends, Saturday afternoons —as we almost always worked on Saturdays during the day or Sunday- we invited Mr. Mike to dinner or something else, since we no longer lived with him, but in the ranchers' farms. Mr. Mike had given us his friendship and confidence; he had helped us a lot, and we were very grateful to him: he was a great person. He always advised us to do well, to help our families and improve our situation.

I have to add something that comes to my mind. The first time we were deported, we went with the two friends of Durango and with Fernando to Ciudad Juárez, Chihuahua, Mexico. When we returned, I wrote to him about the experience we had lived with the American immigration police: they had escaped in a car, armed, fleeing through the plowed furrows and firing. I was told they had been captured because they had asked the police in the village for help; the good thing was that nothing bad happened. Therefore, I wrote a corrido*(song)*. telling this story, but had not had the opportunity to sing it as I wanted, especially with a guitar and someone to make me a second voice. This time, I was with Fernando and his friends, and my brother who could sing. In the song, the three Mexicans were named with an alias, and they liked their anonymous nicknames were used. The thing was impressive. We had a great night, as a new meeting of friends in adventure. Moreover, I felt quite proud and happy because I was the one who closed contracts with ranchers because I knew English, even though these other boys had ventured in the United States more than I had, but perhaps they were not interested in learning the language as much as I was to know more and communicate better.

Things worked great until contracts were finished. The season was very short and there were no more contracts, so we went to ask Mr. Pablo Rodríguez for work. The man happily greeted us and said he had work for us collecting irrigation pipes. He also said he felt very sorry for how we had taken by the patrol the previous year.

"I am the same people as you are" he said, "I just was born on this side of those bloody borders the "Yankees" much care. I know you come to work and not to do evil to this country. I need people here to work and because of them, sometimes I cannot finish my work. It angers me, because it is my people until I die."

What this man said filled us with moral support. He offered us a house that was unoccupied to stay while we were working for him and we did not have to pay since that would go to his payments account. The five adventurers moved to the house since Fernando had his wife, with whom he lived. Mr. Pablo also offered to give us a ride to buy something. Besides, we had a phone for local calls. The ranch of this man was immensely big, and the house he had given us was about ten minutes from his home.

We had been working with him for two months. One day he came home with a pack of twenty-four beers and sat with us to drink because he was happy we were there. He said that the immigration police had reached Cody, Wyoming, and was looking for illegals. He was in the crosshairs of the police: surely, they would investigate his ranch due to report of the last year, so he told us to be careful. My brother and I had bought a car to move, and warned us to be careful about leaving too much to the city. He drank three or four beers with us, and walked away, warning us not to go too often to the town.

After work, we usually went to a river to spend some time until night. One day, my brother and I decided to go to visit Mr. Mike after work. We had to go through the town of Powell, Wyoming. We parked outside Mr. Mike's house, and we did not realize that a car was following us; it was the immigration police sent by Montana. We stopped, and the police's car stopped next to us. They identified and asked for our documents. We did not have any documents; therefore, they handcuffed us right there and told us we could leave the car key in the house of the person we were visiting. Besides, they asked where we were living and they told us we could go there to collect our belongings; however, that was not true. They wanted to get information to go and find other illegals. I overheard the conversation, and my brother and I decided to say nothing, but, of course, they already had information about more illegals in the area. We only got into Mr. Mike's house because we knew there was any illegal there. For a moment, we were left alone with Mr. Mike. We told him that the money we had we would need it to pay the bail since we were not going to sign the deportation to our country. We asked him to put it in the bank until we call him by phone. He shed some tears when he saw us handcuffed and imagined us being expelled from the country, but the immigration police did not know we were Salvadorans. According to them, we were Mexicans.

Those operations were always encouraged by Texans and people from the same origin as us, but they already had their papers, driven by selfishness. They captured several illegals, but William and his Mexican friends were still free. After three days of being looking for illegals in the towns of Cody, Powell, Garlan, Thermopolis and other small villages in the area, we were sent to Denver, Colorado. They are also going to Sheridan, Alamosa, Casper and other towns of the state, where there used to be many agricultural workers in the villages, especially where the ranchers had many sheep to look after. Anyway, we were ready to sign the deportation documents. For them, we were Mexicans, and that at least 95% of immigrants in rural areas were Mexican; for that reason, the immigration police did not ask for information about the illegals' nationality. However, in the county jail we had already had to give adequate information regarding our nationality.

Some Mexicans were deported to their country, and others, "sent" as they called them when they leave voluntarily. That meant that the individual had access to the request for a visa or had not committed a crime within the country. On the contrary, deported people could not apply for a visa or do paperwork associated with US diplomatic affairs for a period of three years, five or more. When I was deported from the prison of central California bound for El Salvador, they stated that I could not return to the United States in a legal manner for five years. However, I signed neither deportation papers nor voluntary departure, since the Americans were insecure and knew that the lives of the deported men were in danger upon returning to El Salvador. I want to add that at that time, I was told that if I paid my flight, I would not travel as a deported man but with voluntary departure. In addition, they told me that in my country I could apply for a visa or other diplomatic documents to travel to the United States. That did not make sense because, as we know, a simple peasant has no record of employment in the country of origin, university profession or economic guarantees so you can never get a visa, unless someone with papers in order in the U.S. backs it. At that time, only the rich or the military, or those who were in contact with them, had "support levers" as we called them, to get a visa.

When the deportation judge interviewed us, we did not sign anything, but they were recording what we said in court. They knew that our country was going through a rather complex and intense war and the United States had to find statutes to justify the deportation of undocumented immigrants to our country, to avoid damaging relations with universal Human Rights Bodies; yet they were still doing it. The White House did not want the whole world realized the atrocities that trained people from its country were doing in El Salvador, Guatemala and Nicaragua, and they were using Honduras as a training base for military in the regional war in the continent waist. The war had become like Vietnam; it was exactly alike. El Salvador was the most affected country due to its size and its density of people as it was overpopulated.

My brother and I were the last to give personal information, after three days of being prisoners and they were already bored to look illegals. Then they would send us to Denver, Colorado, in an aircraft; then, in the city of Denver, a bus was completed, every day I think, heading Mexico. When we were asked to sign the document, we refused, so they asked why, and we told them we were from El Salvador and we did not want to be deported because we were dead men there. The immigration police took that into consideration and did not require it of us. Later we left on a plane bound for Denver. We were three days in a jail in Aurora County and then we were sent to another prison in Pueblo, Colorado. At least, they treated us a little better. Three days later, we were taken to Denver, before a deportation judge, but we did not sign the document he put in front of us and we spoke to him of the danger in our country. The judge was very annoyed because we did not want to sign the deportation and the short story he had heard. Then he sent us to the offices of a deportation officer, and he made us sign a document saying it was the first hearing, if I remembered correctly.

Three or four weeks later, we went to the third hearing. At that time, the deportation officer put us each a bond of $ 2,000. When we returned to the prison in Pueblo, we thought what we could do. Mr. Mike had only $ 1,500 in the bank account. We had sent most of the money to El Salvador, because we were helping our parents and we had bought some land in our village and we were starting to build a house to get our parents out of the place where they lived. The commander of the Civil Defense did not leave them alone and they were facing hell there. Although my younger brother was in the artillery barracks, the commander of the Civil Defense still threatened them: apart from their common threats, now he added that because of us, his brother in law was dead and he would take revenge. That night, we spoke on the phone to Mr. Mike and told him what was happening. We also told him that in a few days we would need money. He told us he did not have the amount of money we needed, otherwise, he would have helped us.

Within two days, we had an unexpected visitor: Mrs. Amelie Starkey, who worked for the Archdiocese of Denver and was a nun came. She was with a Chilean man named Raúl García, who had come from his country many years ago, in the early seventies, when President Salvador Allende was murdered in La Casa de la Moneda, in Santiago de Chile. He, like us, was among the group of people who were in trouble because of the situation Latin American was going through, and his solidarity job was to help illegals in that city, as he was bilingual and was very focused on his personal principles. Until then, I did not know how they heard of us. He told us that the Church could help us providing us a lawyer to reduce our bail and allow us to pay the remaining money later. We were very happy because we would be free soon and would come out with a document so the border patrol would not disturb us. Two days after having met these people, they told us we were going to Denver and the lawyer was about to reduce the bail and pay the rest. The lawyer properly behaved with us, as well as and Mrs. Amelie and Mr. Raul, who was a great man.

The objective was achieved, and left free as asylum seekers due to the problems of the war in our country. Then, these three people invited us to dinner in the city. They were happy either. They listened carefully to our talk since we had much to tell them of our lives. The lawyer was about to start preparing our cases to ask for political refugee. Lawyers were funded and coordinated by the Archdiocese of Denver. In the conversation, Mrs. Amelie came up with that I could start giving testimony of my life, and I accepted. At that very moment, we closed our agreement to defend our ideology regarding politics, peace and democracy. She told me we had to go to a church and talk about what was happening in our country, and I agreed that it was necessary. I did not know enough English to express myself, but I had a translator to help me. I did that many times in a row. The Church was helping me cope with the border patrol and get political asylum to be accepted as a refugee by the war in Central America.

From that moment, I started a new life. I began talking about our country, on behalf of our poor people, who had no voice, in favor of human rights. As Monsignor Romero did when he said: "I speak for those who have no voice." People felt timid to talk about their human rights. Humanitarian values had been lost or exhausted. Somebody who spoke of human rights or religious values could be clandestinely assassinated. Dozens of Catholic priests, people of unions of factory workers, people from the union of women of markets, shoemakers and many farmers who expressed defending their rights had been killed and disappeared. For many, the only thing that had value was survive the severe repression of the military supported by the Americans in Central America.

Many people from the valleys and villages sought refuge in the Evangelical and Catholic Church to save them from that political wave: anyway, they were reached and had to be with the rifle in a stone trench, but they said that if the enemy came they went out with their hands up, surrendering their weapons. Politically, this meant death; they would be taken as traitors. Some peace people only cared about peace although there was no justice. In other words, they were conformist people with the system: even if there were no changes, they were satisfied, but not too much, they could live in war playing with the two political sides that were massively armed. We explained all that to the lawyers of the coalition: we told them it was an armed war with enough political strategy by the United States; the war had greatly intensified and those who suffered were the poor Central American countries, because there was neither work nor food. The only accessible employment was joining the military, if one was young, or the national police, but both were against the democratic system, so the best solution to avoid any trouble to the rest of the family was leaving the country and not having political ties with anyone. That was the only way to save the people you loved. Peasants had left their homes and gone to the villages to avoid having to serve in the Civil Defense, or they had gone to the farms that were controlled by the ISTA. The few who stayed in the valleys suffered more because they lived under repression. Furthermore, they were victims of the fighting and tracking in political and geographical dispute between the two warring sides.

The thing was that with the help of translators, paralegals, lawyers and other people of humanitarian institutions, we managed to gather a lot of information to present to the deportation judge. Of course, the lawyers had to open a political process to present it to the judge with asylum applications, since in the United States people spoke a lot about democracy: we could make that request in accordance with the political status of that country.

Meanwhile, I continued working with the coalition to help more people who needed the same as us. They were in the state of Chiapas, Mexico, and in neighboring states, around Guatemala, on Mexican land. In Honduras, there were three or four refugee peasant camps taken by communists. The military of both countries sacked them and murdered people although they were civilians. They suffered from hunger and needs, as well as the war. Most of them were peasants fleeing their hometowns to survive.

The Border Patrol in Arizona had captured my Uncle John and my two cousins and they said they were Salvadoran, and they were in jail in El Paso, Texas. None of them wanted to return because the situation in our country was hard. They needed economic and legal support, as they had not signed the deportation. They phoned me and told me they needed my help, and I spoke to the coalition, who informed me that, generally, they only helped people who were imprisoned within the state of Colorado. However, in the case of me, they would make an exception and they would help them to come to Denver to continue the proceedings. A few days later, they were with us. Later, another friend was imprisoned in El Paso. I talked about him, and they helped him to come out.

For my part, I made a commitment to the people of the coalition to work with them, considering that there were many people suffering from hunger and wars and they deserved something better. I got involved in talking about what was happening in our country in churches, schools, community centers and universities. There was a great confidence with the people who supported me in a sincere, peaceful and religious way. My brother and I broke the record for all those who had been helped by the coalition; we paid them the money they had given us, so they were satisfied and wanted to do more with us and our political cases to achieve a satisfactory political objective. The lawyers did much more than they could do.

I would also say that being in the middle of the coalition; we ended up living in the home of a church called "The Annunciation." This church had two neighboring houses. The priests lived in the one that was next to the church and the other was empty. The second was a three-story house, and they gave us a place there while we found work and searched for another place to live. There were three Catholic Fathers. They were very nice people and very attentive: we live with them and we were constantly beside them. They asked us about things of our lives, and we told them what we had experienced. The Father who spoke Spanish better was the gringo and the most reactionary: he said there had to be a reason to kill someone. He was not aware of the atrocities that were going on in our country because of the US maneuvers. For him, if a person died it was because there was a good reason.

He thought our country was becoming Communist, and he was not aware that we were victim of many injustices. He said he hated communism and that communism was atheistic, it did not believe in divine things. However, people from my country believed in God and the entire country was almost Catholic. They did not believe in injustices carried out by the rich with American advice, with the idea of controlling the peoples of the continent waist. It is true that in El Salvador, there were few US investments for the Americans to put so much interest. However, we also know that a political change in that country could lead to other villages to radical changes that could affect international policy of the United States. I have to add that Central American countries have a history of political union and consider them brothers of the isthmus of the waist of the continent. Likewise, through a treaty in La Haya in the Netherlands, only a local document is required to move in the five countries that form Central America, either by land or by air. From the border with Mexico to the Panama Canal, you can travel without any passport; it is enough to bring local documents from Central America. However, politicians in North America did not accept the idea of a humanitarian brotherhood and assistance to people suffering and fleeing from countries at war, driven by a need for survival.

It was a little hard and complex to talk to a Catholic Father who had that ideology: it was of extreme right and imperialist, when we know that a Father of the Catholic Church did not have to have any political ideology or favoritism towards any political party. Father Lloyd had been taken to Panama to raise awareness in the US military, and in his religious acts, he had sided ideologies clashing with religious principles. The other priests, however, had a better concept of humanitarian aid and human rights.

Father Lloyd father's answers seemed unacceptable to me. I think God's principles have nothing to do with the imperialist principles, because the empire and politics have nothing to do with the divine or religious things. When I told him about Óscar Arnulfo Romero, the Archbishop of the Catholic Church in our country who had been killed as well as dozens of priests and members of the Church had also been murdered; he replied that if he had been killed, it was for a reason. The reason was that he had released many prisoners from the clandestine prisons; he had freed them from being torture and killed in the capital. He spoke on behalf of the oppressed; defending the civil rights of the people, regardless of race, color or social status. At the time of the talk, I had extended much talking to the Father Lloyd: he listened to me and accepted everything, but he did not say a word, so I kept silent and then told him anything else.

In addition to the empty house that was adjacent to the church and they gave us while we searched for work and a place to live, there was also a primary school, where they gave English classes to emigrants at night. We started attending school. The classes were on Tuesdays and Thursdays, two hours each day. This made us feel very well, as we started meeting new people and learning a little of the language which was much needed. On Sunday, we had to attend Mass in Spanish; the priests were very kind, and they somehow demanded us to attend Mass. After Mass in English, service was given in Spanish. Then we got together with them and we counted the cash from the offerings while they sat at the table and talked. Father John Paul was very friendly and he often invited us to eat at Mexican restaurants, because that food fascinated him. During these outings, he always wanted to know about our lives in adventure and fleeing our country. We always talked about religion and closeness to God. He had a little black blood in his veins. He was from the state of Virginia; he had lived with the minorities and his roots invited him to learn more about racism and social discrimination.

Meanwhile, I was doing presentations organized by the Church. I made people knew what was happening in our country. People liked to know about the actions being carried out. In addition, we asked for donations to the Church itself collected to send to refugee camps inside and outside the country. There were many Salvadorans living in Honduras, Guatemala and Mexico, as well as many other people from other Central American countries living in extreme poverty by the situation.

Shortly afterwards, the coalition gathered all Central American refugees who were in the city and they also invited several refugees of Vietnam, Cambodia, Somalia and other countries facing problems like ours. Although our English was quite limited, we got along very well because we had lived almost the same kind of life because of the war and extreme poverty. That night we had the opportunity to meet with about twenty or twenty-five Salvadorans and Guatemalans, and we decided to found an organization to help our compatriots outside and within our borders. We set a date and venue to start working. Likewise, the Church and other voluntary and solidarity offices agreed to help collaborate with propaganda material and participating in the group. The aim of the group would be to help people from Central America displaced by the war and at the same time, let the American people know the truth of what was happening in the region.

On the other hand, thanks to Mrs. Amelie, my brother and I got a job that was supposed to be temporary, but it turned out I was about five, until almost the end of my stay in the United States before traveling to Canada. The work was provided by the owner of the company, who knew Mrs. Amelie because he was religious and, as we knew, he had a church. The man owned a beer distributor very influential and had many employees that we gradually knew.

Finally, came the day when we met with some colleagues to name the group we formed. Besides, we should define our goals or purposes, our beliefs and our responsibilities. We wrote we believed in the cause and fight that our people were struggling in order to achieve self-determination, to get access to a better life, do not rely on foreign powers and not be enslaved by national and international monopolies or the corruption. We believed in the no American intervention in the war in the region. Therefore, we included a request for "Stop US intervention in Central America." We believed in the civil rights of each individual as a humanitarian value, as a form of expression and freedom of expression that was supposed to exist in any sovereignty. We also had several goals, like letting the American people know the reality of what was happening in Central America, making them understand that it was not about communism, as sources said, but as survival. Poor people were drowning in misery and working as slaves, without basic staple food, without medical care and without education; and it was for that reason that this wave of oppression, tortures, murders and other things came, because people were tired of so much injustice. Another goal we had was to recruit individuals and groups to make orders and get signatures in order to send them to the reactionary bodies dedicated to support our governments that continued making war: we demanded to stop financing them. We also set out to collect monetary funds to help refugees suffering in camps in Central America and Mexico, where there were people who did not have the help of agencies of health or food support. Most were children, women and old people. Another goal was to support radical groups with progressive ideas having to do with abuses, such as movements of the native or the Church, so each individual could be respected regardless of race, culture, religion or political position.

Several attended the meeting, there were about eight Salvadorans, four Guatemalans, Dora García Pimentel and Manuel Hermógenes were among them, a girl named Ana from Dominican Republic and about seven Americans of Mexican origin, or Chicanos, as they are called in the United States. There were three girls of that origin, among whom I especially remember Belinda, whose husband went to the Vietnam War and he died after his return due to the orange agent that fell in his body thrown by the Americans in the mountains of Vietnam. She was a widow, and her life had not been too happy: she told me that after the death of her husband, a motorist who was drunk and was racist had killed his ten or twelve year's old son. The man had been drinking in a bar in the city and there, some people had been saying that because of the Mexicans he did not have a job; as he became violent, they took him out of the bar, and then he killed the boy who was walking down the sidewalk at the edge of the street. Ken Porteisi was there, a Chicano who worked for the city and brought us a lot with his skills and opportunities at his work, doing intellectual tasks. Dennis was also there; another very interesting Chicano who had worked in political movements for the rights of Chicanos in the city and natives from the state. Other members were Ernesto Vigil and Kelly Lobato that were outstanding in the struggle for their race and had worked in political movements in the city most of his life. Kelly Lobato was a great companion who provided us the park and the local of Denver, Colorado to make our events as Kelly was in charge of the community recreation center for many years. Other Chicanos, Mexicans and some few Indians living in the city joined the group later.

In those days, I met a young man from Bolivia. We became friends because I had two guitars and he loved to play this instrument. The second time we met he came to my house and we played. Meanwhile, we talked about the adventure in that country. He told me that in his country they also wanted to kill him because he was in the student movement. Venturing, he had gone and two years later, he had come to the United States. He played pretty, revolutionary, Andean music, and although he was not involved in other things, he did it with his music. One day he told me, "My country is the poorest country in Latin America. Is that a punishment because in my country the Che was killed?"

After the whole agenda, we discussed the issue of what would be the name of the group. We thought "Monsignor Romero," but we had already heard that in that city and other cities in the United States they had used this name for these groups and that the leaders had taken advantage for defrauding followers and benefit themselves, and funds had not reached their destinations. In view of this and we were from different countries, we voted for the name "Latin American

Organization" (Organización Latino Americana), OLA. We made a seal with two hands in an embrace, and that was our symbol, *(logo)*. We started making plans for our next event in order to give talks about what happened in Central America and show videos, sell homemade food and ask for donations to send to refugee camps. We made contacts with groups from California, where we could get fresh information from Central America to distribute among people.

Being in the group, I met Mr. Leo Tanguma, who was a great muralist, quite famous for his work. He had worked in many murals in different cities of the United States and partly joined the group. We also asked us to work with him and give him money to make a piece of work: he had the plan to make a mural. Finally, he did it; it was a work in the form of a cross, made with pieces of almost 35 meters high and about 17 meters wide, which was exposed many times in the city, in different places. Our heroes were painted in the mural: the devastation of the murdered people and the people in struggle. There were also pictures of our oppressors. The man had a great artistic talent and creativity, and this would lead him to be well known in the progressive camp.

THE BARRIERS OF UNDOCUMENTED IMMIGRANTS: RACISM AND SPEAKING THE TRUTH TO THE AMERICAN PEOPLE ABOUT THE WAR IN EL SALVADOR

Meanwhile, work continued well. However, the more I learned English and I communicated with the cultures of the Yankees, Chicanos and blacks, the more I knew what racism and racial discrimination between them in that country. Beginning with the boss we had at work, he felt aversion toward us and there was no reason for it apart from the fact that we were Hispanics. One day, he was so angry with us at work that he said he no longer wanted "those Mexicans"; were we "those". He told this to his superior boss and I managed to understand it. The chief replied that Paul Murray, the owner, had employed us in the company and he had done it for religious and humanitarian principles. By the same time we had started to work there, a young gringo also started working but the man treated him differently. After that conversation, he no longer bothered us; however, we knew what he thought and in the first problem, he would find a way to get us out of work.

"WHO EVER APPLIES RACIAL DISCRIMINATION DOES NOT FEELS IT BUT, WHO EVER FEELS IT, IT'S A REALITY"

I had a friend for years. His name is Murray Law. Born in Courtney, Vancouver Island, BC, Canada. We lived together for a few years. He was educated as a DJ and he had his bachelor degree as a lawyer.

Meanwhile I went to the island to meet his parents to the island. By then he already had told me that from his father's side her grant mother was a Native Indian therefore he don't looked pure white Caucasian. He probably looked a 80% or 90% as white Caucasian. Being my friend and room-mate who goes for the first time Europe. He sets a job in check Republic as an English teacher so, on that trip he goes to England first then after to Germany and travels all the rest of Europe. He told me that that was the first time in his life that he felt discriminated.

One thing that helped him is that he told people that he got related told them that he was from, "British Columbia", Canada. Because when people saw him and got communicated with him they notice his accent that he was not a European.

After getting associated with people in a friendship he told me, that he got a better friendship with the local people.

Sometimes, blacks also came to work temporarily, and we saw how people, other workers and the system treated them worse than us. Then I realized that, unfortunately, the black is more discriminated for racism reasons than Hispanics. In labor departments, expressions of racism were heard. They looked down on them because of their jobs and skills. In the company I worked for, there were several racist, as I said before.

They always were trying to make us do a bad role with the superiors of the company so that we gave up. The issue was of great importance. It represents, firstly, what is experienced in that country. The few blacks who worked for the company had come to my house and they had told me similar experiences. I told a great friend who was black what I had lived with my boss. He already knew how he was, and said, "Do not pay attention to these white boys. Do your job and while bosses love you, forget the rest."

Through the organization, I had met many very smart people, like doctors, broadcasters, teachers, lawyers, singers, musicians, and journalists from different areas of the country, writers and poets. In addition, of course, religious people -especially, Catholics- as nuns, priests and others who were linked to the Church and also worked in the political environment and helped the victims of war in Central America. Those people were constantly looted by the military of Honduras and El Salvador, and often disappeared through the political game of the United States. When I met a person from any country or of other color different from mine, I always wanted to know what he could tell me from his country, although he had reactionary ideals. In general, they were poor people hurt by the capitalist system of their country. I met many from Asia, Africa, Eastern Europe and Latin America. I have never belittled anyone: I feel the need to share my life with the world, but there are people who do not even know one and they are already despising and hating one, simply because of his color.

In all my jobs, I have had about three bosses. One said, "I'll make your life impossible until you quit your job." Sometimes, officials or the same owners in the companies do not believe or do not see what is going on among workers. In another job, I had a boss of French origin: he did not like me at all and he treated me badly until one day he told me to go to my house. To corroborate what I had heard, I asked him if he was sure he wanted me to leave work, but this time he told me not to go. The following day, he apologized because he realized his attitude was absurd. Later, he even gave me a ride to my home and while we were in his car, he told me that he had come to British Columbia almost accidentally, because of his father, and he hated the English. I thought, "If he does not like white and Canadian people, what about me...?" He ignored me when I spoke and pretended not to understand me. He did not tell me everything so I committed a mistake and then he had the opportunity to embarrass me. In some cases, he felt jealous because he knew as much carpentry as me. The trouble was that he did not hide his silly ideologies. The man always tried to humiliate or embarrass me, for no reason, regarding my work. This is often seen in some jobs.

My father, called Juan Serrano Figueroa, told us that he was already 12 years old when the insurrection of 1932 occurred and told us that Maximiliano Hernández Martínez, who had given a coup to a Democrat Mr. Pio Romero. That insurrection murdered more than 35,000 citizens in a few days, including our leader Farabundo Martí who was executed in the firing line together with his two university "companions", Luna and Zapata. The executioner made many changes in the decreed of the constitution. In that decade the National Guard entered the country bringing contingents from Germany to give doctrine and "Hitlerian" training in the country because he "felt Nazi disciple," he also made another great feat. He forced "little black or colored race "to go into exile. Many were battered, tortured and even killed and they had to leave the country; some went to neighboring Central American countries. He also changed the laws in the Constitution: no black person could become a citizen in the country.

A new friend told me that. His name is Prisciliano Zamora, he is black and we are partners at work: he told me years ago he had to travel via El Salvador and had to wait at the airport of Comalapa, El Salvador for several hours to continue his trip to Colombia because he is from that country. After waiting for a while, my black friend was at the airport knowing and thinking of these changes, racial, illegal and totalitarian that occurred in the country over eight decades ago and I think that persist. Personal, I am ashamed that a developing country like ours practices such phenomenal inhumane norms.

In my life, I have met many highly intelligent and highly educated white people, and they had told me: "In these countries also have people who have narrowed mind", that is to say, reduced mind.

In the company, there were some few blacks that served only to cover the distribution of beer in black areas. A few others were sales agents and distributors. So it was with Hispanic or Chicano. They hired only enough to cover the areas of Hispanics in the city. Of course, the boss knew this pattern, but it was a business strategy. Although there was a lot of work for the minorities, the work for Chicanos and people of color was harder, with fewer opportunities for improvement and less income.

There was a Chicano named Adolfo. He was very friendly with and a good worker. He spoke a little Spanish, and I sent them to distribute beer with him. He went to the places where he had to deliver a lot of product and sometimes we had to return to fill the trailer of beers. Then, the company changed the statutes in sales. Motorists had a base salary and earned extra money by the amount of product distributed: the motorist who distributed more products earned more money. At that time, Adolfo could no longer go to such places and the whites did those areas to make money. Adolfo told me, "I am the next in hierarchy within the company; therefore, I am the one who deserves the post that comes from supervisor". However, they did not give it to. They gave him twenty-five dollars and a cap, because Adolfo made the best slogan for the company, "Murray Bross is people with Pride". The company owner sent for him and let him know his admiration. Mr. Paul Murray was a millionaire and made hats with this phrase for his company, Murray's distributing... There was no gringo or white that said something bad about Adolfo; he was a worker totally dedicated to his work and he liked it, but in the end, they did not like him. He taught me a lot at work and made me see many things. Two great friends, whites, were stealing the company Cash on delivery (COD). Before I knew it, Adolfo had already noticed it and told me as a friend on good terms. When they caught them, they had already stolen the company hundreds of thousands dollars. This man could do things like that, but he was not a bad person at work. The supervisor post was given to a white man who had fewer careers than Adolfo did but he was the protegé of the chiefs and gringo; he was also a great rider, those in high positions liked him and he longed for that position. Such maneuvers were frequently seen in the work, as I had many Salvadoran and Latin American friends that told me similar stories. I imagined that the same happened in another companies, throughout the country, as such stories were always heard.

Then, I got accustomed to the city. We got an apartment to live and we kept visiting priests and going to church on Sundays. We collaborated in the group that we formed, we went to school and we kept meeting people through the Church, in class and at work. Besides, we already had a car for transportation.

I took the driver's license and started visiting friends, Salvadorans and no Salvadorans, in order to join them to our group, OLA, or at least give them information about our humanitarian cause. I focused more on Central Americans, but Mexicans also got involved; however, I must say that Mexicans were more asleep than awake to this political ethics. Many Salvadorans had already been several months or years in the country, but when I told them about organizing and helping people in worst conditions, especially in Central America, some told me they had already been organized and the collected funds had disappeared without reaching their destination. Because of that, they no longer wanted to work with any group, because all were corrupt and they would not feed those ambitious people. Others said they did not want to know anything happening in our country, and others said they had no time to do it. Salvadorans always contributed: although they did not participate in movements of support for the country, they helped financially. As a matter of contribution, then came the Guatemalans, since in their country there was much social confusion than in ours. People from Honduras and Nicaragua came then; they were much interested neither in their families nor in their homeland or political beliefs. Given those mediocre convictions, one feels confused.

I would like to add that the Mexicans almost never cared about these ideas. In their ignorance, they began talking of their presidents and the corrupt people in the country, without realizing what the medicine is: that of the Che Guevara. When I spoke to them in political terms, they said that was another ideology. They heard about what the revolution meant, but ended up saying: "All are equal: miserable and corrupt in politics." The truth was that they had no interest in volunteering: there were no benefits and they were already in the United States and did not care about the others. Definitely, they had no social or political principles. Of course that, on many occasions, in many places in the United States, there were groups who committed fraud of this type with the same fellow citizens and even churches that were in solidarity with the Central American people, but that did not last long, because we have to know it immediately. Our intention was to work honestly to help those who needed to survive in the midst of a very complex internal war. Occasionally, we one ran into with Central American individuals who were reactionaries. For them, talking about that was an offense, just because they were former ex-military who had been brainwashed or they were far-right civilians and had no reason to be in that position. They said that the people had taken wrong turns in their decisions. They often thought that because maybe they had a military relative or from ORDER, or they had been executed. These damaged the process because they told the people who were in extreme poverty that if communism came, they would lose what they had. We are talking about people who had nowhere to live, nothing to eat, with naked children, living on the streets, in a small hut they had done to defend themselves from the water or they had been given permission to do one hut of grass in the countryside. And those people sometimes had two or three chickens roamed around, and that was all they had; and some ignorant people had made them feared the arrival of communism and the losing of their belongings. Moreover, as the poorest people sometimes were the most faithful and devoted, they told them that the Communists did not believe in God: they did not want people to realize how wide the road of the struggle for human rights, universal rights is. They did not want them to ask for better living conditions as people were enslaved and lived in a world of extreme poverty and subhuman social conditions. Nobody had the chance to hear anything about their rights as citizens, as all media were swamped with capitalist, right wing and reactionary information to have people deceived.

All new presidents promised, painted the glory with their big promises and criticized the Democrat party. José Napoleón Duarte and his democratic leaders played with the military and the CIA. The soldiers were in front, behind was the CIA and the Democrats were in last place. For that reason, Democratic votes were not many, since those who supported them had radicalized by other political paths.

Many Salvadorans in the United States no longer wanted or speak to us because they may be had their papers, their cars; maybe they spoke little English or they had married an American, or perhaps they had a good job and believed that war was for fools or that it was unnecessary. The causes were not worth it. Some fellows had escaped thought from war and extreme poverty. When they reached North America, they became big headed, as we say, because they no longer wanted to hear a single word about our people. Others told me that the people had the fault of suffering and they, thank God, were alive and out of that hell: many were aware of the poverty in which our country was but they did not want to accept that, they never matured. It was a bit depressing the topic of the boys with reactionary mind.

In those days, we had a hearing in the building of the Migration Court. Of course, we had two lawyers who wanted to help us to obtain permission or status of political refugees, but things were not easy: if the judge accepted our cases, he was automatically accepting the damage the United States was causing in our country. Obviously, this judge would not accept such a thing. The agreement was long and our stories were well described. One of the lawyers, -who, if I remember correctly, was called Chely Dodge, and she was a great person- assured the judge were in danger of losing our lives if we returned to our country. The judge replied that the United States was there with its democracy, and that nothing could happen to us. In the end, he told us we could go and take the identification of the state, but not the social security.

We went with my brother to do the written test to the engine and vehicles offices, as we wanted to get a driver's license. We went three times. A fat white woman always served the public, and she always disapproved us. She treated us in a hard way and showed a racist attitude. We did the written test in Spanish, but since she did not speak it, to qualify in that language she used a model. The last time, marked wrong one of the first questions, which said: "In a high, you have to stand up: 1) behind the line of pedestrians, 2) above the line of pedestrians, 3) in front of the line pedestrians. It was a very simple question, which obviously we answered well and yet she had marked as incorrect: she had made the mistake, and not only that time, but also the time before. That day, she showed those papers to the woman who was with us, Mrs. Amelie Starkie, and there we saw that she was wrong. Mrs. Amelie spoke to her, and only then, the woman realized she was using the wrong model. Then Mrs. Amelie gave me the car, I took the test and passed it. My brother passed the written exam. Then we went to celebrate at a restaurant in town that I already had driver's license.

Things were going well at work, because most people liked us due to our attitude as workers. There were a few gringos that did not like us and they were always trying to create us a conflict with the heads of the company. Although we did not know English very well, we could understand when someone was talking about us. We went to school to learn the language, and that helped us a lot. They called us *Mexicans*, and used that word to discriminate us. We did not care being called Mexicans, but the tone they used. Nevertheless, we continued working, as the company owner knew us and thanks to him and the nun, we had gotten the job.

The same day we got the job, a man began working; he was a young gringo called Deren, whose father had retired in that company. They did not want to give him a steady job, and he would only work temporarily. He was a very good person, and always wanted to know how our family was in El Salvador, in the midst of war. One day, he asked me,

"How is your family in your country?"

I said that was fine, and he kept asking me.

"Do they have any economic problem?"

I said that in our country economic problems never ended. When he heard that, he thought for a moment, and replied,

"Listen, I have saved some money because I come from a good family, and would like to help you and I want to send money to your relatives there."

I thought of those Central Americans who had used the struggle of Central America as a shield to strengthen themselves. That made me think, and I said,

"If you want to help my family, I thank you very much. If you want the address and name of whom you would send the check, I can give them to you."

The young man had a very caring heart and really wanted to do it, and he asked me for information about what I had to do. I said,

"Buy the check to this name [the name of my older sister] and write in a note what you want to say to my people. I will translate it into Spanish for them to understand."

Therefore, he did, he bought the check in the bank on behalf of my sister and sent a note with words that came from his heart, their feelings, and I translated it into Spanish. In the same letter, I spoke to my sister of this young friend who sent them the money. Our old aunts, my grandmother, my mother and my sister used the money that fell as rain in May. My sister wrote a letter in response to my friend. The old ladies gave many thanks and sent their "God bless you". The boy felt like crying when I translated that into English and he felt very flattered and pleased with what he had done with his gift.

The ladies also gave me the thanks for what I was doing humanely for them there, but I felt more than that. I wanted to do that with all the people of my country, which was very difficult because of the conditions in which we lived in the United States, either for political differences or for the lack of the necessary documents to succeed in jobs. Moreover, people who were in the refugee camps were controlled by the military; and we knew that they often took people to torture and kill them. People in those places could not be saved from the military. Likewise, it was more difficult to send aid to those fields that were in the midst of war within the country.

I continued working with the coalition and the group we had formed. With the coalition, I went to talk to many places, such as churches, religious centers, community centers, elementary schools, high schools and even universities in the state of Colorado. The responses of college could be both interesting and captious, especially when it came to law or history students.

In the following years, the emigration of Salvadorans to Mexican and American lands was terrible. Despite being a small country, the Salvadoran group was the second largest in the United States, after Mexicans. It turned out to be the group that sent more money to their families; so El Salvador became the country receiving more money per capita. I want to emphasize that even though we lost many people by social weaknesses, the people from our country have always been very determined.

Before the twentieth century, the United States did not have much interest in the political and military manipulation of those countries, but then, they began to make investments as the Panama Canal and purchasing a whole department in Honduras, where they created the United Fruit Company. In the fulfillment of both works, most of the workers were Salvadorans. From the Monroe Doctrine and its investment in Latin America, everything changed. The first day I spoke to the public without a translator was facing some university students, and I only told them that if they did not understand what I said, they should raise their hands in order to corroborate or clarify what I was saying. That day I felt real independence, I was happy. Students were interesting and wanted to know much about the political atmosphere we were living in my land. First, it was about a political dynasty dedicated to keep the growth of the exported products. After that, the American intervention came. In the 1910s, the Meléndez family was in power;

they had countless farms and ranches throughout the republic. Then, the Quiñones family came to power; they were also extraordinary chiefs and owners of much land in coffee farms and ranches. These Quiñones had so much land to make almost a quarter of a million of small farms. About fourteen families that came from Europe were the owners of the riches of the earth and politically manipulated the country. On the other hand, two-thirds of the farmers had nothing at all: they did not have anywhere to live; their children did not go to school because they had no money and there were not nearby schools. They lived on the banks of the streets in places made of cardboard tents. They kneeled in front of the landowner's supervisor or overseers to beg a place to live.

Some students asked questions that were very smart about the political games of Latin America, and what was the percentage share of the rich, the military and the United States. Thus, the speaker had to be updated to the statistics of the past and the present. Sometimes, those people ignored the reasons for the American intervention in the war in Central America, which was regional, and were not just about overuse. However, some students discussed the idea that had anything to do with economic control, as they are small countries. Of course, we must accept that the countries of the region are not big but they produced many products to the United States. El Salvador was in eleventh place among the countries that exported coffee worldwide for decades. It was also important the export of sugar cane, cotton and paper. Then, there were manufactured products that were exported to the United States, as fabrics and clothes, as there is a large textile factory across the country. A friend who had already worked for many years in the industry told me, for example, they manufactured the American military uniforms. Central American countries also export marine products. On the other hand, the United States was exploiting uranium mines in the west of the country, in the department of Morazán to use it in the nuclear bombs industry to continue killing my people. It was also vital for the United States to maintain its control and that El Salvador does not become another Nicaragua or another Cuba. First, because the waist of the continent could be more dangerous in geopolitical terms: the area where these countries are located is called the waist of America; it is the bridge between southern and northern of the continent. In addition, they could not let any country become autonomous; if improvements arose in any Latin American country, all the other countries might seek the same path; and if those countries develop and have access to a better life, the United States would lose their income in Central America and in the countries of southern of the continent.

Some people only attended these talks to criticize: they considered the United States a God who did not need these third world countries and they said they could not take economic advantage from these insignificant countries. They did not know the position of the United States in these countries and that there were many interests. The biggest reason for the intervention was geopolitics, and they wanted to avoid the self-determination of the peoples.

Thanks to the job Mrs. Amelie Starkey got us, my brother Manuel and I were able to finish our house in El Salvador after nearly two years of construction. By coincidence, the place became one of the best neighborhoods of the town. Thus, our parents went to live to the village and could be out of that hell camp where the commander was. We sent them money to live and feel happy their last days in the midst of a war. My father did not feel the taste of life; he liked being in the piece of land, planting cornfields, beans, vegetables and fruit trees.

Sometime after, there was a mission to El Salvador from the Catholic Church of the United States, and nuns travelled there, in the midst of war. Mrs. Amelie and other nuns who knew us took part of it, and they went to visit our parents to the house we had built them. It was a dangerous time because the place reeked of Civil Defense. On the other hand, the nuns who had been murdered in our country were known and friends of this great lady, Mrs. Amelie. However, the group managed to visit my parents and women realized I was not lying to them about what I told them about my life and my work. This time, they could check that with a letter written by my brother-in-law, who was a national police officer, where he said to me: "Your nuns friends are just a guerrilla".

Meanwhile, we continued with our problems concerning our legal situation. Ralph Dellinger, the supervisor of supervisors of the company, wanted to help us, as well as the other young supervisor named Dan Cehura; both were very nice people. I told them we had to fight hard: we had to pay fortunes to lawyers and spend a lot of money with American immigration police. At that time, the sponsor system no longer existed in the country, and that was what they thought they could do. Whenever we went to see the judge, he only spoke of deportation.

In the company, I also met a great person, whose name was Bob Redd. He was a person of color, as they are called in the United States. This man was a soldier and when I told some passages of what life was like in El Salvador, he was sad and remembered the Vietnam War, where he had been some years ago. He told me that people in North America was wrong because of the information provided in that country. No one took into account the great needs of the people from that extremely exploited Third World country. He said that they only incited them to kill Vietnamese without taking into account the value as human beings, without exception, and that black people and Hispanics were put in the firing line during combat. Moreover, many of the people who returned had great difficulty in getting a job, besides their mental problems, and having a normal civilian life.

He told me once,

"Here, we, black people, have no value; we are discriminated everywhere. Note that we could not vote some years ago; schools for blacks and whites were separated; we were not accepted in any social place; they wanted to send us back to where we belong after having been slaves and then sold us like dogs." In addition, he continued, "We cannot be with a white female down the street at ease, because they even see that. I have some young friends and two of them have white girlfriends, and they tell me they are happy neither. In this country, we are asleep; we have no principles regarding fight for our rights. My people think of racism in the same way as them. They are engaged in drugs, because they do not find a direction in life, and they ruin their lives and those of their children. Of course, frustration is serious, because 99% of black people live a life with social blockages, lack of improvement, and that usually leads to total ruin, especially in the cases of those who have been military and those who get a good job and then quit because of racism."

My brother and I were his friends, and in the afternoons, after leaving work, he took us to our house when we did not use car for not having a driver's license. He was sick at heart; he had already told us about this problem. After three years, he died. He could not resist the surgery. The boss of the company said we could all attend his funeral, and we accompanied him from the chapel to the grave. Almost all the employees attended his funeral: we went from the chapel to Logan Cemetery in Denver, Colorado, which is a military cemetery. There laid soldiers of the First and Second World War, as well as Vietnam. That was the first time in my life that I personally saw the ceremony made to a soldier in his last moment. Mr. Bob Redd had told me on several occasions about the great hero Martin Luther King Jr., and he had told me that his people needed another man like him. Coincidentally, after Mr. Bob's death, the blacks were given as holiday the same day this hero was born.

Once I went to work with another individual. This young man was white and named Rich. One day, while we were going down the street in the truck, we saw a young couple walking down the street. It was black with a pretty white.

"I hate to see that", Rich said as he watched them.

I asked him what he meant, though I had perfectly understood what he meant. Then he asked me if I liked niggers. I told him that if a person had not hurt me, then, I had no reason to hate him. Then he added, "Did you know you that niggers could not vote before and they were slaves here in this country for a long time?"

The young man did not know I had studied it in elementary school, in my country, apart from what I had read in some books in North America. I had also read about blacks who live in Latin America and the Caribbean. This guy, obviously, did not know me, and the racism in his heart would not allow him to know more about life.

Finally, he added,"You're a good person because you're not Mexican, but there are other Mexicans… I do not know what to say…"

A few weeks later, he wanted to throw my brother from the truck to kill him.

I met dozens of white men like him in my way of life or my adventure. Besides, I used to smile when they said they disliked seeing a couple of a black with a white female walking through the streets of Denver.

Precisely in those days, I was introduced to a young Yankee girl named Laura Schaeffer. She was born in Ireland but grown in Pittsburgh, Pennsylvania; she had Irish roots and had lived in Europe during her childhood. She was studying in one of the best schools there, called Grinnell in Iowa. We met because during her holiday she came to visit her sister who lived in Denver. She played the piano very well and had taught classes for a while. She was white and blonde and was only nineteen. Soon, we began a courtship.

Laura spoke and wrote in Spanish without difficulty, and some other languages, such as French. I translated my poetic verses into English so when I recited them in public, they were in both languages in the same paper. We got along very well, and we ended up living together when she finished school: we moved into an apartment and she took a job as a bilingual teacher. We had the opportunity to do things together. She collaborated with our group, and we attended the meetings together, and she made us suggestions. Furthermore, she translated documents and material we would include then in our monthly pamphlet, where we published fresh information coming from El Salvador. Everyone admired her and praised her for being smart and having good humanitarian principles.

We had contacts in El Salvador and in Los Angeles, California, with an office called Casa El Salvador. Thanks to them, in that monthly paper we could show the greatest atrocities the army committed against my people and the misdeeds of the members of the CIA in El Salvador. We could also show the needs of refugees inside and outside the country, different things of the local community and a poem written to touch the hearts of the fellow citizens who were insensitive.

When we went out together, either to restaurants or to other places, young whites stared at us and they even said things directly or indirectly. They looked at her greedily, and me, with contempt. She spoke to me in Spanish and made me some comments- smiling in a sarcastic- about them watching us. She was extremely nice. She also said to me, "But when they see a white man with a black or Hispanic young girl, it is not the same, because they like to see that", she laughed.

It was true, I saw it many times in the United States, and it looked more interesting if it was analyzed as a sign of male chauvinism in the society.

The relationship was very good. Her parents were separated, but they still visited us from the east of the country. His father was a film artist and his mother a university professor. They really appreciated me. We thought of getting marriage because we got along very well, but one day my ideas changed: her paternal grandmother -which already passed the seventy years - was wealthy and lived in Long Beach, California, in a mansion on the edge of the beach, as they told me. Once, the girl told me,

"If my grandmother knew I live with you and we are thinking about getting married... I am sure she would have a heart attack!"

That made me changed my marital plans with her because the whole family loved this girl as well as her grandma.

But her grandmother's case was not isolated. In the United States, I met elderly ladies who told me, even crying,

"In this country, we are being invaded by Mexicans. I only meet Mexican when I walk through the streets of Denver."

Of course, she said that to me because I am Salvadoran. I also met in Canada ladies with that way of thinking. They were all white. Some from Vancouver, British Columbia, told me in tears, sobbing, that the city was full of Chinese. As I am a Salvadoran, I was not in the list of discriminated people. I kept my sobs in my heart; I did not show how much it hurt me. Sometimes, people cannot contain these weaknesses and somehow they bring them out, especially when they speak from their hearts, trying to make invalid justifications for racist attitudes.

I want to add that these acts were commonplace; they happened just around the corner, every day, at every moment. After traveling to Canada, I realized that racism also exists in that country. In this regard, Canada has some things greater than the United States, because to solve problems with racism the government system intervenes, although on many occasions they also become deaf and ignore the affected. In other words, the conflict always exists, although the government procedures might help a little in some situations. In my own experience, I can say that sometimes I was offended because of this prejudice.

Once, when I lived in London, Ontario, a friend told me, "Let's go to the inn. I drank a little last night, and I feel bad. I would like to drink a beer and then eat something. I know in which inn good soups are sold to eat."

I told him I would go with him and that I was interested in eating something similar. As soon as we entered the place, two men pushed us out, and we fell on the street. They were two men who looked like gorillas, very large and heavy, and they told us we were not allowed to be there because we had the wrong color. We just got up and, and without saying anything, we left the place.

Many times, I had to leave places because I felt things like that could happen. However, there have been other situations. In Ontario, I did a course on interior design and carpentry for construction and as forming carpenter as well. When you finished it, you automatically entered the union, but in Ontario, there was no work. As I got bored of looking for a job there, and since I was already in the union and paying monthly installments, I talked to them to see where I could use my training because I needed to work. They informed me that the only place where there was work was in Vancouver, British Columbia, so I asked to be transferred there. They organized my papers and talked to the people in Vancouver, and everything was ready for me to undertake my journey of several thousand kilometers.

Days later, I was in Vancouver. I got maps; I searched the union building, I saw it was in Westminster, and I went to visit it. I went to one of the two managers and I told them I was the person who came from Ontario and I brought all my papers in order and I was ready to work. More or less, I knew what they were doing and where: they were building shopping centers. The man, who I assumed was the local chief, just stared at me, he did not know what to say, he choked with his words and could not find excuses. After having me standing there for a moment, they sent me to take a sit at a remote place at the end of a corridor. From there, however, I heard the conversation, or rather, the argument held by each other: why they did not give me the job. I understood perfectly what they were saying. At one point, the man whom I had talked to told the other;

The truth is that this man will not have a job here.

"Why?" Replied the second.

When I heard that, I got up from the chair and went to where they were. The man who refused to give me the job could see me approaching them and went to another office. When I asked his partner to tell him I wanted to talk to him, he told me he was busy at the office. I replied I wanted to clarify what I had heard; when he asked what I had heard, I said that he had heard it better than me because he was closer to the person who had said that. The man said nothing and got into the office. After a while, he came out and told me that the other man would not leave the office for a long time because he was busy talking on the phone.

They even refused to see my union documents. After that, I left the place and I even thought about taking the case to someone who would listen to me, like a lawyer, since I was offended. However, I chose not to visit the local again.

There are times when one is very conformist and that is not good. After, in less than a week, I got another job in the same work rubric, but it was not a union and I forgot the litigation. Besides, they were two against me. My word against theirs and they were white. Racism affected people and sometimes we never forget some things. I lost jobs in my life being a professional carpenter with a workout I had during six months to make it, but as I have a white, slow and chatty partner who did care little about the production or working demonstrations, I was fired and my partner kept the work.

However, I stayed in Vancouver. Later, being in that city, I studied television and video production, since I liked it, and I like nowadays, things related to the arts. The course lasted over a year and it cost me a fortune: $ 12,000. All my savings went there. At that time, they said they were going to turn Vancouver into another Hollywood: they were going to call it North Hollywood. However, after graduation, I also found work in the field. This took away all hope and motivation to progress through education, as these possibilities were not equal for everyone in terms of races. The victim feels frustrated seeing that sometimes the person who got the employment had no knowledge; but as he is white, he has priority in employment opportunities and sources. It had happened to me, and you have to live with that.

After all this adventure, I have met many people from all over the world: from Europe, Africa, Asia, the Middle East and many people tell me they have felt racism on their shoulders, in their hearts. My instructor in Ontario was from Yugoslavia and told me countless times he was victim of racism but the American white people have never felt that, because they only had discriminated. I have met many NATIVES, "first nation"; they also tell me the same thing: they were and still are discriminated in their schools, in their works and in all social areas.

BEING A CARPENTER

As I mansion before that I come from a carpenter's family from my dad side: They were, lumber makers, house builders and furniture makers; of course that all the tools being used were powerless but they had all the tools to do fine furniture so the kids of all them we inherited the same thing since we were kids. We started doing toys like a two wheels like a bike, three wheels, four wheel and 6 wheels carts and also we did a big one to bring fire wood and other provisions to the house. We did the wheels out of big logs chopping the big round logs up to 3 feet in diameter and at the evenings or nights we used to like to go on the down hills driving with head lights at the front up to seven kids on seven trycicles in the property that was six hectacres and on the street going to the neighbourhood store to groceries with all having fun that we had, and we end up doing this toys for another kids.

But one day the brother of dad told us: Don't stuff like that to bother people during nights. Do something like, chairs, tables or another things that are good for people.

My older brother and I started our own "*little business*" besides our other responsibilities: Doing, chairs, tables, benches, etc. So whatever they wanted needed in the community/valley. It was funny and interesting, I felt quiet important with our little business because the people came to us and tell us:" I want a table with four chairs". By then we were already ordering lumber from lumber makers to make orders from peasants of the community.

In this passed years that I have gone to El Salvador and I visit some of my people in my village, some of them ask me: "Remember this..?: "This something that you guys made me long time ago." They steal have thing that we did long time ago.

Years passed; I came in to Canada, I came to Ontario and the first time I became unemployed in Canada I had the opportunity to take the course of carpentry trough training allowance for being unemployed. So far most of my life I have been a carpenter in construction. I have met ordinary people/guys from all over the world; some of them nice, some of them not to nice. Some of them look people like me but they think they are in a higher spot just because they are white Europeans but at the end we do the same thing and we have the same value and the same experience about the trade or maybe they never had the training and they feel jealous because me, as a immigrant is doing the same money like them.

So many times I have had co-workers that are white, from Canada and from different European countries of the world and they have asked me for so many times:" What do you think Max about a guy that is racist". I have been asked this question so many times in over than 30 years that I have been in 2 countries. My answer have been the same: *"I think that a person who uses the racism is a narrow mind"*. Because, they know that is the truth. Most of them who have been my co-workers they agree with it, but I have met so many ordinary guys that probably they will never understand. In construction is where you can met the most ordinary guys and where they put on practice the racial discrimination. I have being in the union of carpenters and is the same thing.

ANOTHER EXPERIENCE

My Ex-Wife

For the first time I went El Salvador for Christmas. This time I went with Canadian documents; this was December of 1991. I met this girl in the same neighbourhood where I had a house: We met and talked about future so, in 1993 I went again and we got the engagement. We got married for Christmas of 1994; I brought/sponsor her to come to Canada in February of 1996.

And then came the time when we met/know each other so. She told me that she was 6 and half years old of age when she saw that about 300 revolutionary peasants came to her house and killed her father. Her father was the administrator of tree fincas of the Alvares Cordova of El Salvador; one of the 14 richest families of El Salvador and some of the workers told me that this man used the gun point at people, workers of the finca and that was why he got killed by revolutionary fronts.

I made the mistake of telling her what I knew about her father from friends that I met. That's why she always had her believes in the right wing party of the country. After this, our relationship became a night mare after this, until came the separation between us.

At that time, I met a man with Nazi mind, and it was like an adventure. After two or three days in Vancouver, I went to the Greyhound station to pick up a suitcase I had left there. The place was almost empty because it was too dark, and I saw a guy sitting and scratching his head as if he was stressed. Suddenly he looked at me and said, "Hey! Can you do me a favor?"

I asked him what was it about, and he asked if I could look after his luggage while he went to the toilet. I said I had no problem, and I sat there until he returned. Then, he thanked me and told me he had come from New Scotia and he had already come to work, but his friend lived a few blocks from where we were and he did not answer the phone, so he wanted to go to the hotel to see what was happening. Then, he asked me to look after the bags again while he went to try to find his friend at the hotel. I said I could take care of them until he came back. He returned forty minutes later. In the hotel, they told him that person had left the place a few days earlier. He scratched his head nervously and said he did not know where he was going to sleep. He did not have any money and the friend was no longer living at the address he had given to him.

I arrived a couple of days ago and told him,"Listen, I am staying at a hotel on Granville Street. If you want to stay with me, you can, but the problem is that there is only one bed and the room is small, so you would have to sleep on the floor."

He was pleased with the offer and we immediately called a taxi to take us to the place with the suitcases. Once in the room, we talked and he told me he was qualified in tinsmith and somebody was already waiting for him in a company. I also told him why I had gone to Vancouver, but I did not tell him the reason they had not given me the job. Then, he said he wanted to save money to travel to Germany. I replied it was a great idea and he almost invited me, but I said I still had my parents in my land and that in case of travelling; I would better go to visit them.

The following day, he went to the company where he would work and when he returned, a little drunk, he asked if he could smoke marijuana in my room; I said he could. Then, he told me that the main reason for him travelling to Germany was to visit Adolf Hitler's grave. I asked him why, and he replied that the man was his idol and that he considered himself as his disciple: he had indoctrinated for several years with some people of his town. At that time, I wanted to know why he had befriended me, since I was the kind of people they despise, and he told me, "Yes, it is true, but you are a good person. In my village, we mistreat, hit and even kill people like you and the niggers. However, if you came to my place, I would stand for you. Some Mexicans had gone to my land and we do not like them: and there are some niggers too and we hate them. That is why I don't like being in Toronto, because there are many niggers."

He was for three days in my apartment. Finally, he received money from social services and he got his job, so he ended up renting another room in the same hotel where I was. He usually visited me almost every day, and he always talked about the same subject. He invited me to his room to spend time with him, but I was not the kind of people he wanted to have as a friend. He said I was the only non-white friend he had, and that he neither understood why.

When he was a bit drunk, he always told some racist jokes. I remember only one he told me one day, "Do you know why in the United States they capture blacks and us, in Canada, the French?" He added.

Since I did not know what to reply, "Because it was a *free trade*"

Almost every time we talked, he said he would not die without visiting the grave of his idol in Germany. Once he arrived drunk at my apartment. I welcomed him and told him to go and take a seat, and we started talking. After a while, he began talking about racism and other obscenities, until came the time he told me he wanted to fight with me because I was a person who belonged to the group he hated. Then he insulted and put me in the dock. I did not want to fight: I told him to go to his apartment. The next day, he returned and apologized to me, but I knew that in his heart he was so; he thought that way. After about two months, he disappeared, and I no longer saw him again: he did not tell me goodbye. Maybe he went to Germany to visit the "saint" he loved that much or maybe he went to the state of Texas where he had many colleagues and where he wanted to enter the so spoken Ku Klux Klan.

With all this, I want to note that racism also exists in Canada, and this is very hard for immigrants. So far, in Canada I have lost three jobs because of Canadian racism. They start making the worker their life impossible, until the person ends up leaving the work: they made them quit. Although the person knows the job, bosses sometimes abuse and discriminate employees. As a worker, one can feel the pressure they exert to make us quit the job. There are those who see and hear, but do not feel it, and others who do not care. Nonetheless, there are those who know inside what is right and what is wrong: they analyze and realize that the boss is being racist. There are white friends who told me things like, "This man does not like you because you are an immigrant". I always answer that these people are racist to me, but not with immigrants from countries like Germany or Switzerland. I do not see that are racist with fellow workers in these European countries. However, I also met Europeans who told me that sometimes, they had been victims of racism, and I said to them, "If thou have experienced it yourself, ask me how many times I have had to live it..."

On the other hand, when someone is racist, he does not see any value in the other: one is devalued, despised. Facing that, no matter you have the necessary qualities and skills for a job. That is where the outcast feels frustrated and clings to living a life with low incomes.

Once, also in Canada, I got a job in construction, as I like it and I have worked in this industry for many years. When I started, the senior chief just told me I had to go with my basic tools and an electric screwdriver drill. I did not have that drill, so I had to buy it with my credit card because I had no money. It cost me $ 270; two weeks later, somebody stole it during a work. While I was looking for it, the supervisor saw me and asked what I was doing. I replied that someone had just stolen my screwdriver drill while I was putting large screws in metal structures. This man, who was a Yankee, told me almost shouting and in an extraordinarily aggressively and contemptuously way to look for it until I found and to hurry with my work. It was about eleven o'clock. I kept looking for my tool for another twenty minutes until the supervisor looked at me and asked me if I had found it. I said no, and he just told me to go to my house. I went to my house, very disappointed, unemployed and without my tool, which I had not paid yet. The next day, I went back and told the supervisor I had no other tool, but I wanted to work on whatever he had. He replied he already had another in my place and that there was no more for me...

Of course, they tolerate white people rather than Latinos who make mistakes at work or who does not show up. At the drop of a hat, we are fired; if we have not made a mistake, they make them up to dismiss us from the job. I have felt despised in many cases, have gone through a lot of stress, it has not been easy to get new jobs and start again. After that, the curriculum is never satisfactory to the new employer, because if you put you have been fired for racial discrimination, they do not believe it; and if they investigate in your previous job, bosses deny it all because they will never accept. Those are complex cases and officially a little delicate; however, they occur very often in both countries in North America.

Moreover, I want to add that the preferential treatment I saw in Canada towards European immigrants is with those individuals who are "white". I met many people from Romania, Poland, Czech Republic, Italy and Portugal that had also been victims of some kind of discrimination. Concerning Africans and Asians, they are as discriminated as us.

Many whites have told me, "I hate Mexicans! But you do not worry, because you're not Mexican..." How much ignorance in that comment...! As if people of Mexico and Central America were so different... Likewise, I have met people from different nationalities that even discriminate traditions, customs, and the culture of Third World countries. I have seen dances and other cultural demonstrations in some European countries, and they seemed to me extremely interesting, but there are people who despise such things.

There is another detail I realized, it is that the Chilean and Argentine immigrants –I worked and lived together with them- in the United States were very friendly and had to fight just as we did in the work field and to obtain their documents. However, in Canada it was different: there, they felt superior and some were intellectuals. Of course, most people in those countries are of European origin, and there was no doubt they also felt the superiority in color, in contrast with Central Americans. These immigrants discriminated us: this is obvious due to the arrogant way in which they talk to you, as if they were in a higher position. Nevertheless, it should be added that most still keep in mind that they also are discriminated and remember talking about the issue that has brought them to these countries: policies and oppression waves they have lived in their home countries.

When I lived in northern Mexico, in Sonora, people though I was from Oaxaca, because people of that northern state are large, generally high, and a little white or ladino, and they called me "Oaxaco crappy". People from Oaxaca are the most discriminated against across the

Mexican land even by Mexicans themselves, and they do not want them to work neither. I liked being confused with an Oaxaco because, in other words, they said I was Mexican. I had some friends in Oaxaca in northern Mexico. One of them was called Atilano; he was a good person and we got along like brothers. He told me that he was always treated with discrimination wherever he walked: he did not speak Spanish very well and had marked features of an Oaxaco. We worked on the same ranch and we usually went out together for a walk, and he said he wanted to do one of two things: either go to the United States, or enter the military barracks in Mexico, as his older brother there was in the state of Sinaloa. He felt very Mexican from the heart and he loved his homeland in a faithful way. I told him to feel proud of his people, as the best president in the history of Mexico was Mr. Benito Juárez, who was an Indian from Oaxaca, Mexico primitive state. He was a man of ideals who said, referring to foreign invasions in Mexico: "The respect to somebody's rights and nations is peace." In the southern states of Mexico, such as Chiapas, Oaxaca people are called hogs, meaning "pigs"; in northern Mexico they are called turkeys, meaning idiots".. Both words are used as a form of racial discrimination, as an insult, and with them, they mean "clumsy and ugly." I think, however, that are the sincerest hearted people I have ever met in my life or in my adventure in Mexico and the United States.

I remember another individual who also lived at the ranch, with which we worked together every day: he was from Guanajuato, he was white, and he liked neither Atilano nor me. We had several clashes, but he respected my uncle Juan. Atilano was tired of so much social and racial discrimination, so came the day he felt to fight this guy in front of the whole group we were working with. Atilano hit very hard the Guanajuatans; he had some bruises for a couple of weeks. That was the remedy for such man to stop being arrogant with him. He looked and felt humiliated the rest of the time we lived at the ranch and at work. Already living in the United States, I was still communicated with Atilano, but eventually we lost touch.

In Denver, Colorado, immigrants who are in the street or at work are mostly - almost in their totality-, Mexicans. Many of the Salvadorans who have migrated to this state have already forgotten their land and even their loved ones; they like to meet Mexicans only, and as they had generally lived in Mexico, they have a Mexican accent. When you saw them in their meetings with Mexican, they secretly whispered on their ears, "Do not say that I am Salvadorian, for them I'm Mexican" since -I must add- the Mexicans, who represent the majority of immigrants in the United States, discriminate against other Latin Americans. Some Mexicans despise the Central American, without realizing we shared the same social conditions. In my personal life, I have lost three jobs in the United States; I lost both for not being Mexican. In those jobs, there were only Mexicans, and they did not like that I was not one of them. I have been a rebel: I spoke with a Mexican accent only when I needed, in Mexico. This is the reason why many Salvadorans say they are Mexican and they interact more with them than with their own people.

I have met hundreds of Mexicans in my life and I can say that most of them were poor and workers, fighters. There has been no one who said something good about the political system of their country: they all know they have a great, beautiful and productive country, like few in the world, but they also know that Mexico needs a political change, needs to do something to end corruption. All Mexicans speak of in their talks. We had only one Mexican in the OLA group. I went to his land, in Chihuahua, to meet his father, who was one hundred years old and had walked along with Pancho Villa in the Mexican Revolution. Sick and very old, he told me some passages he lived during the revolution: he talked about the political game, the Institutional Revolutionary Party (PRI) and the political and economic relationship between the United States and Mexico. The United States controlled not only the sales of Mexican lands but also the agricultural and industrial manipulation of their people. He also told me that they were just a round table for the United States: the table of delicacies and exploitation. In contrast, near where he lived, there was the siege of borders more care in the world and he assured me it was going to get worse one day. He would die soon, but things would be even worse.

I met his son in a job. I was wearing a shirt with a picture of Che Guevara, and thanks to that, he approached me and we started talking. Then, we knew ourselves better and became very good friends. Julian Quezada is his name. He was already in his sixties, liked to join us, and worked voluntarily in the group. We gave us courage, made suggestions and contributed ideas to move further on. He said among thousand Mexicans, there was not a single person who had thoughts or revolutionary will, as his people were asleep in a vacuum; all Mexicans knew what the problem was their country, but nobody did anything about it. He knew a lot about Mexican history: I talked about things that happened in the past and things that occurred in the United States, as the treaty of Guadalupe, in which it was said that all Mexicans could enter without any problem in the American territory. He told me about the four land sales that made Mexican politicians to the United States and much more about the political system of his country. He said: "Our country has everything: oil, mining, industry, agriculture, good weather and two beautiful oceans with many riches. The only thing that does not help us is our political system". He always said he wished to see a change in his people because there could not be so many poor people in a potentially rich country in the hemisphere.

Racism and social differences in the United States have changed or canceled many goals for improvement and education, because that problem is present every day at work. Sometimes even the immigrant workers become themselves infected with this phenomenon. Chicanos discriminate against Latin American immigrants; the person who already has documents discriminates and exploits the undocumented. Almost all immigrants are Mexicans, but they called them wet backs, or Mexicans. When somebody spoke to them in Spanish, they said they did not know; though they spoke it, they said they could not. They felt socially inferior if someone heard them speaking their own language; they felt ashamed. Blacks also have racist attitudes. Minorities discriminate against other minorities as a way to counteract the disease that affects them.

Personally, I loved talking to any immigrant from anywhere in the world; I would like to hear about their countries of origin, geography, culture, customs, traditions, etc.

I also realized that when parents behaved that way, then the children repeated those same attitudes. There was a time when I heard some teenagers telling racist insults. Of course, if a child does not grow in that environment, he will not grow that way; I also met families of that kind, in which neither parents nor children had racist attitudes. Generally, racism is more frequent in the lower classes, like among construction workers or between those who have underpaid or hard jobs, because there are people with less education and they have been treated that way. However, it is also common among bureaucrats, for I remember a young friend I had who was very intelligent and spoke three languages, but when she graduated from secretary and had to look for a job, she could not find any. She wanted to work where perhaps only white worked, and she could not get it for being Latino. Once, I told a black friend I would have liked to work in some company where we were well paid and I could have all the benefits given to the worker, and smiling, he replied: "You have to be a white boy to work there ".

In those days, I also remember that my Uncle Juan and my two cousins went to work for a white man who owned a small landscaping, gardening and home renovations company. When they asked for help, they said there was no problem regarding the situation in the country; it was enough if they had desire to work. They had applicants' permissions for political asylum, which was in process. After the first two weeks, there was no payment, and the man said he had had a problem with his papers and names. After four weeks of work, he told them he needed their social insurance, but this was a lie, and he ended not paying them the four weeks of work to any of the three. These stories were common, as one was closely related to people like us hat shared the same problems with documents and English, which was vital for the undocumented.

I also noticed something unusual among Latin American immigrants. When I was at school, I realized that the percentage of Mexicans who attended classes was very low, even though this group represents 90% of the immigrants in the United States. If there were twenty-five students, four or five were Mexicans; the others were from different Latin American countries. Perhaps this is partly because Mexico is near the United States; if they deported them, the next day they are back -that is much more complicated for other immigrant- in addition, there still exists among Mexicans the idea that these lands are theirs and, therefore, they do not care to speak another language. Most people migrating from Mexico has virtually no studies, they are those who like to work in agricultural fields.

I talked to some that told me I did not have to speak English; however, the system requires it, since in fact this is no longer their land; they lost it long time ago. When was signed the Treaty of Guadalupe between the United States and Mexico, in Hidalgo, Mexico, it was said that the United States would respect the sovereignty of Mexicans who emigrate. However, they did not, and Mexicans are unhappy with this act, they feel harmed by the treaty -which is not fulfilled- and this makes things more complicated among the people of both countries.

While I was in OLA and worked with the coalition, I had the chance to meet Dr. Charles Clements personally. We talked almost in private, because the people of the coalition wanted me to meet him and talk to him. He spoke Spanish very well and told me he was a pilot in the United States in the war with Vietnam. There, he realized he was on a humanitarian error. After he returned from Vietnam, he got his medical degree and went to Honduras. Then, he made an incursion in El Salvador and was working and healing war fighters and children, women and elderly wounded by military invasions launched by the Government. He brought several films about life in the country and traveled throughout the United States collecting funds to help these people. The film was called Guazapa and was focused on the guerrilla and the people who fought for change. In this film, I could recognize several of my neighbors, young peasants who were in combat. He told me about the invasions of the military where they operated the Atlácatl Atonal and Belloso battalions: all were against the insurgency. In addition, there could be seen several military invasions of up to 5,000 troops and helicopters strafing with 50 and M-60, and planes bombarding areas. This man wrote a book called Witness to War, where he speaks of the great abuses of the war that the United States was causing. His book is very rich with respect to information on this political war.

In those days, we discovered the great abuses that were been carrying out by the armies of El Salvador and Honduras in Salvadorans refugee camps settled in Colomoncagua and Mesa Grande, Honduras. There were refugee camps in Honduras, Mexico (Chiapas) and in El Salvador. The most affected were those in the border with Honduras; the survivors had fled to that country, but the armies of both countries had pestered them with military operations: they captured people and then made them disappeared. The Sumpul River, which marks the border between Honduras and El Salvador, witnessed many massacres performed by the armies trying to stop the people who were leaving the country. All of them were considered subversive / communists by the military of both countries. In the refugee camps, there were mostly children, women and old people. They felt that it was no longer life. They took them out; made them disappeared and they said in the media that they were guerrillas.

In Vancouver, I met an ex-major of the air forces of Honduras. He told me he had studied at the military school in Honduras because all his family was of high rank in the military leadership of that country. He told me that after being in the Air Force he had come to Canada because corrupt politicians had ruined him. He said they ordered him to bomb the Salvadoran refugee camps in Honduras and people who were walking or leaving El Salvador. He said he only took orders from their elders, and he had gone to bombard towns and villages in Salvadoran land. We know these were decisions coming from the White House.

They wanted to move the refugee camps to the interior of Honduras, to make it more difficult to people that were fleeing. During the hardest part of the war in El Salvador, the United States would no longer train Salvadoran troops in North Carolina. They also began to train them in Panama.

A friend who was part of the Atlácatl Battalion told me he had to go there, and there were soldiers from Bracamonte and Atonal barracks: all trained for immediate reaction by the Americans. Salvadoran military were mobilizing in a political and military way, helping Americans in a filthy and dirty war, but the high military commanders had their financial rewards. They wanted to earn a lot of money. The United States trained them next to the war in Honduras and Panama and thus remained in conflict Guatemala, El Salvador and Nicaragua.

The Sandinistas were victims of invasions by seas, war and political infiltrators were used to disturb people; they made an international blockade, and sabotaged their ports and other national resources. The CIA said, "The fish without water dies." On the other hand, the United States supported the Contras with the idea of recovering the power in the country. In addition, it closed diplomatic and trade relations with other countries, starting with Honduras, the country that most helped the Americans, with the purpose of drowning it in misery and for people to say that the revolution was useless. They use the following image: you put a live frog in a pot with cold water and put it to heat. The frog does not detect the heat is going up, because it sleeps, until it dies. They want to do the same with the people, starting with the third world countries.

Nicaragua is the largest country in Central America, but also the poorest, and there was the second richest man in the world at that time, Anastasio Somoza Debayle, supported by the United States. Historically, his family had been given the power to rule in all fields: political, diplomatic, military and economic, and to make with the people what they pleased. They were the owners of the country; the power came by inheritance. Most of the land was this man's property. Nicaragua was the fourth country in importance in the production and export of coffee, and in meat exports abroad: all belonged to a family. They owned other industries as well: fishing, mining and textile, whose products were heading north. To keep order, they copied Hitler and created the National Guard and other security forces.

The United States has never cared to know who the corrupt politicians are: those from the industrial oligarchy, from military cupolas, etc., all they want is to keep the political, geographic and economic control in the region. For that, they have their trained military and their puppets to control the region from a distance.

In our group we were aware of the series of negotiations meetings that had begun in La Palma, Chalatenango, and then were held in Costa Rica, then in Guatemala, later in Mexico and finally in New York, where the peace agreements were signed. This negotiation did not satisfy the Salvadoran people, since changes were few, and the people who died were a lot. The principles of this war were many more and foreign interventionists political manipulation continues. In conclusion: the thirteen years of war and the people who died were insignificant; they did not deserve the right to self-determination. The military were the least that wanted the end to the war, because they were getting profits from money sent by the United States, "eating at two cheeks," as we say in El Salvador.

Americans, on the other hand, had already lost some intelligence advisers and spent one and half million daily in the struggle for that part of Salvadoran land. People said that Americans were feeding gorillas and military buzzards with that war. Besides, they also had the dirty war between Honduras and Nicaragua, with the famous Iran-Contra.

In the negotiations, they had made up efforts to break the Salvadoran territory. This did not work because our country is very small and has the highest population density of all of Latin America. They wanted to split it from east to west, leaving the people who fought the north side, next to Honduras: something similar to Vietnam. The enemy would take over the other side to drown people from the adversary part until they starve to death, as in Nicaragua. They would also use war and political infiltrators.

The latest offensive launched by the people was in the end of 1989, when the guerrillas took the university by force. First, there was a big shooting: guerrillas caused some losses in the military and in the National Police. When they were already inside the university, the military could not bomb or shell, because the hostages were the military and political brains of the country. The guerrillas took those hostages for several hours together with other advisers of the United States, gathered, according to them, to combat the phenomenon of the revolution, and the Americans that leave the country, that leave the people in peace. They also said that there, in that time, they could kill them all, but that was not the solution to the problem. It is said that many cried being humiliated and realizing the great skill that the guerrillas had to know that the meeting would take place there. Several advisers had already died in Cuscatleca land. It is claimed that day there were about 250 gathered.

In those days, they killed a group of six Jesuit priests along with the house cleaner who worked for them and a teenage girl, daughter of the woman. This was done as retaliation towards the people. Moreover, the Catholic Church was separated as well. With the assassination of Monsignor Romero, some other Catholic priests and other members of the Church, they had managed to divide it. Then I realized that in many churches the catechist doctrine had nothing to do with the spiritual, but with the reactionary politics. In those places, the catechist said Monsignor Romero was a communist. Sometimes, the institution suppressed these acts, in other occasions, they let it passes, depending on the ideals of the headquarters of the town or city.

One weekend, we received a call from El Paso, Texas, from a neighborhood friend of my town. He said he was imprisoned in the detention center of that city; the immigration police had captured him and they wanted to deport him. He said that on that path toward the United States, he had suffered a lot and he almost died, and some people nearly killed him in Mexico, the police on one occasion and some thieves on the other to steal his money. They had killed half of his relatives that lived in the countryside in the department of Chalatenango, since this department had been attacked by the government with its military, exterminating every living thing. The man asked our help to walk free and seek political refugee. I told him to call me in about two days to see the resolution of the coalition. The next day, I talked to Mrs. Amelie and I told her about my friend. She repeated to me in a very generous way that the coalition would not normally help people outside the state of Colorado. In my case, they had helped my uncle and my cousins, who were in California, and they would help this boy because my brother and I had paid the debt with the coalition in the shortest time. Besides, I was very in touch with the staff of that institution. It was said and done; in less than two weeks, we had another adventure with us.

He was highly grateful to the people of the coalition that had helped him to be free him instead of being deported to El Salvador, where he risked being killed upon arrival.

In my adventure in the United States, I met another Salvadoran peasant who had fought the guerrillas for six years and then he had left the revolutionary lines because of an illness. Due to that, he was forced to leave the country since given the circumstances; he would not be alive for a long time. He went to Honduras and studied at the university. Then, because of student political problems, he walked in mass movements of students in the capital.

He told me that the National Guard had gone several times to his house to kill him; but, fortunately, they had not found him. Finally, he had to abandon his studies for fear of being killed, and joined the revolutionary forces: the FMLN, which met five groups of armed wing, including the Popular Liberation Forces (FPL), which was the largest group, mostly, peasants. He told me he was in that organization for four years, but then he left because of some differences within the organization, and joined another organization called People's

Revolutionary Army (ERP). He said that was the most prepared arm of the FMLN, even the soldiers feared. He said that during the time he was there, they had destroyed twice the Atlácatl and Atonal battalions: the immediate reaction battalions trained by the United States. It was the most feared by the military barracks. He also said he had the opportunity to kill a US advisor through an ambush on the road when he was traveling in one of the jeeps of a convoy of seven military trucks.

He also told me that once they had to take hostage an old rich and bad man. Because of this man, many poor people had died and they were asking one million colons for a ransom. The air force, the artillery and the troops constantly attacked them. He had made an underground cave to hide in times of bombing. He said that after the attack, they were going to get him from where he was, and all the times they realized he had taken crap because of fear and he was crying.

He told me dozens of passages of his life as a guerrilla. He was also Military Political Chief; he commanded a section of 45 fighters. He belonged to the party: that is, the group that is informed about the plans to be executed in the future days, information fighters have just before they leave. This is done to prevent infiltrators know the plans and make them fail.

He also mentioned that when a city, town or township was taken, he was the one in charge of giving the talk to people. First, they gathered the inhabitants and let them know the causes of the struggle, why they were fighting, and what the revolutionary principles of struggling town were, who the enemies were including the organizations and countries with interests in that war, and what they dreamed for the future of the people when the target was achieved. The person who fought or contributed to the fight, with money, propaganda or demonstrations, he did it voluntarily. There was never any pressure, as the reactionaries said. People wanted the change, but the aggressor had the weapons, the media manipulating, and the money of the wealthy and foreign intervention. Of course, people were afraid of losing their lives and their loved ones. That made them be aware they were between life and death, and many preferred to live in extreme poverty instead of dying.

He said that the United States had to choose between Roberto D'Aubuisson and Álvaro Magaña as president, and the CIA chose him as the puppet.

Since D'Aubuisson had all his pages in red on his career as a military and as political leader. Roberto D'Aubuisson with his German blood in his veins died with the dream to give to the country, (*a wipe out*) as he told to the pentagon of USA. Magana, however, did not because the man was always behind the screen. This man told me that they could annihilate Roberto D'Aubuisson, but they did not because it was a political strategy and to give the whole world know they still had the psychopath leader who wanted to exterminate everyone.

The arrival of this veteran in the group helped me to know more about it, since he had lived all these things. As he was used to give talks and to work with groups, we went together several times to speak at schools and community centers. Of course, he always carried the M-60 and a handgun.

We always talked about racism together, and we had an experience of racist action against us in the United States.

One Sunday, he phoned me and told me, "Notice that I got drunk last night and they do not sell beer in liquor stores today; let's go and drink a beer at a bar to cure me, because I feel bad."

He invited me, and I wanted to drink some beer either. We walked to a nearby bar. It was located on the famous Santa Fe Street in Denver, Colorado, in an area of Chicanos. In the trashcan of that bar, some people had appeared dead, at the back, in the alley, and it had been closed several times because of that and because it was forbidden to serve beer in bottles, as they did, since they only could serve beers in aluminum cans.

I had never been to that bar. We arrived, ordered two beers, we got them, and we paid and sat at a back table. In the counter, there were two men and three women, sitting, apart from the bartender, and they all were Chicanos. As soon as we had taken the first drink, the bartender came and kicked us out because he heard us speaking only Spanish.

He said, "You, Mexicans, get out of here. We do not like wet backs around here. Out!"

I replied in English that we would. I begged him to give us five minutes to drink the beer, and he said it was fine...

Then, he went to serve those who were sat in the counter. They continued talking quietly, and we hurried to drink the beer while we wondered what we had done to them. After two or three minutes, when we least expected it, the bartender came back and kicked our table, and all leapt on us: two women and one man took out knives and wanted to stab us. At that time, I was practicing martial arts and my friend had agile movements, but they blocked the exit, which was a corridor about a meter wide, and knives passed close to us. We took the chairs and we defended with them. Surely, many chairs were broken. For a while, I managed to put the side of the foot on the throat of one of the women who had a knife in her hand and was stationed on one side of the wall, preventing us from reaching the exit, and that helped us escape. I do not know how we could avoid the two men who were at the door with knives. We managed to get out and ran down the street.

It had snowed heavily the night before, and there was about a foot of snow on the streets, which were empty, without traffic. My friend had been given two slashes, one in the chest and another in the stomach, but they were not serious. They gave me one on the left side of my chest. After having run half block, my friend felt dizzy and fell on the snow. I picked him up as I could and I told him not to leave me and to remember the moments he had lived in the war. Finally, it was not necessary to receive medical care. He was a strong man and he liked that kind of duels, because he had enough courage and vigor. Then, we joked remembering what had happened to us with those racists.

Making events and many community efforts, we could save some money in the bank account of OLA and we could send funds to refugee camps in Chiapas. Beside the news of abuse in those places, we knew there were missions of foreign groups, but official sources did not listen to them, they called them guerrillas, too. One day, the colleague Ernesto B. Vigil told us there was money that an association of eastern United States wanted to donate to a humanitarian group that was doing things, whether inside or outside the country. We had to attend a meeting, where other groups who also wanted that money for similar things would be present. Ernesto told us the date, time and place where the meeting would be held. Of course, we had to wager everything to get the money. The organization only asked a monthly report of the things we would do with the money. We were working in complete good faith, it was all for our compatriots who were there, suffering directly or indirectly the consequences of the war. We got ready for the occasion, we went there, together with five other groups, and we were granted the donation. Thanks to that, we worked with more desire to perform other important works and continue raising awareness to the people of the United States.

By then, I had already participated in some interviews on television. I liked to read my poems over exploitation, racism and the difference between social classes. I had also spoken on the radio and to the newspaper I had published some of my poems and my talks about my country. I thought the CIA already had my name. When we did some events, there were a woman and a man, who obviously belonged to the CIA, writing, taking notes of what was said in the sessions. We had a clear record of that. While things were getting better, they got worse in that sense. We were under the magnifying glass of US control. I began to feel afraid, because a person told me my phone was already intercepted and an intelligence source listened to my conversations, so we tried to avoid telephone conversations. The CIA was watching us; it was taking notes of us, the immigrants. My life was a bit miserable in that sense; that was not a place to settle down politically. I was in the air; I had no certainties about the future of the refugee people in Central America. I spoke on the events that happened there, and added poems, wrote songs and sang.

In Los Angeles, California, they had killed two girls and two boys that were activists from El Salvador. According to the information we had, they had already imported to Los Angeles the Death Squad to fight there activists of our country, with the promise to give them status in the USA, whose aim was to let American people know how was the reality of Central America.

The war had been conceived and it had affected Central America in a very subtle way. They had taken a part of our lives, family welfare and community well-being. Many relatives had died and hundreds had left the country forever. We were no longer fully satisfied with life. I wanted to go back to my country with my parents, but I could not, it was a matter of life or death. I thought about going to live the war wielding a rifle in the front lines, fighting against the oppressor. They had already killed many peasants, who were some loved ones in rural areas. At the same time, I wrote to my brother, who was in the Civil Guard. He was a kind of official and he was with eighty officers taking care of the antennas of the peak of San Salvador volcano, where all communication is handled in the country. I told him to leave, and he answered me that the commander could kill our father. He said he was not afraid to be there, he was lucky because it was said that the same guerrilla preferred to attack a military barracks and not the place where he was, since the peak is very steep and an attack was a waste of men. In the midst of the desires I felt about returning to my country, I also thought about my parents and the help I gave them, and they were going to worry more about me being there in the war...

I would also say that when they killed someone or made them disappear, often this fact was not officially registered and therefore, it was not part of the statistics of the country, much less the world's ones. There were times when the Death Squads, the Police, and the National Guard or military were looking for individuals they had in lists to kill them, and some of them had already been killed or were missing. In many cases, someone appeared dead but they did not identify him, there were doubts or no one could give the report to the municipal authorities since it was dangerous to leave the house because of the war. For that reason, the guerrillas began to burn mayoralties from villages and killed many mayors because they collaborated with acts of war, but they especially sought to destroy files documents as identity cards, marriage certificates, birth certificates, etc. from the civil records of this city, as the ultra-right obtained hence the names of the citizens. That saved the lives of thousands of people: in those villages where the guerrillas did those things, it was more difficult to the extreme right to have a detailed control of the place.

We had also heard that when the guerrillas captured soldiers and they surrendered, they made them prisoners for a few days, and meanwhile, they indoctrinated them. They made them know there were no Russians, Cubans, or Sandinistas in combat and they told them: "As you can see it, here there are only Salvadorans, mostly peasants wielding this rifle." Wounded soldiers received medical treatment until cured. Many who changed their minds stayed with them, and the others were sent to the Salvadoran Red Cross to leave for their homes. The uniform, the rifle and the projectile stayed in the camp, and they sent them in civilian clothes. Instead, when the armed forces or other "security forces" captured a fighter alive, they burned him or mutilated him. For that reason, when the fighter was about to be captured, if he could kill himself, he did it, and thus avoided a painful death or being interrogated under torture before death. Many military officers said they liked to capture fighters alive to torture them.

With the events, we brought people the message of what was happening in Central America and we raised money to send aid to the refugee camps. Every month, we made a report of those collections. Besides, we supported groups of professional singers who came to the United States.

On one occasion, I met the Salvadoran group called Yolocamba ita, which in Lenca language (a Mayan language) means "sowing rebellion." After the concert in Boulder, Colorado, I talked to the members and they said they wanted to enter the United States for a tour, but the country had denied their entry because of the message conveyed in our music, until they succeeded saying this music was a cultural expression of their land. My job was to record on video tape such events. They told me how their lives had been in wartime. They told me about their exile in Mexico, they had already released their third album to the public, and they always came up against reactionaries who were against the revolutionary music.

Roberto Quezada, one of the group leaders, together with his brother Franklin, told me, "Sometimes, there are reactionary people at concerts that want to hear Salvadoran music, but reactionary, music of the bourgeoisie or of the oligarchy of the country. We do not do that; we sing to give people the message of those in need."

At that time, for example, an individual yells he wants them to sing "The coalman".

"The coalman" is a song for the oligarchy of our country" said Roberto. We do not come to sing to our oppressors, but we come to sing to our people. That sounds like when at school they taught us poems of Alfredo Espino, Miguel Ángel Espino, Vicente Acosta and other poets and writers who only write pretty metaphors, but they do not speak of the people that are dying of hunger and the tyrannical oppression.

271

The first time they went to the United States, they performed in the Church of Guadalupe and sang religious songs related to the Church and Monsignor Óscar Arnulfo Romero, like that song that includes the words "Reforms are useless if they are covered with blood".

This is a recent monument of our great hero, Monsignor Oscar Arnulfo Romero. Other monument added to El Salvador square of the world in the capital.

THE FINAL CASE

Then came the day when the case of my situation in the United States could no longer be brought to court with lawyers of the coalition. Either the judge accepted me as a refugee and gave me political asylum or deported me to my country. The lawyers of the coalition looked for a good lawyer for me, Anne Smith: very nice people, apart from being very progressive. The affidavit she had prepared was extensive. She had included newspaper clippings of my appearances in newspapers and interviews I had done on television. She also added the letters where our sister told us the commander of the Civil Defense wanted to kill my brother and I when we returned and letters from our parents where they said it was better we were away but alive.

The lawyers advised me what I should do with my life. Lawyer Anne Smith took my case. One month before the last meeting in court, she took the documents from other lawyers and prepared them in detail. By then, there was new information that would be vital for the case. The day of the last hearing came, and I took my friend Ernesto Vigil as an official translator. The judge did not like me; I knew it because of the way he stared at me. The man was a veteran of Vietnam. According to what they said, after being in that war, he had achieved his position as a judge specialized in illegal immigration and he used to take the decision to deport people.

That morning, my lawyer, my translator and I arrived at court. On the other hand, were the judge, the district attorney and a woman who wrote in shorthand what we talked about, more so everything was being recorded in a device. The lawyer exposed to the judge, among other things, all documentation of my case I had mentioned before. She explained that I worked as a volunteer member for a group whose aim was to help refugees inside and outside Central America. Likewise,

273

she also let him know what we knew about the Salvadoran activists murdered in California. The judge believed that nothing could happen to me; well, it did not suit him to believe it. He also said I had been deported from the United States; that was the other issue he used. In this regard, my lawyer and I made the judge aware that I was still alive because I had some relatives who were military. However, that was not useful anywhere in the country, as in the valley, with the commander, who only had to talk with another Civil Defense in the area to come and arrest me; and the man did not seem to be involved, he would intervene anonymously.

At times, the judge contradicted; he got up from his seat, spoke in an angry tone, hit the desk with his hammer, told the district attorney to make me questions, etc. The prosecutor, who was also a deportation officer, sometimes did not know what questions ask me. We took short breaks, of about twenty minutes, because the judge needed them. That day, there were eight to nine hours of questions and answers about my case.

The following day, we returned, seated in the same seats to treat the same subject. The lawyer had information about many Salvadorans deported upon arrival or after few days of their return to El Salvador had been killed. Things worked that way there, usually anonymously. The judge did not accept it and he always hinted that if someone died in that war, it was because there was a good reason for that.

Monument of "El Salvador del mundo"
"The saver of the world"

In the afternoon of that second day, the judge was upset again and the court adjourned: slammed his hammer and said I could be deported from that moment on. If they had accepted me as a refugee or had given me political asylum, the judge would have accepted the harm US intervention was doing in the region with its dirty war. The lawyer told me:

"Note that when that group of Salvadorans died in the Arizona desert, the survivors were also denied this request. So, do not feel bad, because there is no jackpot for anyone."

The lawyer also told me that she could make an appeal of the case and start another trial. However, these cases are much more expensive for the client and almost never win. She meant it was useless to seek the solution on that side.

Some days later, I had an appointment with one of the lawyers of the coalition. They asked me what I planned to do; I told them I did not know yet. The lawyers advised me to look for another country;

they mentioned the possibility of traveling to Australia, Switzerland or Canada, by the United Nations Convention and they gave me enough information about the countries. They told me about government benefits and that they would give me the migratory statutes so I could live in peace. The idea seemed great, and started to process a request for political asylum, to which I got an answer in a few months. I had an interview with the Canadian consul, who had come from San Francisco to Denver, Colorado. Then I had to get my police record of three states of the United States and a general health report as priority requirements to be accepted in Canada.

After many struggles with the English language, I had managed to get the GED Diploma in Denver, Colorado, and I had already gotten a scholarship to study at the Community College of Denver. I liked philosophy, history, and math; of course, I took two different English classes. I was studying to be an architect, and enjoyed it very much. When I was in the midterm of my studies, I got the papers from Canada, approved to travel to that country. They gave me three months to enter the country. I called them, told them I wanted to finish what I already had paid at school. They told me to send the documents back and they would send them later with other date. They did so; they sent me another documents, with longer terms. Soon, I traveled to this country.

THE END OF THE WAR IN EL SALVADOR AND POST WAR

Casualties

While being in the United States in the eighties I had to meet some guys that they were also in the refugee program. Two of them told me that both of them were recruited to be in the army and they had to escape. They told me that for being wounded they had to be in the military hospital of El Salvador. They told me that in that hospital I could see things like: Guys with no arms and legs and blind; Blind because of bombs of gasses that they used in the war.

A lot wounded from mines on the trails. They told me that very often some wounded soldiers/patients that arrived from the battle fields to the hospital and had a wounded foot or arm once they were they asked that if they were going to get treatment for his foot or arm but they just put them to sleep and the next day they were without the foot. The military regiment was not paying/spending for treatment. Washington was not giving money for treatment or may be the top military voltures/slugs were eating that money.

"No treatment, just the chopsaw"

That's why we have a lot of umputaded, ex-combatants or ex-soldiers in El Salvador that still survive now these days, begging for money because they don't get an income.

Christmas of '96, I went to El Salvador to bring my wife (now my ex-wife) to Canada. I married her in Christmas of 1994 and it was September that year when I got my Canadian citizenship. The flights were from El Salvador to Los Angeles, from Los Angeles to Vancouver, Canada. Once landed in Los Angeles, I had to go through Customs and Immigration. One of the agents took me directly to the immigration office where they arrested me and my wife. Despite that, I didn't feel nervous, but curious about what was going on. I started feeling unconformable and upset at the same time. I started asking questions of what's going on. "Why was I arrested? What's the reason?"

Two officers told me they couldn't divulge the reason why. The only thing they kept on telling me is that I was not welcome in the USA. Two hours later the big boss of the immigration arrived. He said, "You are not welcome in this country, therefore we are going to deport you - back to your country, El Salvador". I answered, "I came from my country, El Salvador and I am going to my new country Canada; I am a Canadian citizen since 1994, so what's wrong with that? So which country is going to deport me?" He continued, "You were deported from the USA in 1994, and so, you are not acceptable here!"

By then the lady flight attendant showed up in the office and told me, "Don't worry Mr. Serrano you will get into the next flight going to Vancouver - you and your wife".

She could get into the office and once I talk to her I could see and talk to my wife through the glass wall. But still the immigration officers thought I was trying to escape because they ran towards me. I wanted to explain to my wife that I didn't even know what was happening. They even told me, they could have handcuffed me for the reason that I was not wanted in the country.

I answered, "Do it if you want!" I told them. "Listen, I traveled from my country, El Salvador to Canada, unfortunately, I have to make this stop in the USA, and I don't even have the slightest interest to stop in this country – a country that does not give any security of my life and that all the time it is looking for war! The truth is - I hate to be here!"

Later on the officers were discussing that I got my Canadian citizenship in 1994, why their big boss came over and said that I was deported in 1994. That simply means I was not allowed in the USA. I knew that the immigration big boss had all the information about me and of what I did in the past - the newspapers in Denver, CO and when I was on TV with people in the city carrying the signs saying to the CIA, "STOP U.S INTERVENTION IN CENTRAL AMERICA".

Finally, I said to them, "deport me anywhere you want. I came from my country and I am going to my new country - Canada". I knew that if they'd send me back to El Salvador, I'd be forced to go back to the Canadian Embassy in Central America to give this information for a Diplomatic attention.

When I told them that it was neither my choice nor desire to step in the in the USA because it does not bring happiness and that somehow I kind of dislike the country, the immigration officers just scratched their heads and didn't say anything.

Due to the circumstances that has been happening with this corrupted political system in Latin America, dictatorships (puppets) bought by the USA to lead these countries the way they want - century after century, decade after decade. We are having these waves of uprights of people particularly in Central America after we had an internal war in the region for more than a decade.

After this war the delinquency has gone up to a very high degree. Firearms have been the toy for kids and teenagers after these conflicts. These cycles of society have been a product of too much exploitation. We have been under exploitation in the local industry land owners of the regions and foreign countries. All they cared is the plus value on their sides, leaving misery and starvation on the other side – the third world countries.

Nowadays, we are having these waves of people coming up north, looking for a better living with peace and tranquility because the product of the war did not leave a good result even though it was necessary by the people that were fed up of it - dictatorships were not alone, they were supported by the empire and now we are a (shithole). That's what the US President, Trump, said on the TV once.

But for others, they don't think what the reality of these phenomena is. We have to look back to many years of history, of political manipulation, of political and military occupation, and political puppets bending their knees to the empire.

Alfredo Cristiani one of the 14ᵗʰ richest families of the country and in Guatemala and also has been the president of the National Association of the private Enterprise of El Salvador, ANEP to conserve the wealth for the wealthy families of the country.

Now in these days we are facing other problems that were germinated due to the war but we now have a better government system, fighting against injustice, corruption and other issues that affect the people of our country. A new government that is assuming the task gathers with our ex-militants that have been the vanguard of our people who needs it in this small country. The people of El Salvador, Central American countries and the rest of the third world countries starving for social dignity, equity and the lack of fraternity. While these problems prevail in the world: Wars, unhappiness, sadness and starvation for justice we will have in this world.

A message to the world from:
Máximo Serrano Hércules.

ACKNOWLEDGEMENTS

I want to thank the people who have helped me in my life and who have changed their path; starting with David Marroquín, the veteran of the war between El Salvador and Honduras. He always wanted our valley to have a school, safe water, electricity and a better road to the village. He even dreamed of a health care department. He could never see it come true. He fought against right-wing extremists and the landowners of the country. He gave me information on many passages of the war with Honduras from his own experience. The Death Squad murdered him without any particular reason.

I also thank Mr. Mauricio Canales, one of my professors, who is still alive in El Salvador. He is now retired; he gave me a lot of motivation and information to make this work possible.

To the school principal, Mr. Manuel Figueroa Bonilla, still alive and now retired.

To Mr. Julio, who was murdered by the National Guard in the beginning of the war together with other teachers who taught in the area and were engaged in the movement of professors and students.

To university students of the village that later became warriors of the people against the national oligarchy.

To Ovidio Orellana, son of the woman of the community, I thank him for the information about his mother. A woman beloved by the surrounding valleys, who is always remembered for what she did, that was very important for the community. Today, Ovidio is a leader in the valley when it comes to voluntary work to help the community.

To the Mexicans like Julian Quezada and other compatriots who gave me information about their country, their policies, the poverty in which they also lived by, the beauty and the non-acceptable in their land, and their reasons for migrating northward.

From the Coalition, to begin with, I want to thank Mrs. Amelie Starkie, who was in meetings in New York and spoke in the New York Times denouncing what they were doing in Central America and informing the public about our reality.

To the other people of the coalition, who helped me so much, lawyers, people from the Church, teachers and all those who worked for the community of that city, people from the Coalition who not only helped me, but also helped my relatives in my country.

To the members of the OLA group, we worked together making a small contribution for those who needed it in Central America, particularly, Manuel Hermógenes García, Guatemalan, for giving me his sincere friendship, for having been so close.

I thank Carlos Antonio Contreras and his wife Eugenia Mira Hernández; both are teachers and helped me with the final editing of this work, my greetings for them.

To Leo Tanguma, Texan of Mexican origin, a great muralist who performed and exhibited his works in several places in the United States, including that mural denouncing oppression in which lived El Salvador, my personal and special thanks to this man. To care about and raise awareness in those in need with an artistic, historical and political message, full of true creativity.

I want to thank Saúl Platero, for providing me with the photos shown in this work, to show how we live now and how we lived some time ago, in our school days.

Thanks to Canada, for giving me the opportunity to enter a great and sovereign country through the Convention of the United Nations, for becoming a citizen. Thank you for the opportunity to enjoy the privileges I could not get in the United States.

I want to thank my friends from Latin America, Asia and Africa. All my friends from underdeveloped and Third World countries, for sharing with me things of much political and social interest, bearing always in mind the potential we have and the idea that we are a family with many natural charms, with our customs and traditions, and with our particular political principles.

Photography: Elsa Yolanda, Mira Hernández, Eugenia Mira Hernández and Rosita Díaz.

This is the volcano, Izalco, named by the Mayans. For so many decades this volcano had a huge flame on its peak after the Spanish came to America in the 15th century and still in activity when earth quakes happen with fire inside. The sailors called it "THE LIGHT HOUSE OF THE PACIFIC", to lead their way to come to Central America.

CPSIA information can be obtained
at www.ICGtesting.com
Printed in the USA
BVHW031532120919
558177BV00020B/51/P